BLOODSHOT

WRITER
TIM SEELEY

ARTISTS
BRETT BOOTH with
ADELSO CORONOA
TOMÁS GIORELLO

COLORISTS
ANDREW DALHOUSE
DIEGO RODRIGUEZ

LETTERER
DAVE SHARPE

COVERS BY
DECLAN SHALVEY
DAN BRERETON

**ASSISTANT
EDITOR**
DREW BAUMGARTNER

EDITOR
LYSA HAWKINS
KARL BOLLERS
(FCBD Special)

GALLERY
SIMON BISLEY
BRETT BOOTH
ADELSO CORONA
ANDREW DALHOUSE
ERNIE ESTRELLA
TOMÁS GIORELLO
DAVE JOHNSON
MARC LAMING
JAE LEE
FELIPE MASSAFERA
FRANCESCO MATTINA
AMILCAR PINNA
DIEGO RODRIGUEZ
TIM SEELEY

**COLLECTION
COVER ART**
DECLAN SHALVEY

**COLLECTION BACK
COVER ART**
TIM SALE
with BRENNAN WAGNER

**COLLECTION
FRONT ART**
JONBOY MEYERS

**COLLECTION
EDITOR**
IVAN COHEN

**COLLECTION
DESIGNER**
STEVE BLACKWELL

 **VALIANT**

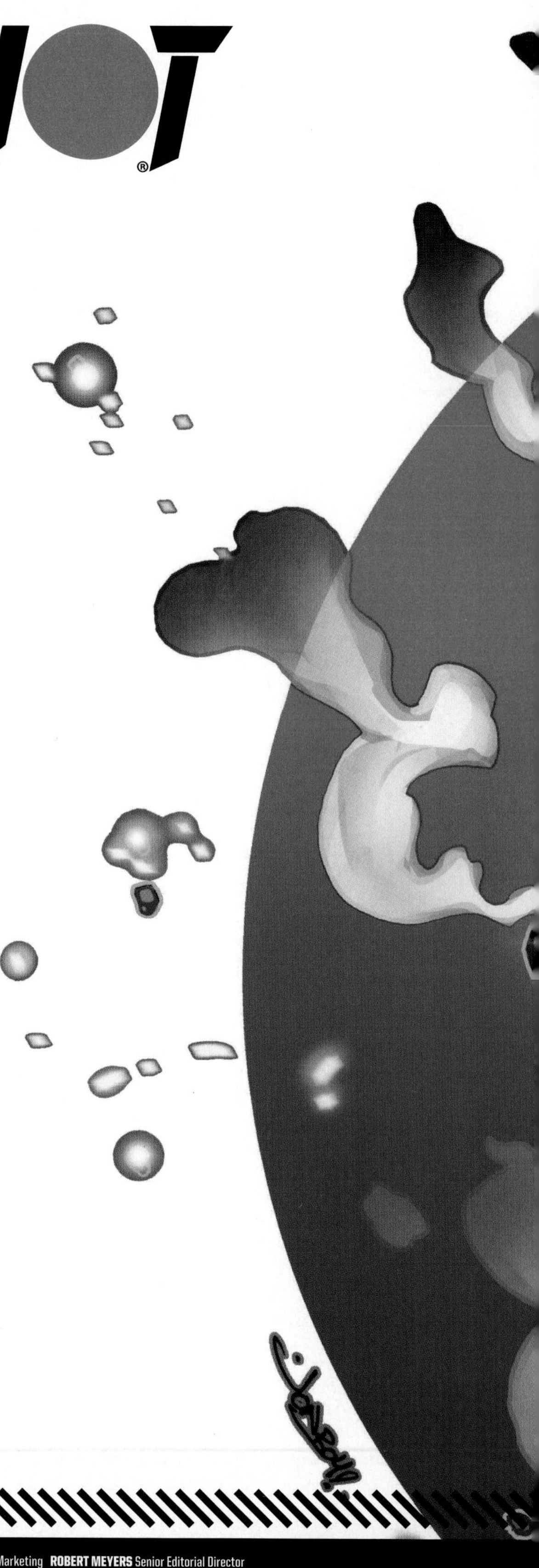

DAN MINTZ Chairman **FRED PIERCE** Publisher **WALTER BLACK** VP Operations **MATTHEW KLEIN** VP Sales & Marketing **ROBERT MEYERS** Senior Editorial Director
TRAVIS ESCARFULLERY Director of Design & Production **PETER STERN** Director of International Publishing & Merchandising **LYSA HAWKINS, HEATHER ANTOS** & **GREG TUMBARELLO** Editors
DAVID MENCHEL Associate Editor **DREW BAUMGARTNER** Assistant Editor **JEFF WALKER** Production & Design Manager **KAT O'NEILL** Sales & Live Events Manager
CONNOR HILL Sales Operations Coordinator **DANIELLE WARD** Sales Manager **GREGG KATZMAN** Marketing Manager **EMILY HECHT** Digital Marketing Manager
RUSS BROWN President, Consumer Products, Promotions & Ad Sales **OLIVER TAYLOR** International Licensing Coordinator

Bloodshot® Book One. Published by Valiant Entertainment LLC. Office of Publication: 350 Seventh Avenue, New York, NY 10001. Compilation copyright © 2019 Valiant Entertainment LLC. All rights reserved. Contains materials originally published in single magazine form as Bloodshot (2019) #1-3, and Valiant: Bloodshot FCBD 2019 Special. Copyright © 2019 Valiant Entertainment LLC. All rights reserved. All characters, their distinctive likeness and related indicia featured in this publication are trademarks of Valiant Entertainment LLC. The stories, characters, and incidents featured in this publication are entirely fictional. Valiant Entertainment does not read or accept unsolicited submissions of ideas, stories, or artwork. Printed in the U.S.A. First Printing. ISBN: 9781682153420.

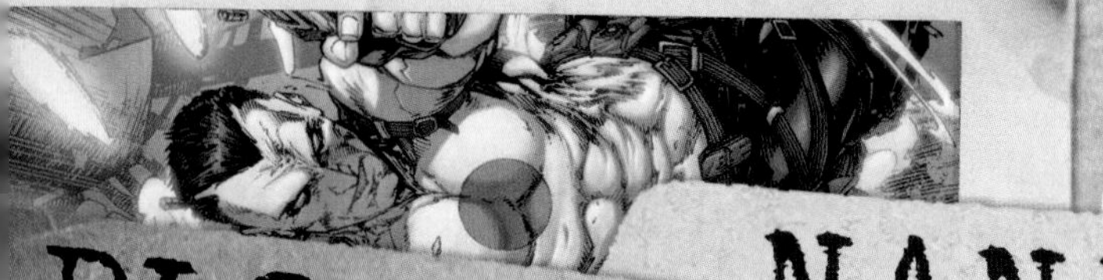

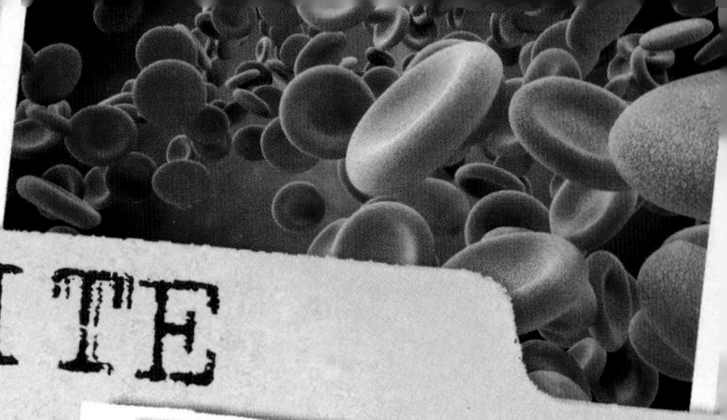

BLOODSHOT NANITE

VALIANT

CLASSIFIED [redacted]

23 AUG 19

RECORD COPY
DO NOT DESTROY OR MUTILATE

SUBJECT: Bloodshot

ALIASES: [redacted] Ray Garrison, Angelo Mortalli, The White Ghost, [redacted]

D.O.B.: [redacted]

NOTES: Created by now-defunct military contractor Project Rising Spirit (PRS) for covert special ops, "Bloodshot" served for years as a near-unstoppable killing machine. He is infused with billions of "NANITES," advanced nano-robots giving him a rapid healing factor, enhanced strength, speed, endurance, and the ability to temporarily alter his physical appearance. Now free of his former masters, Bloodshot pursues his own directives, aiming to rectify the perceived wrongs he did while under the control of PRS [redacted]

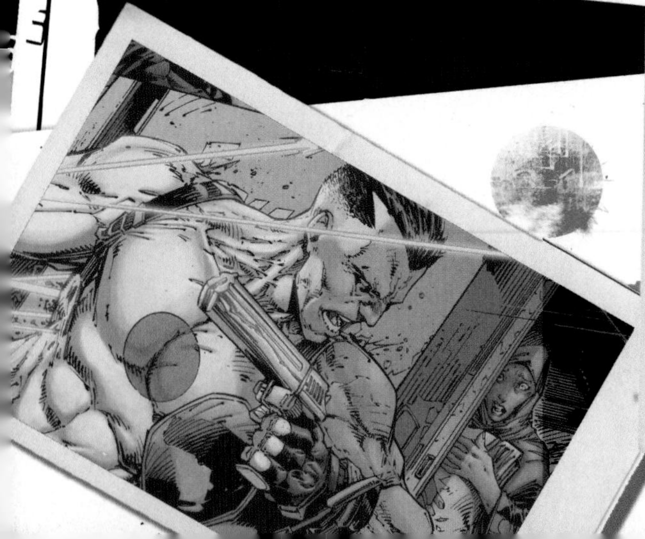

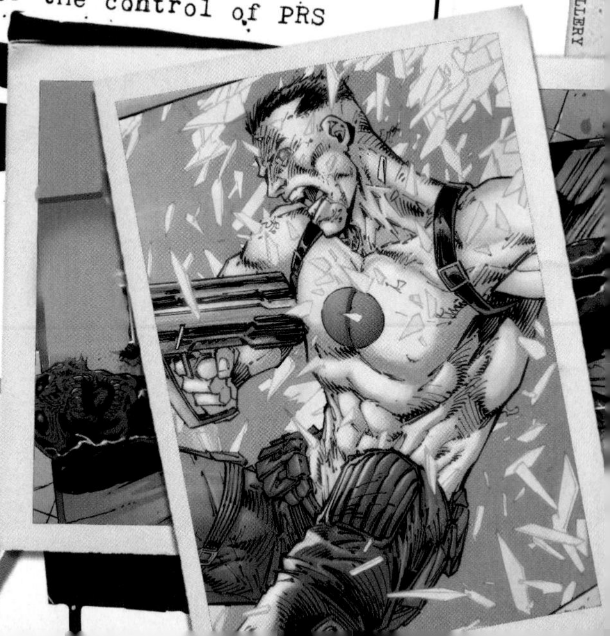

RECAP DESIGN BY TRAVIS ESCARFULLERY

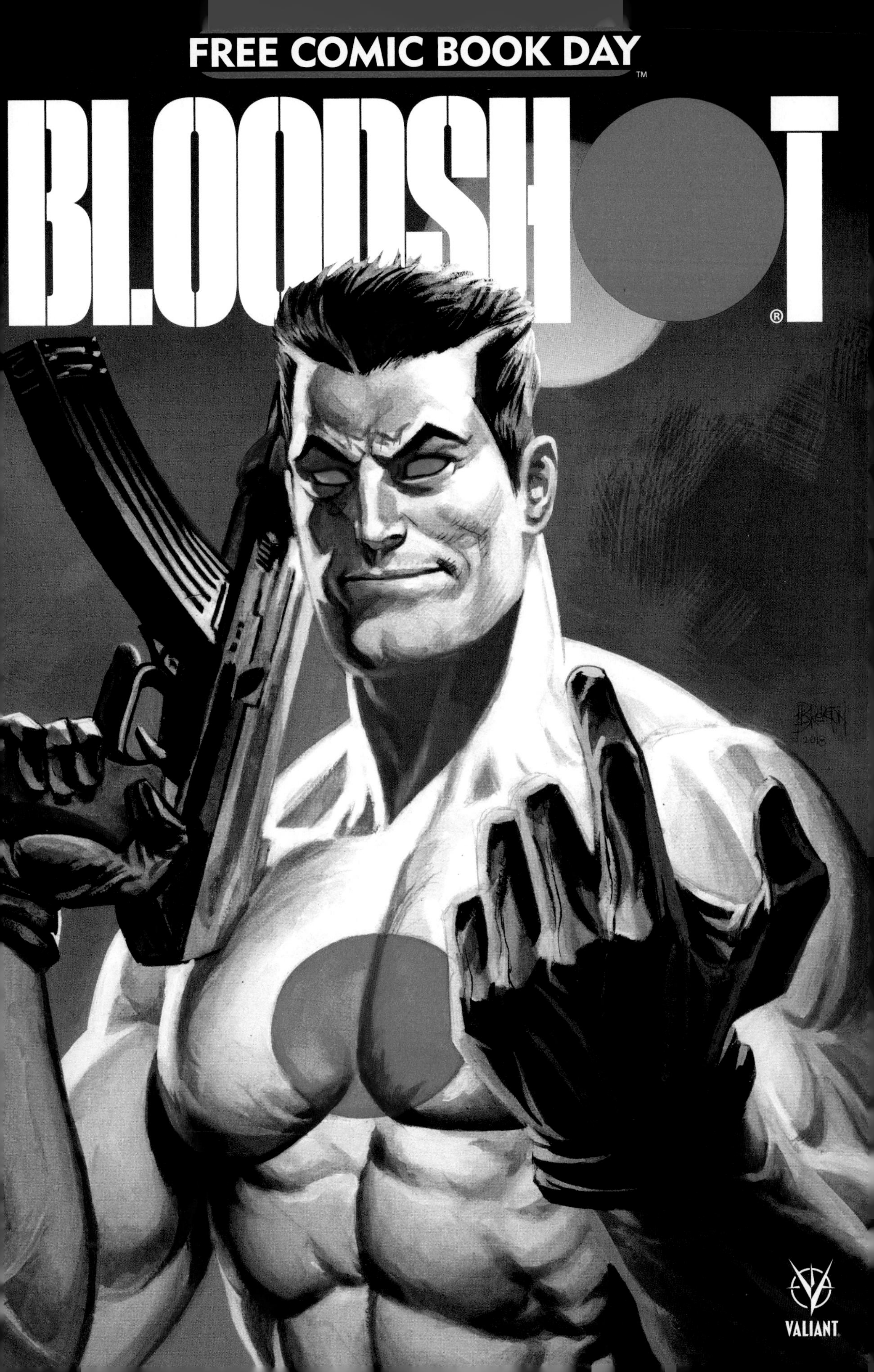
FREE COMIC BOOK DAY™
BLOODSHOT®
VALIANT

"BLOODSHOT: PRELUDE"

VALIANT: BLOODSHOT FCBD 2019 SPECIAL
WRITER: Tim Seeley
PENCILS: Tomás Giorello
COLORS: Diego Rodriguez
LETTERS: Dave Sharpe
SENIOR EDITOR: Karl Bollers

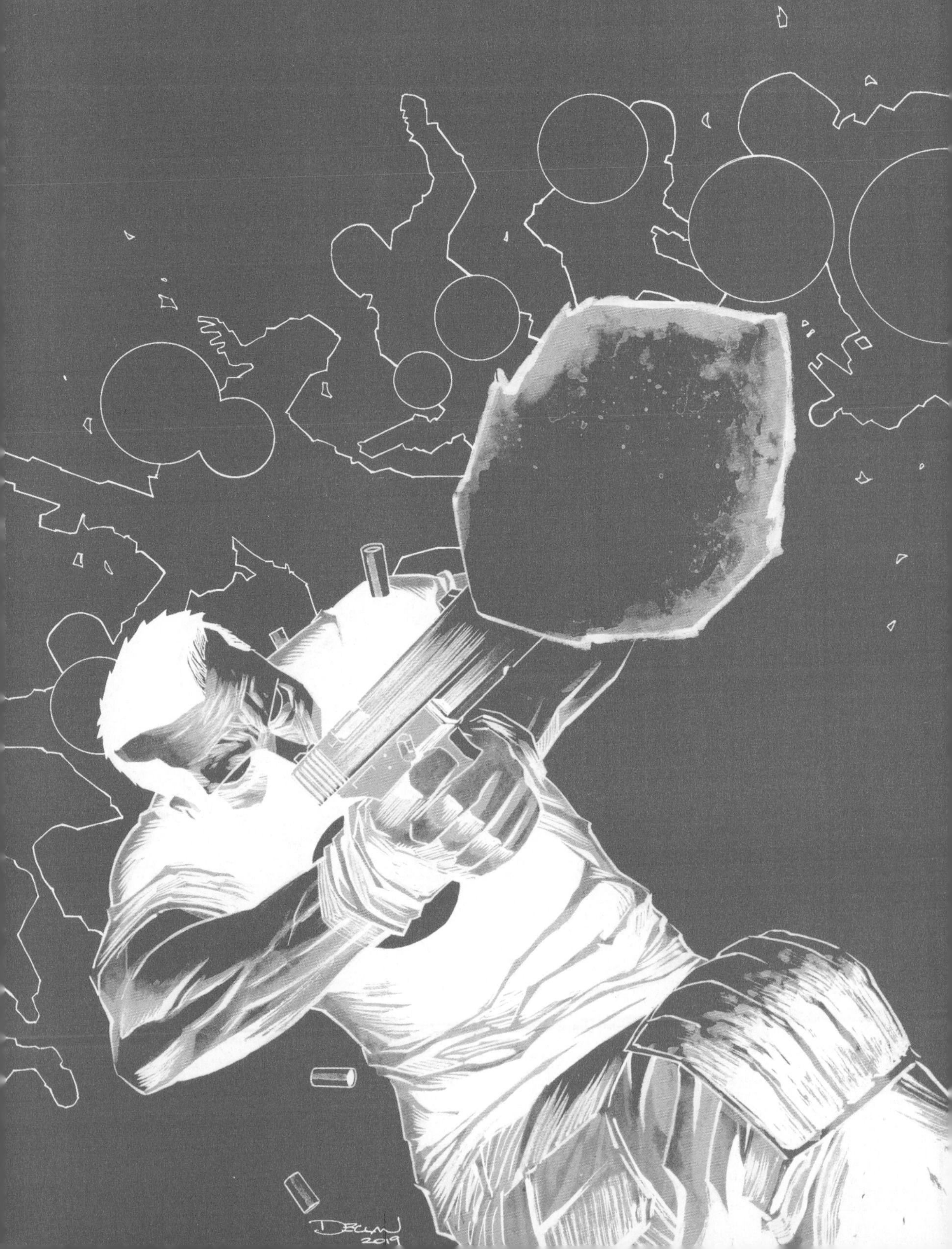

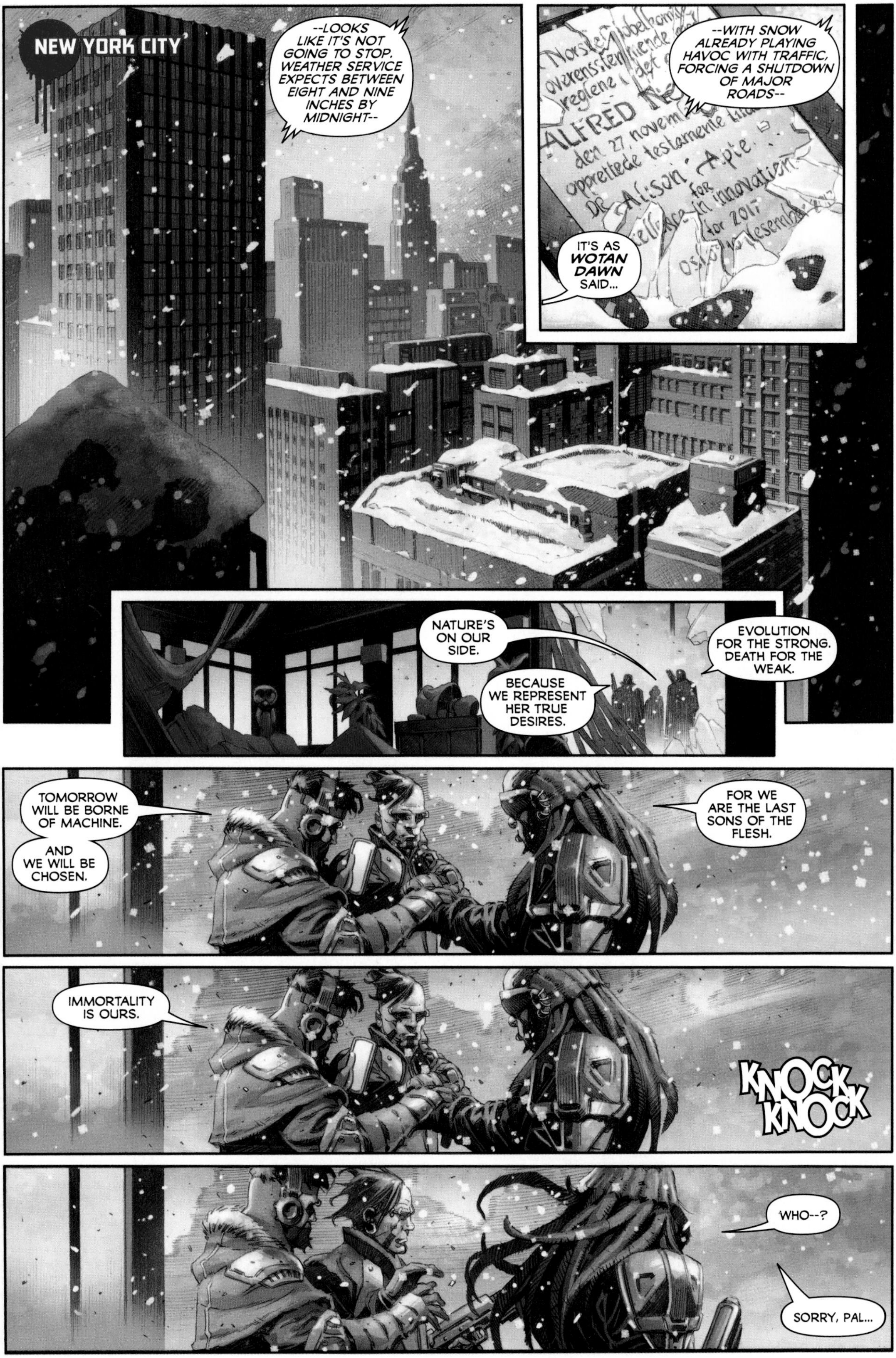
NEW YORK CITY
--LOOKS LIKE IT'S NOT GOING TO STOP. WEATHER SERVICE EXPECTS BETWEEN EIGHT AND NINE INCHES BY MIDNIGHT--
--WITH SNOW ALREADY PLAYING HAVOC WITH TRAFFIC, FORCING A SHUTDOWN OF MAJOR ROADS--
IT'S AS *WOTAN DAWN* SAID...
NATURE'S ON OUR SIDE.
BECAUSE WE REPRESENT HER TRUE DESIRES.
EVOLUTION FOR THE STRONG. DEATH FOR THE WEAK.
TOMORROW WILL BE BORNE OF MACHINE.
AND WE WILL BE CHOSEN.
FOR WE ARE THE LAST SONS OF THE FLESH.
IMMORTALITY IS OURS.
KNOCK KNOCK
WHO--?
SORRY, PAL...

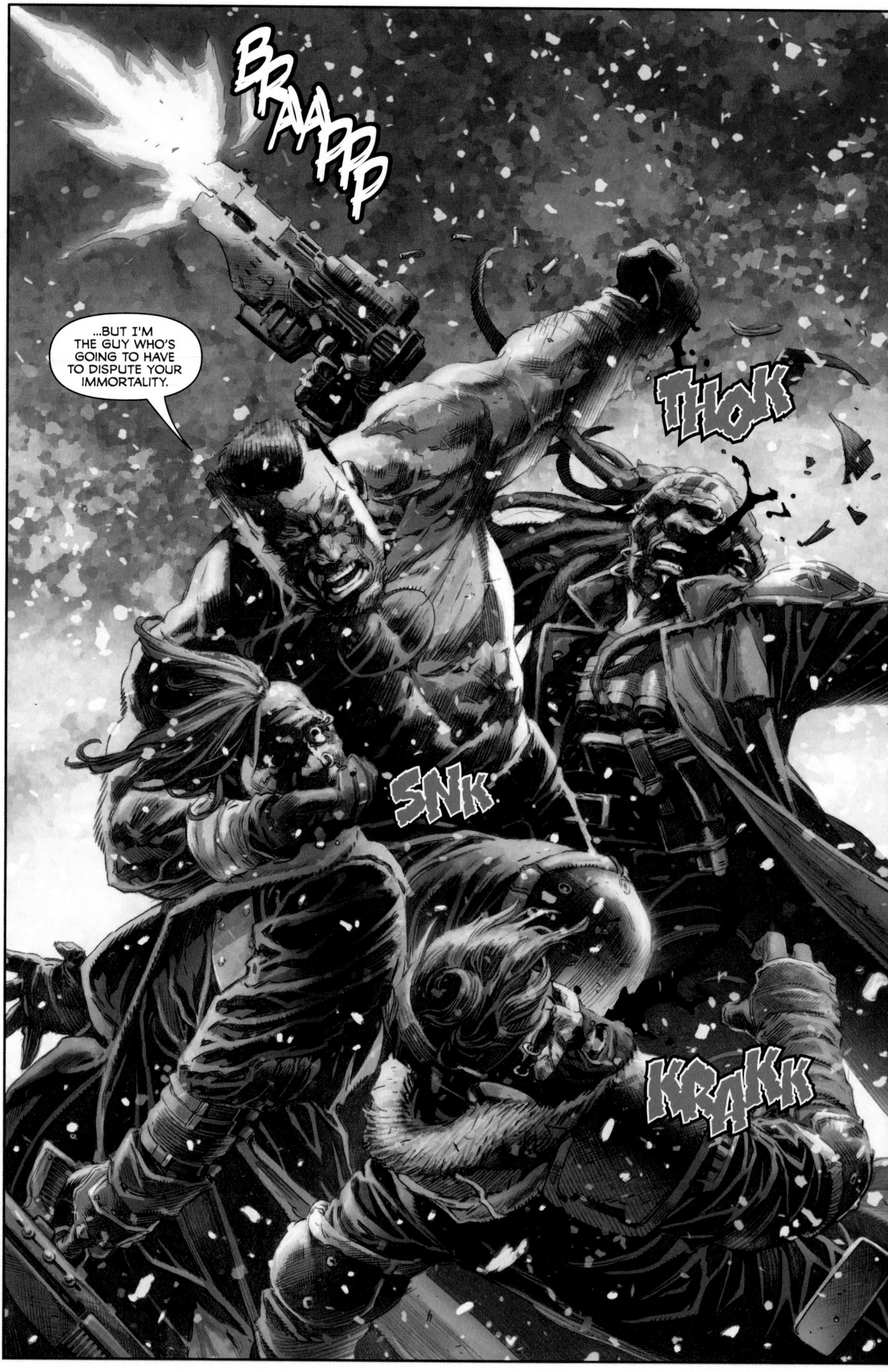
BRAAPPP
...BUT I'M THE GUY WHO'S GOING TO HAVE TO DISPUTE YOUR IMMORTALITY.
THOK
SNK
KRAKK

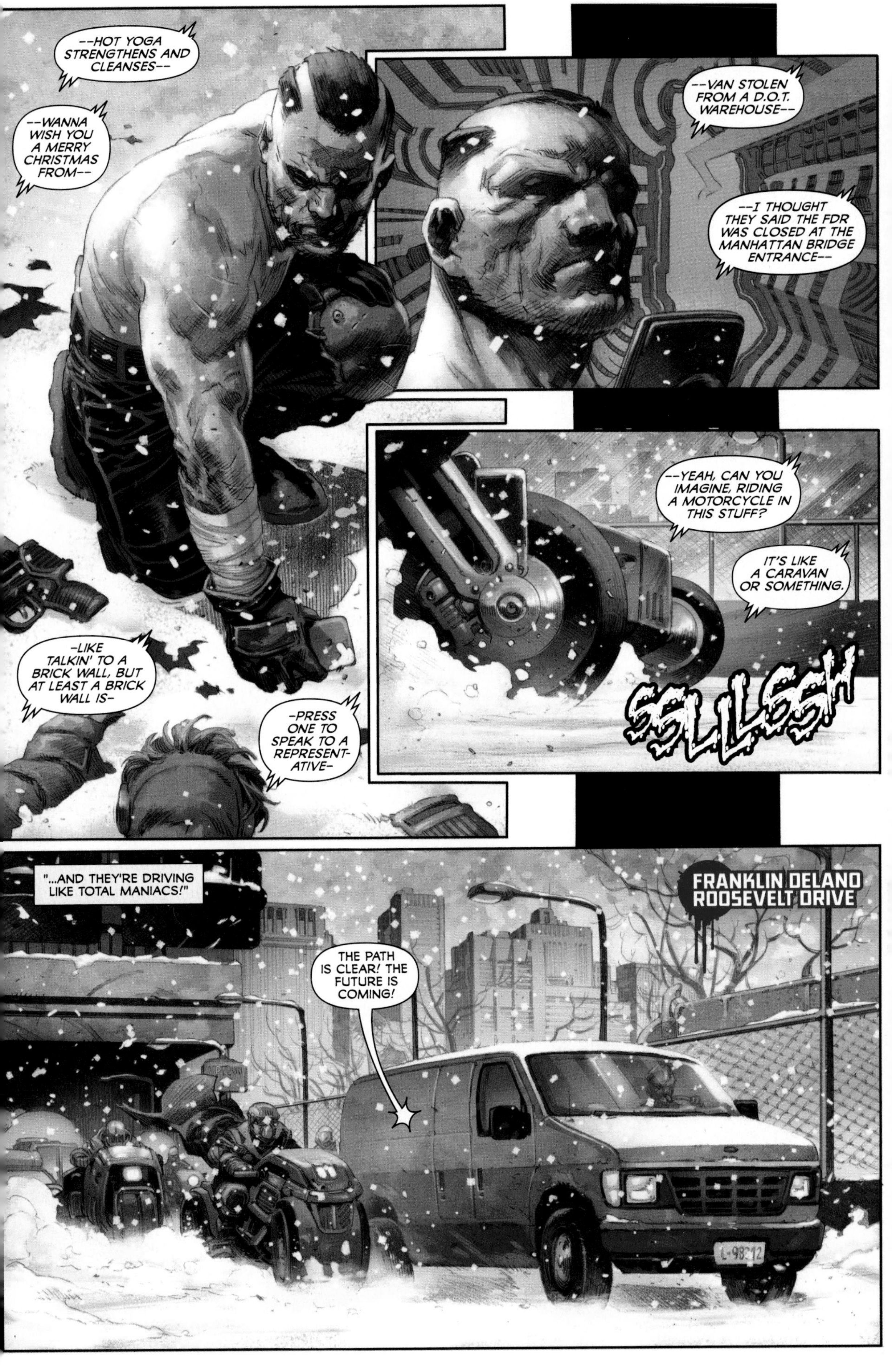
--HOT YOGA STRENGTHENS AND CLEANSES--
--WANNA WISH YOU A MERRY CHRISTMAS FROM--
-LIKE TALKIN' TO A BRICK WALL, BUT AT LEAST A BRICK WALL IS-
-PRESS ONE TO SPEAK TO A REPRESENT-ATIVE-
--VAN STOLEN FROM A D.O.T. WAREHOUSE--
--I THOUGHT THEY SAID THE FDR WAS CLOSED AT THE MANHATTAN BRIDGE ENTRANCE--
--YEAH, CAN YOU IMAGINE, RIDING A MOTORCYCLE IN THIS STUFF?
IT'S LIKE A CARAVAN OR SOMETHING.
SSLLLSSH
"...AND THEY'RE DRIVING LIKE TOTAL MANIACS!"
FRANKLIN DELANO ROOSEVELT DRIVE
THE PATH IS CLEAR! THE FUTURE IS COMING!

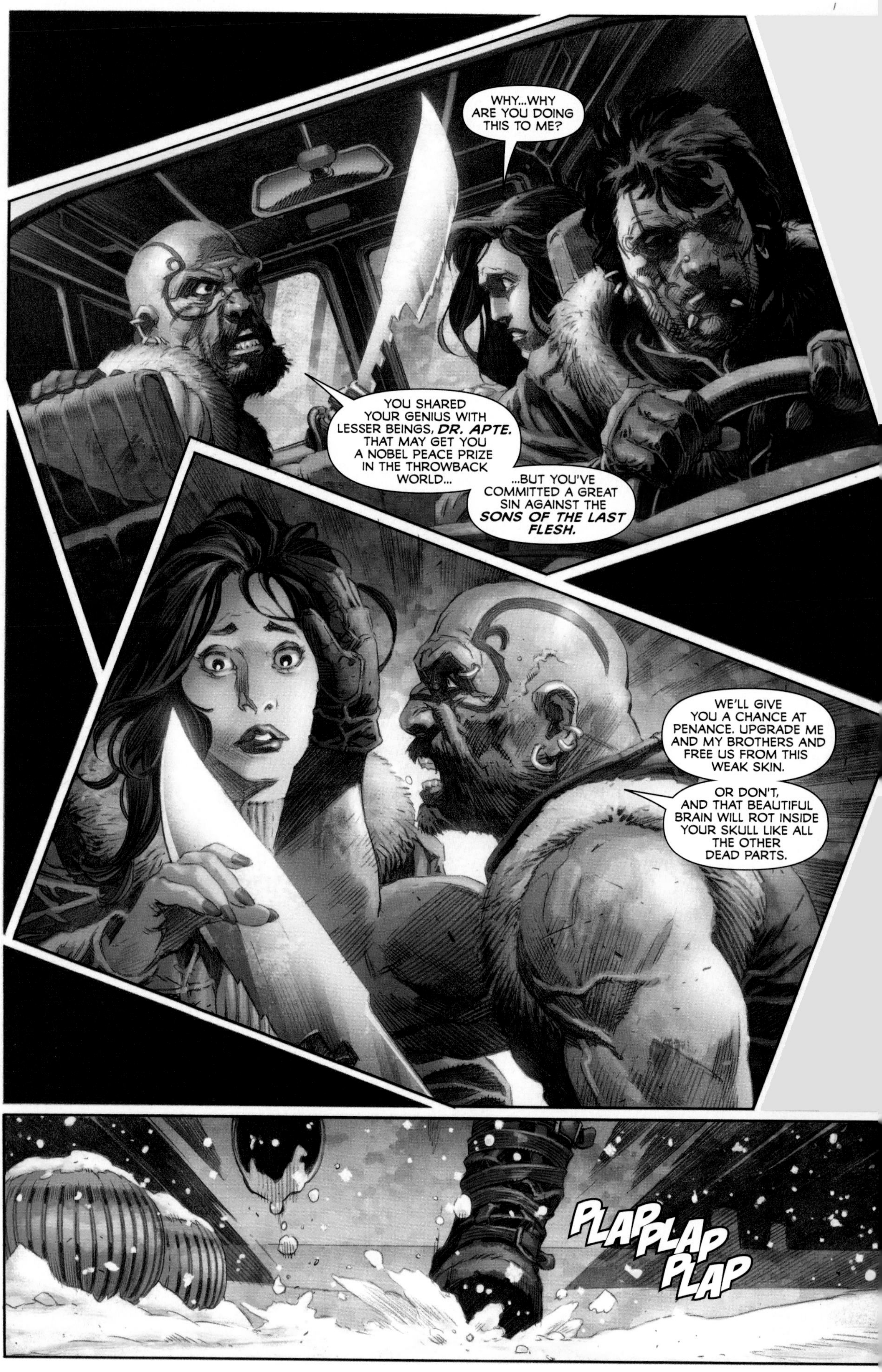
WHY...WHY ARE YOU DOING THIS TO ME?
YOU SHARED YOUR GENIUS WITH LESSER BEINGS, *DR. APTE.* THAT MAY GET YOU A NOBEL PEACE PRIZE IN THE THROWBACK WORLD...
...BUT YOU'VE COMMITTED A GREAT SIN AGAINST THE *SONS OF THE LAST FLESH.*
WE'LL GIVE YOU A CHANCE AT PENANCE. UPGRADE ME AND MY BROTHERS AND FREE US FROM THIS WEAK SKIN.
OR DON'T, AND THAT BEAUTIFUL BRAIN WILL ROT INSIDE YOUR SKULL LIKE ALL THE OTHER DEAD PARTS.
PLAP PLAP PLAP

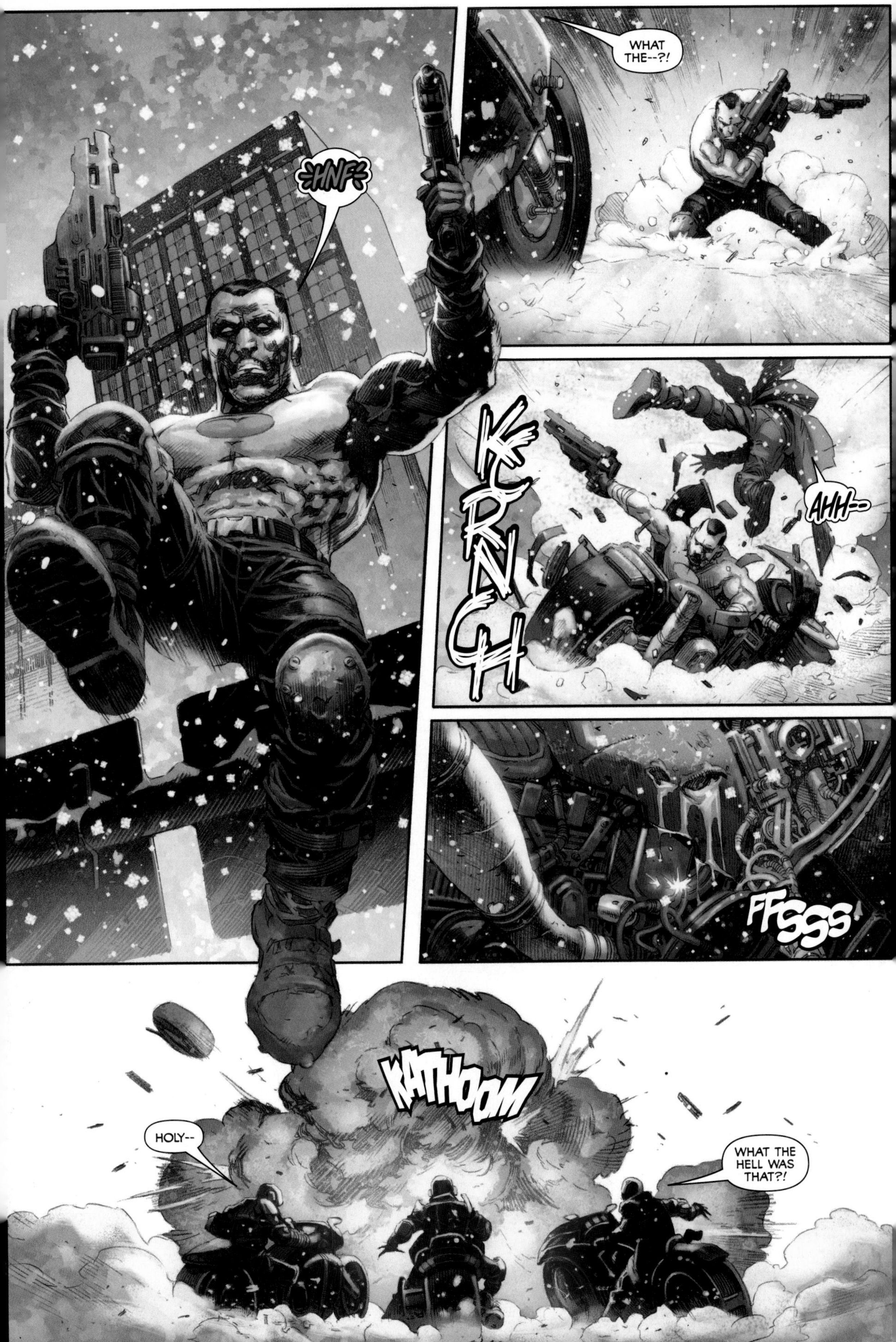
HNF
WHAT THE--?!
KRNCH
AHH--
FFSSS
KATHOOM
HOLY--
WHAT THE HELL WAS THAT?!

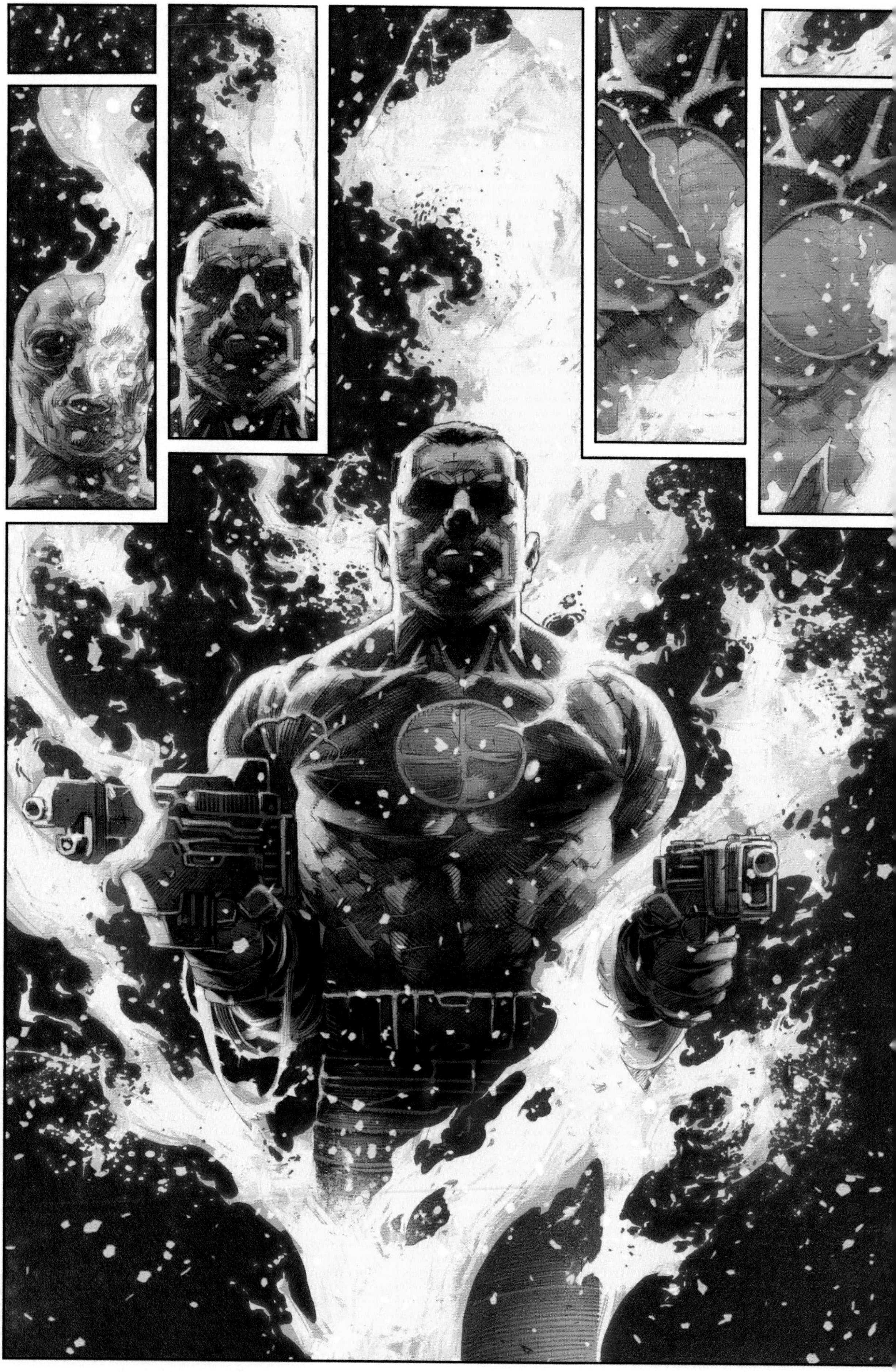

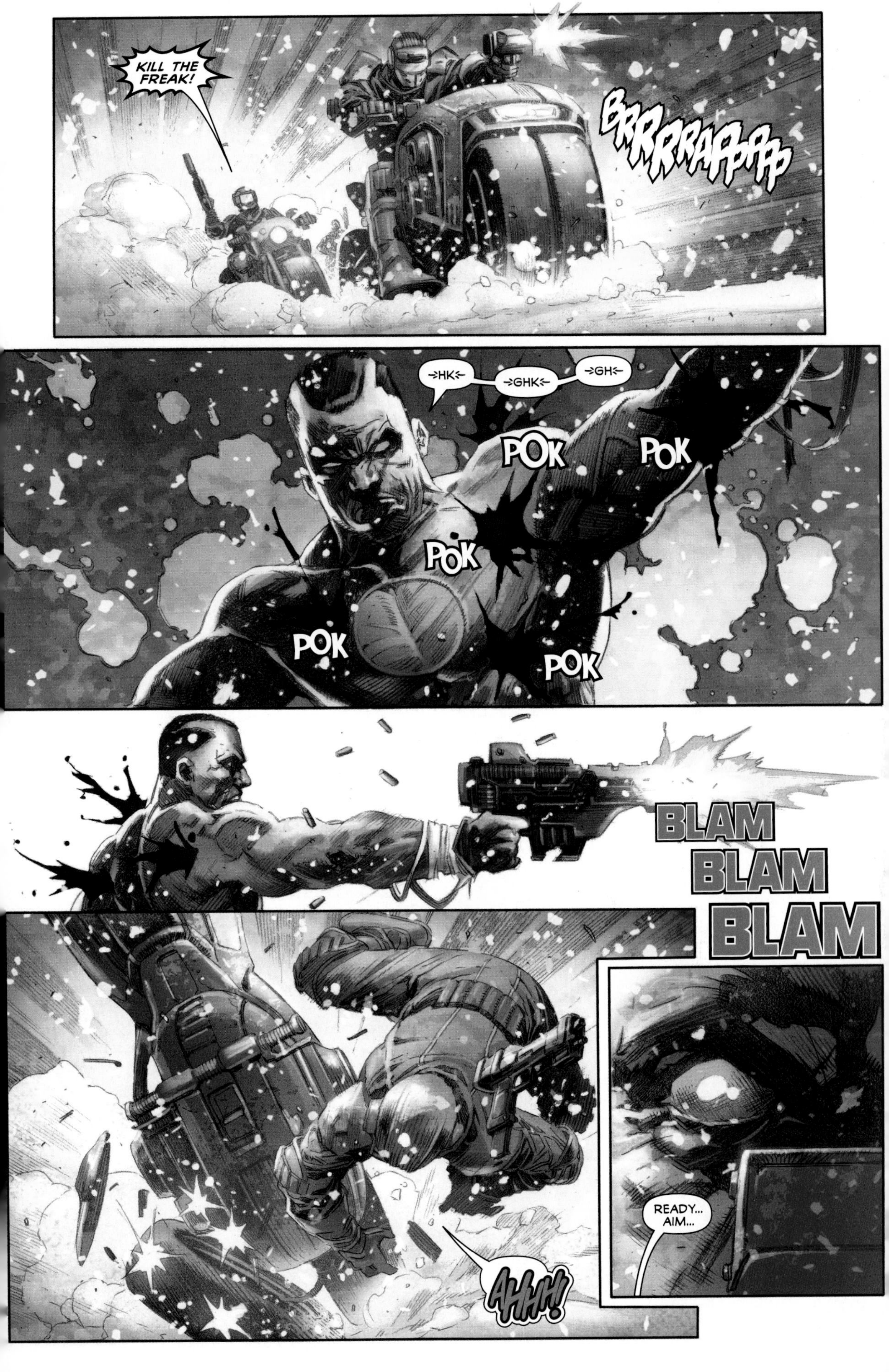
KILL THE FREAK!
BRRRRAAPPP
HK
GHK
GH
POK
POK
POK
POK
POK
BLAM
BLAM
BLAM
AHHH!
READY... AIM...

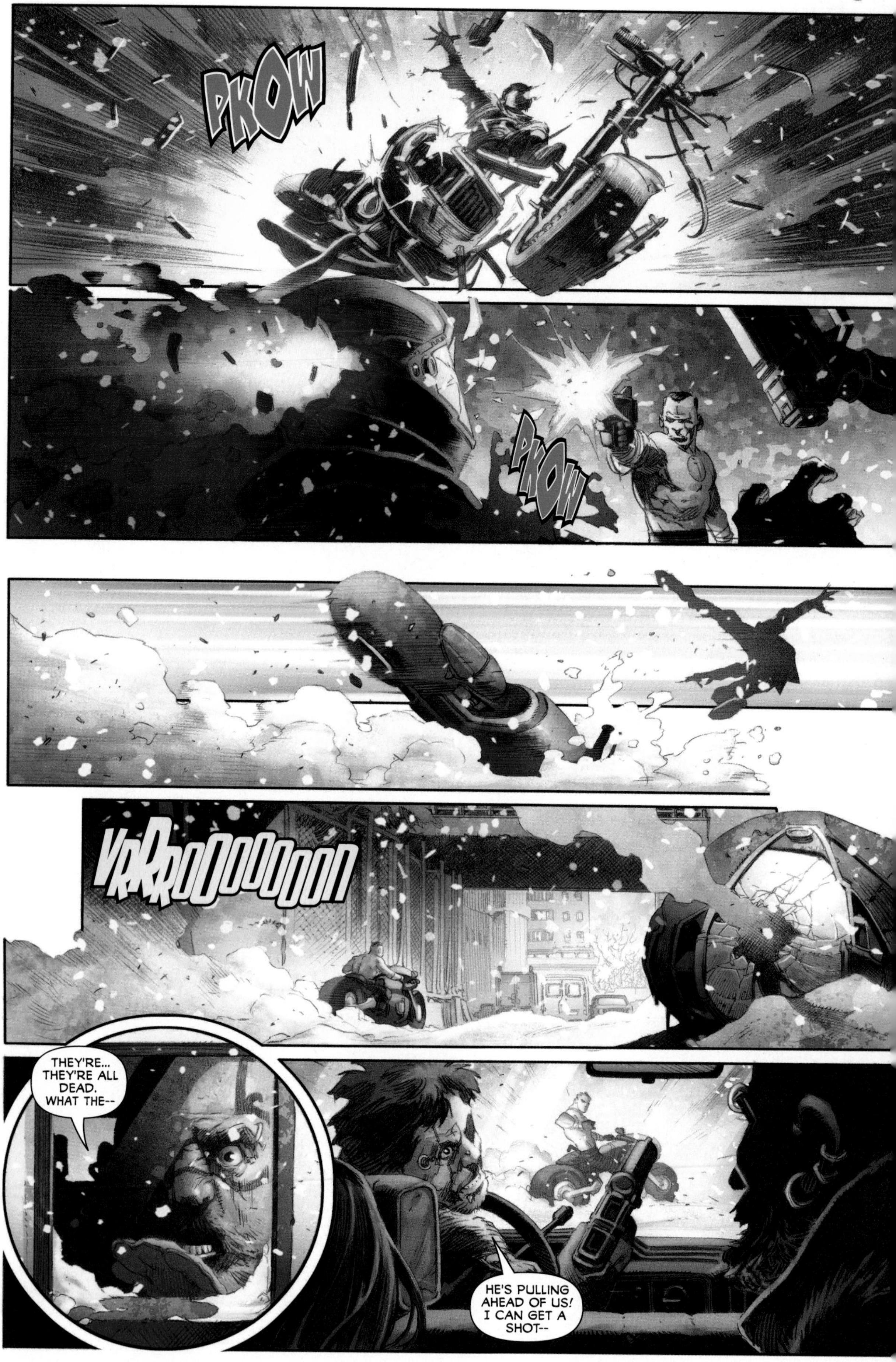
PKOW
PKOW
VRRROOOOOOOOOOOM
THEY'RE... THEY'RE ALL DEAD. WHAT THE--
HE'S PULLING AHEAD OF US! I CAN GET A SHOT--

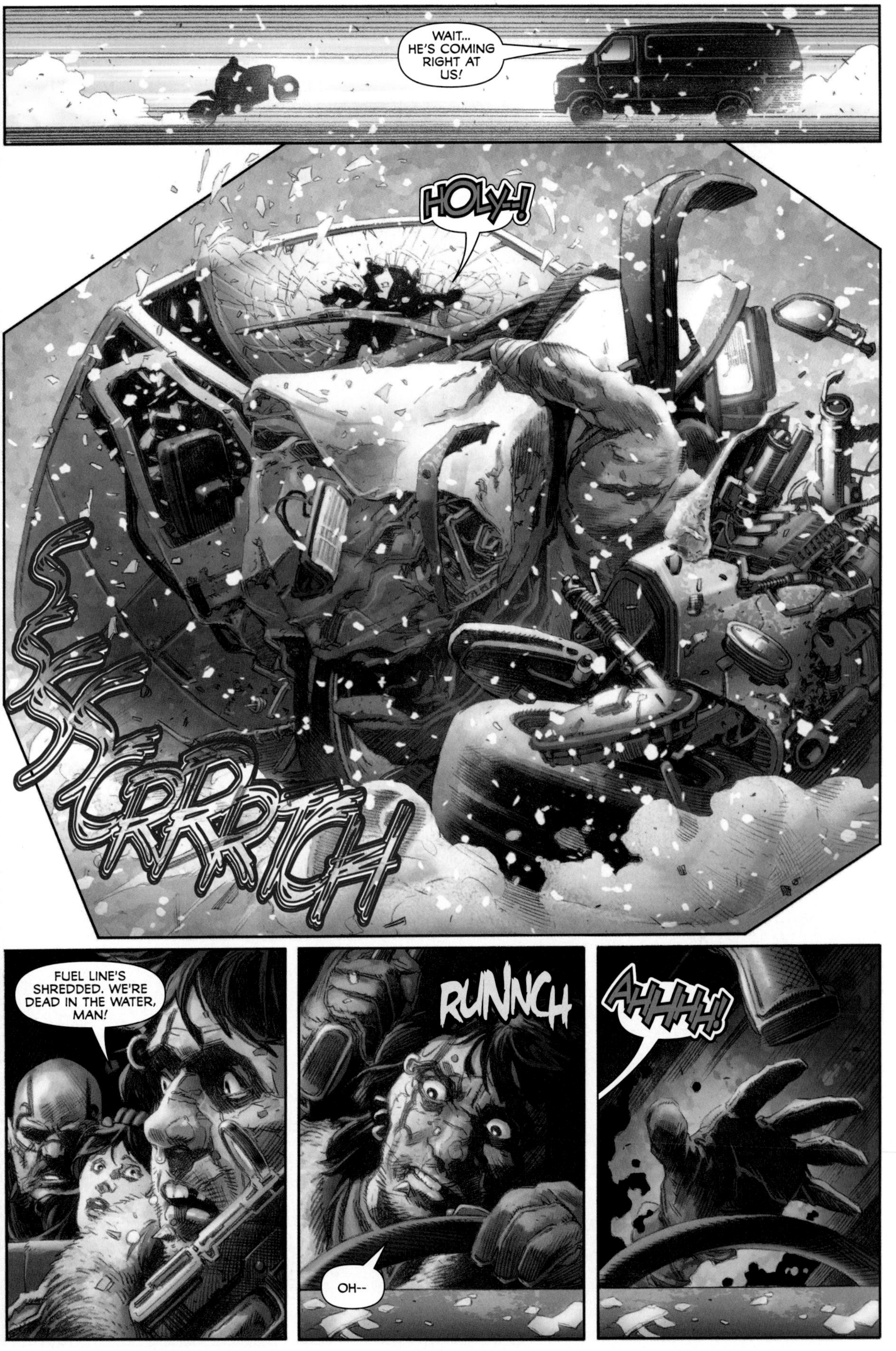
WAIT... HE'S COMING RIGHT AT US!
HOLY--!
SCRRRRRTCH
FUEL LINE'S SHREDDED. WE'RE DEAD IN THE WATER, MAN!
RUNNCH
OH--
AHHHH!

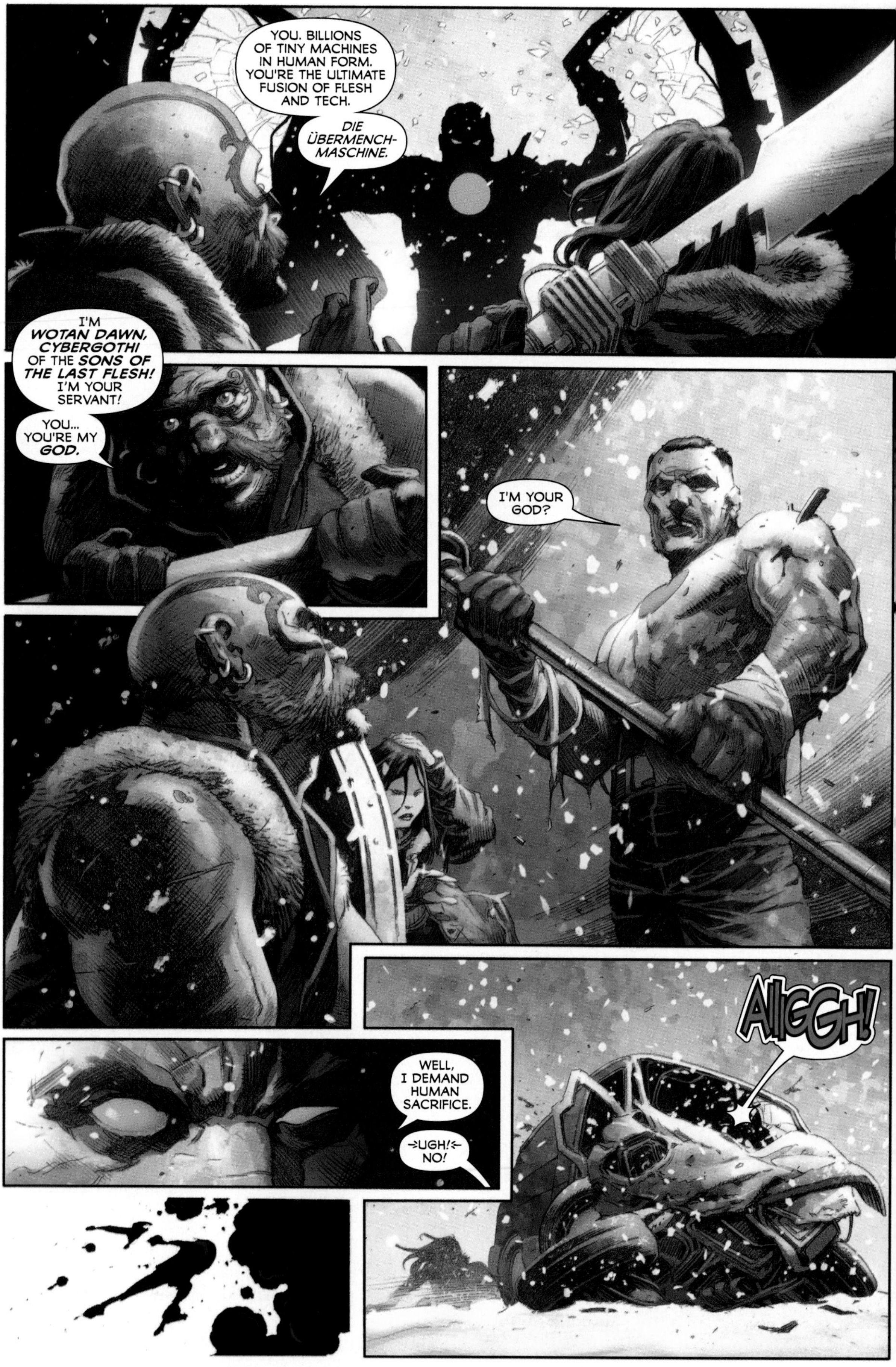
YOU. BILLIONS OF TINY MACHINES IN HUMAN FORM. YOU'RE THE ULTIMATE FUSION OF FLESH AND TECH.
DIE ÜBERMENCH-MASCHINE.
I'M WOTAN DAWN, CYBERGOTHI OF THE SONS OF THE LAST FLESH! I'M YOUR SERVANT!
YOU... YOU'RE MY GOD.
I'M YOUR GOD?
WELL, I DEMAND HUMAN SACRIFICE.
UGH! NO!
AIIGGH!

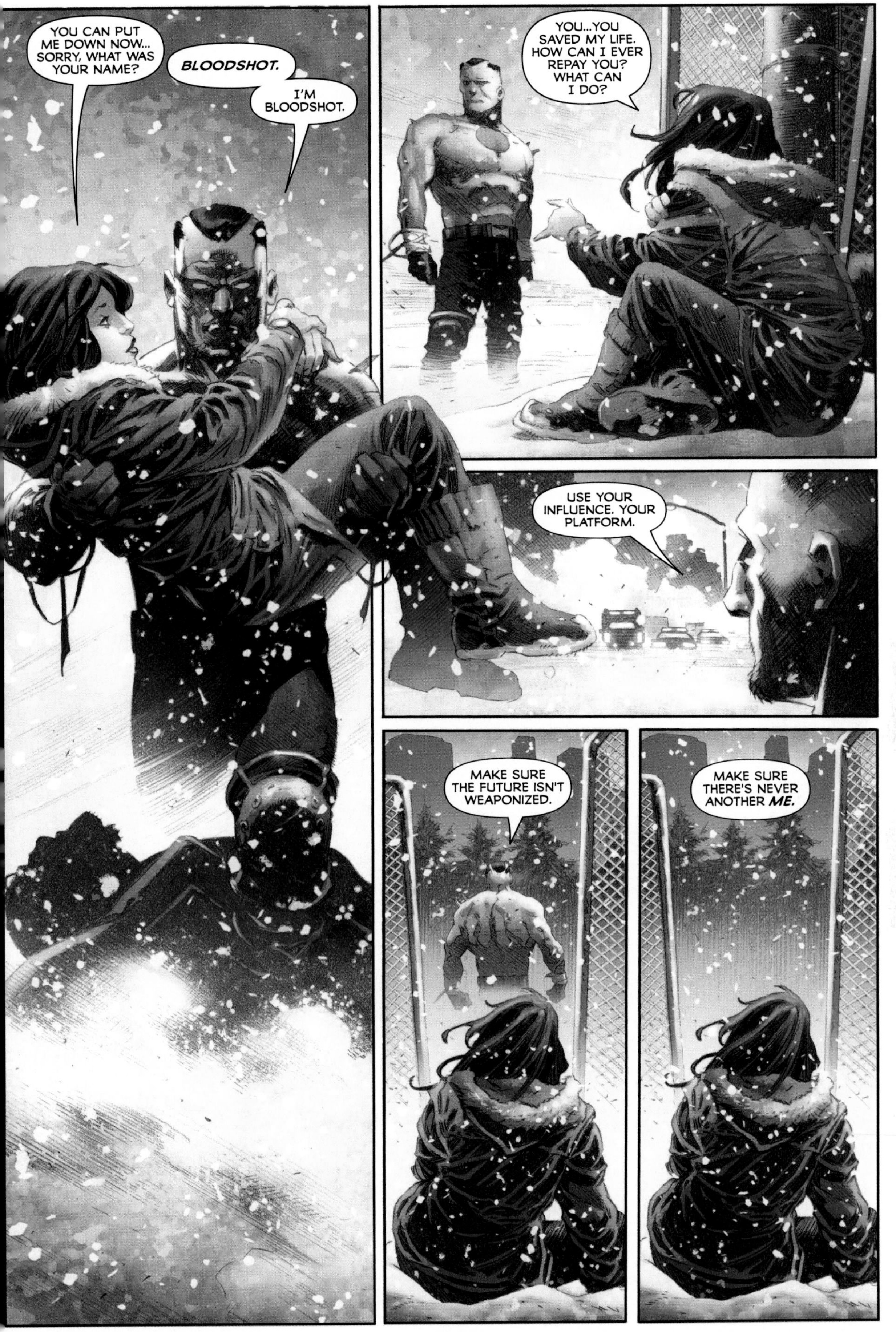
YOU CAN PUT ME DOWN NOW... SORRY, WHAT WAS YOUR NAME?
BLOODSHOT.
I'M BLOODSHOT.
YOU...YOU SAVED MY LIFE. HOW CAN I EVER REPAY YOU? WHAT CAN I DO?
USE YOUR INFLUENCE. YOUR PLATFORM.
MAKE SURE THE FUTURE ISN'T WEAPONIZED.
MAKE SURE THERE'S NEVER ANOTHER ME.

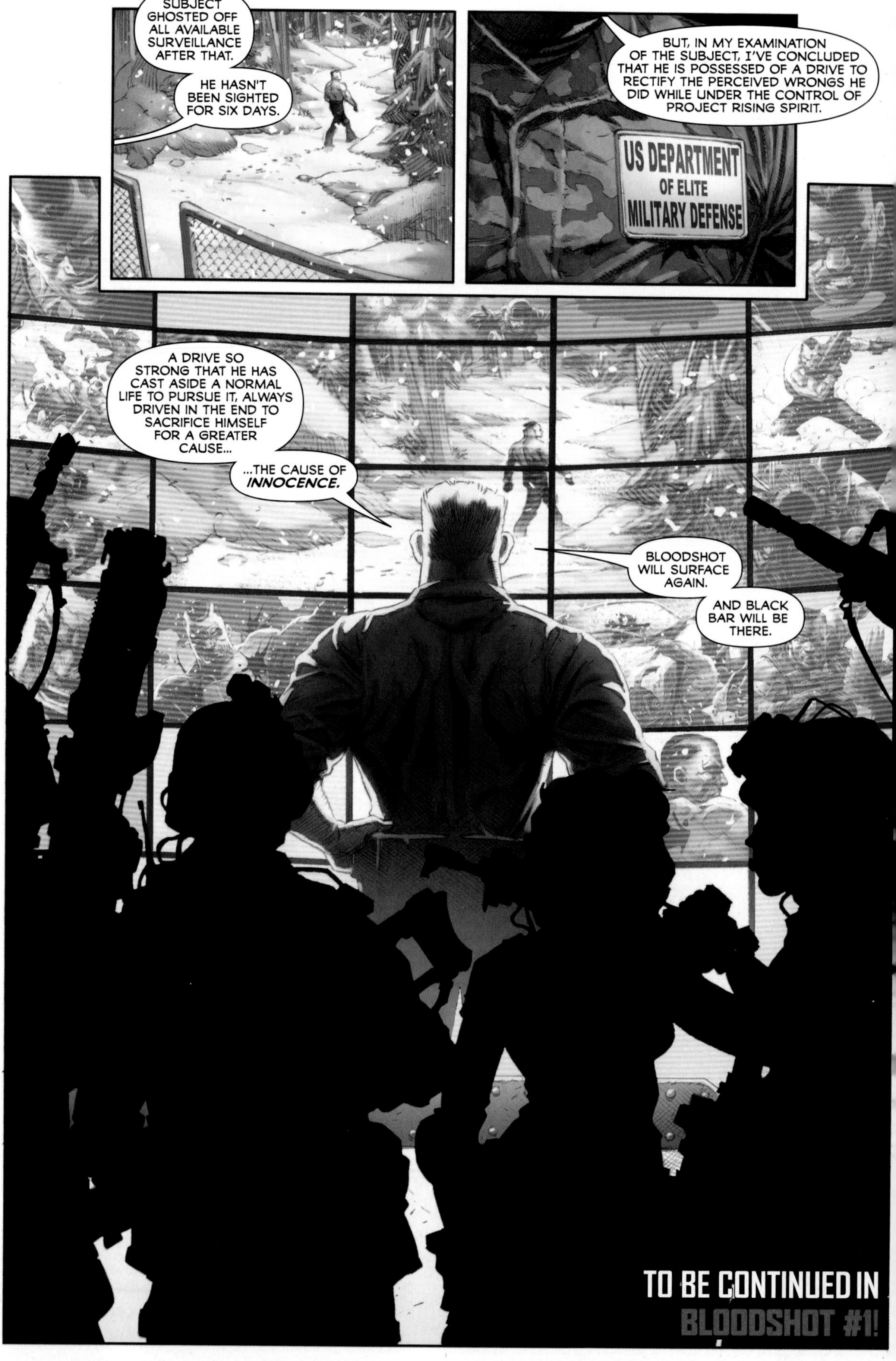
SUBJECT GHOSTED OFF ALL AVAILABLE SURVEILLANCE AFTER THAT.
HE HASN'T BEEN SIGHTED FOR SIX DAYS.
BUT, IN MY EXAMINATION OF THE SUBJECT, I'VE CONCLUDED THAT HE IS POSSESSED OF A DRIVE TO RECTIFY THE PERCEIVED WRONGS HE DID WHILE UNDER THE CONTROL OF PROJECT RISING SPIRIT.
US DEPARTMENT OF ELITE MILITARY DEFENSE
A DRIVE SO STRONG THAT HE HAS CAST ASIDE A NORMAL LIFE TO PURSUE IT, ALWAYS DRIVEN IN THE END TO SACRIFICE HIMSELF FOR A GREATER CAUSE...
...THE CAUSE OF *INNOCENCE.*
BLOODSHOT WILL SURFACE AGAIN.
AND BLACK BAR WILL BE THERE.
TO BE CONTINUED IN
BLOODSHOT #1!

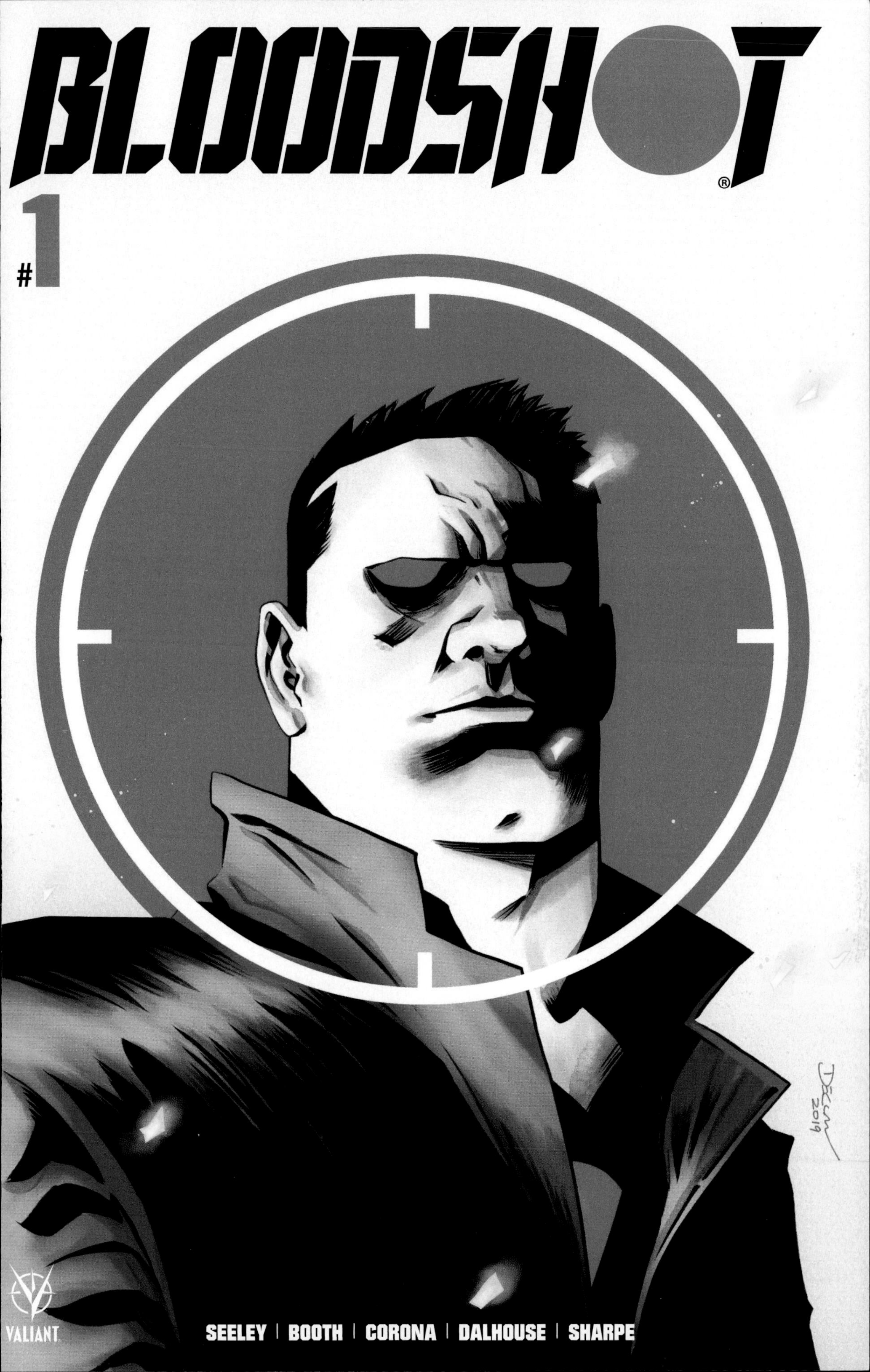
BLOODSHOT®
#1
VALIANT
SEELEY | BOOTH | CORONA | DALHOUSE | SHARPE

BLOODSHOT #1

WRITER: Tim Seeley
ARTIST: Brett Booth
INKER: Adelso Corona
COLORS: Andrew Dalhouse
LETTERS: Dave Sharpe
COVER ARTIST: Declan Shalvey
ASSISTANT EDITOR: Drew Baumgartner
EDITOR: Lysa Hawkins

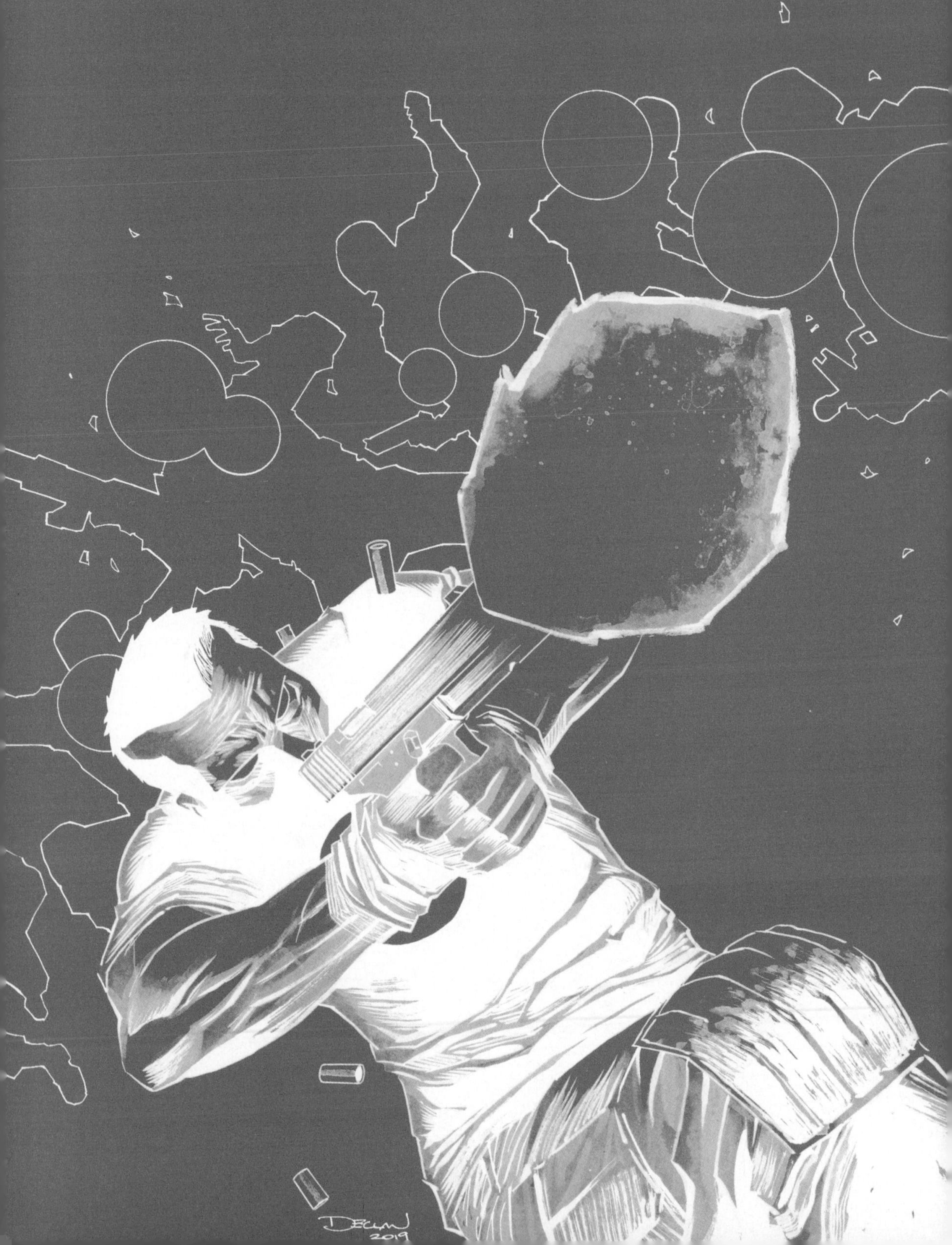
DECLAN
2019

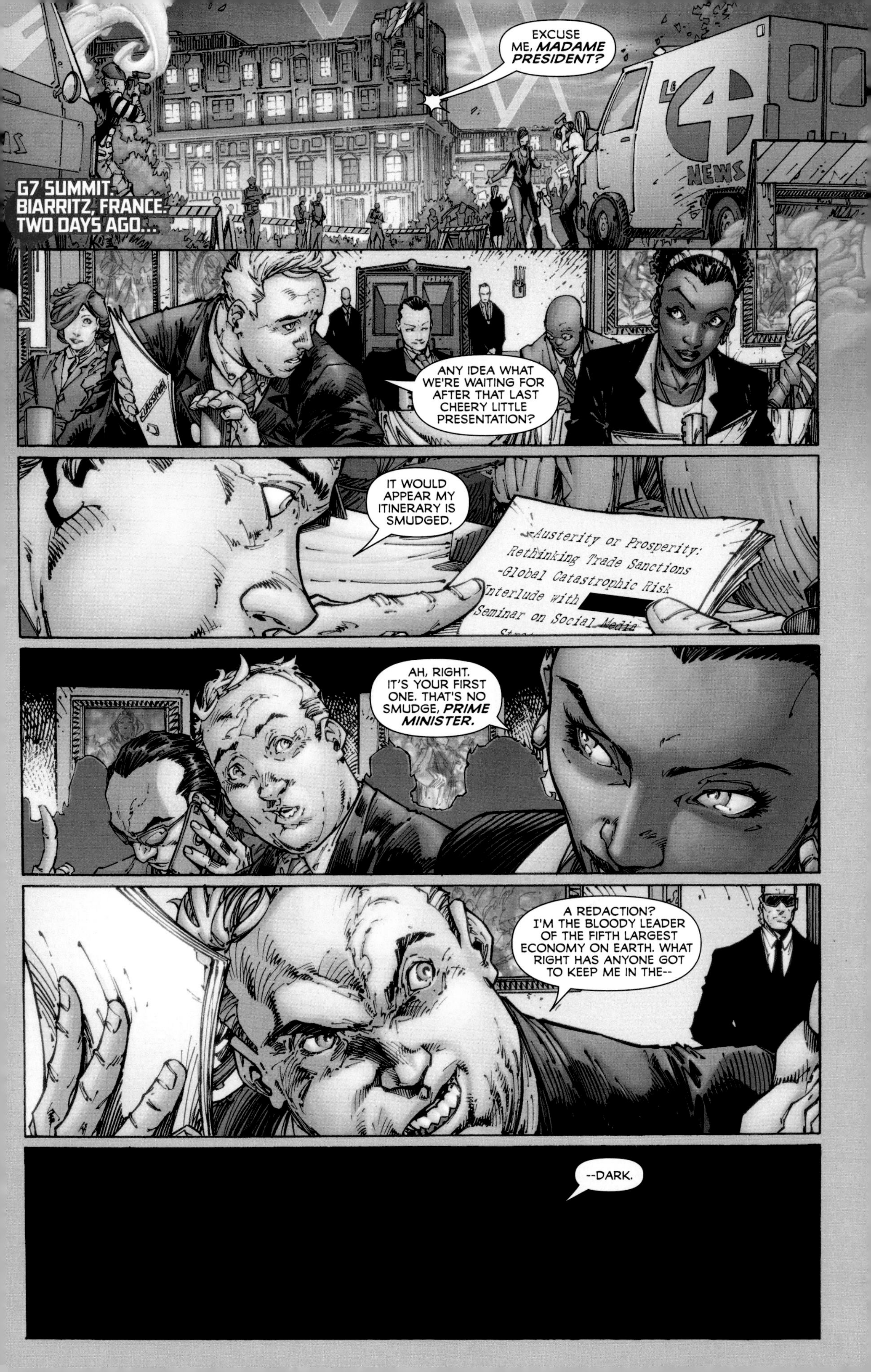
G7 SUMMIT.
BIARRITZ, FRANCE.
TWO DAYS AGO...
EXCUSE ME, *MADAME PRESIDENT?*
NEWS
ANY IDEA WHAT WE'RE WAITING FOR AFTER THAT LAST CHEERY LITTLE PRESENTATION?
IT WOULD APPEAR MY ITINERARY IS SMUDGED.
-Austerity or Prosperity:
Rethinking Trade Sanctions
-Global Catastrophic Risk
Interlude with [redacted]
Seminar on Social Media
AH, RIGHT. IT'S YOUR FIRST ONE. THAT'S NO SMUDGE, *PRIME MINISTER.*
A REDACTION? I'M THE BLOODY LEADER OF THE FIFTH LARGEST ECONOMY ON EARTH. WHAT RIGHT HAS ANYONE GOT TO KEEP ME IN THE--
--DARK.

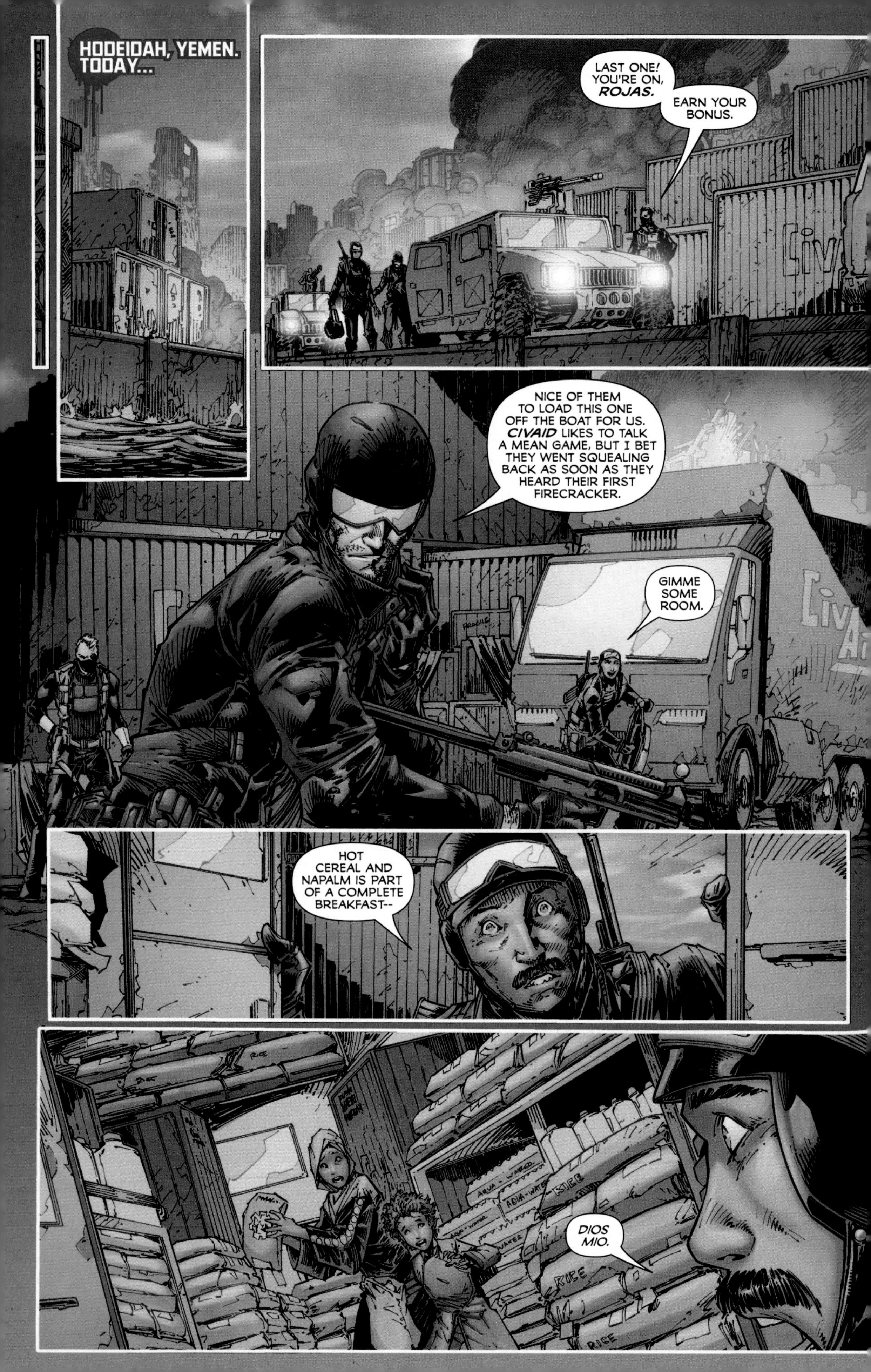
HODEIDAH, YEMEN. TODAY...
LAST ONE! YOU'RE ON, *ROJAS.*
EARN YOUR BONUS.
NICE OF THEM TO LOAD THIS ONE OFF THE BOAT FOR US. *CIVAID* LIKES TO TALK A MEAN GAME, BUT I BET THEY WENT SQUEALING BACK AS SOON AS THEY HEARD THEIR FIRST FIRECRACKER.
GIMME SOME ROOM.
HOT CEREAL AND NAPALM IS PART OF A COMPLETE BREAKFAST--
DIOS MIO.

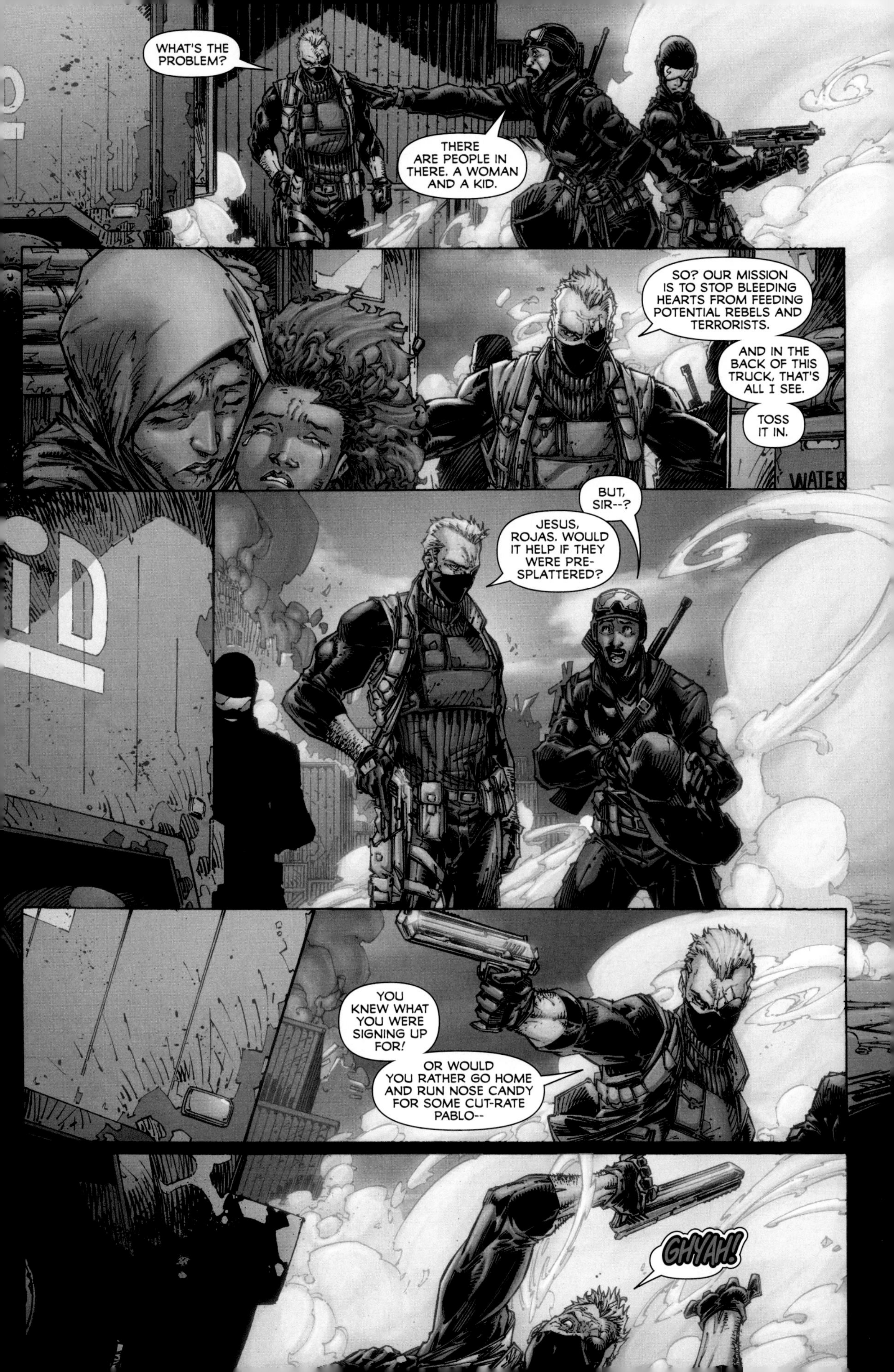
WHAT'S THE PROBLEM?
THERE ARE PEOPLE IN THERE. A WOMAN AND A KID.
SO? OUR MISSION IS TO STOP BLEEDING HEARTS FROM FEEDING POTENTIAL REBELS AND TERRORISTS.
AND IN THE BACK OF THIS TRUCK, THAT'S ALL I SEE.
TOSS IT IN.
WATER
BUT, SIR--?
JESUS, ROJAS. WOULD IT HELP IF THEY WERE PRE-SPLATTERED?
YOU KNEW WHAT YOU WERE SIGNING UP FOR!
OR WOULD YOU RATHER GO HOME AND RUN NOSE CANDY FOR SOME CUT-RATE PABLO--
GHYAH!

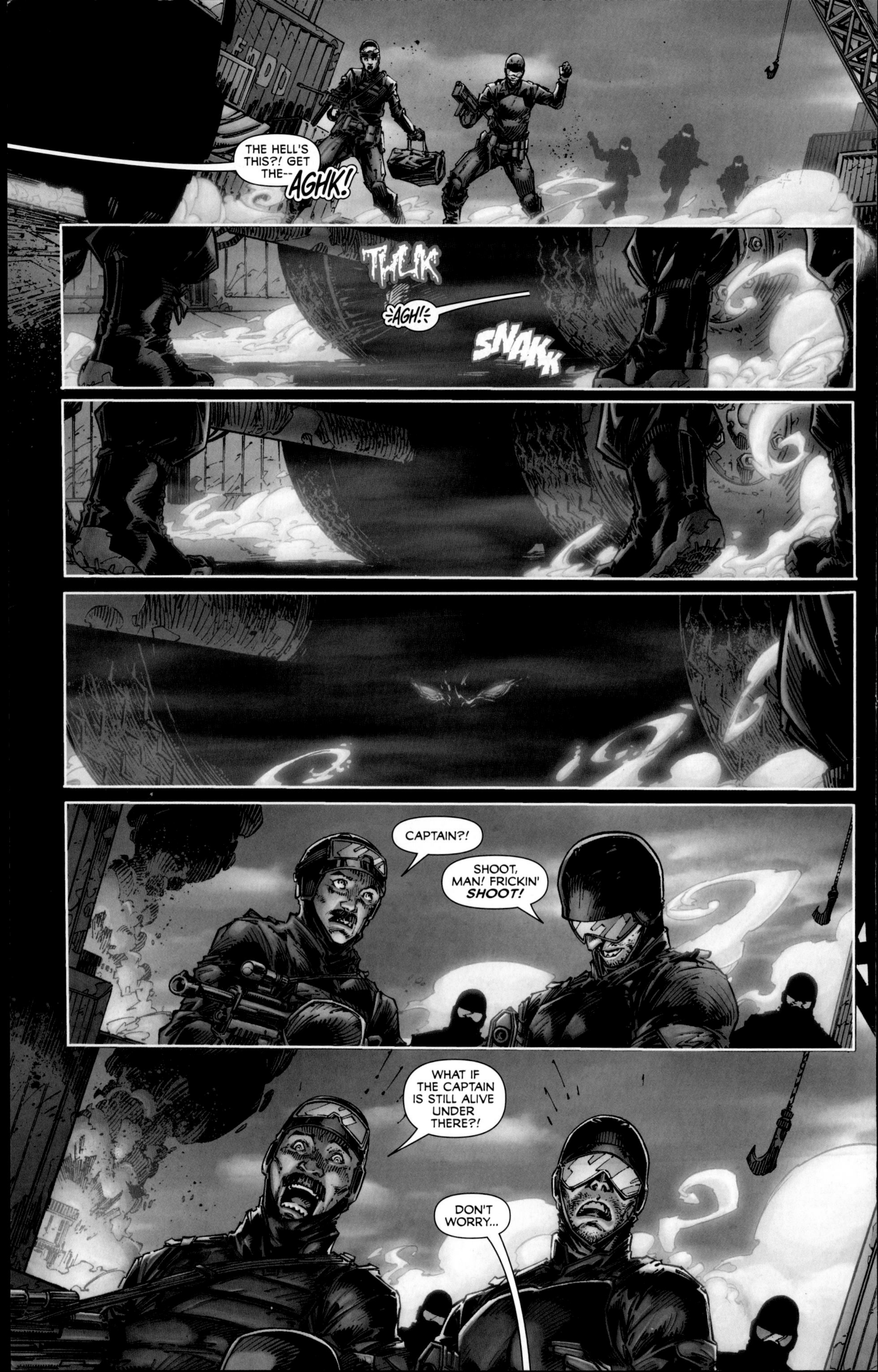
THE HELL'S THIS?! GET THE-- AGHK!
THUK
AGH!
SNAKK
CAPTAIN?!
SHOOT, MAN! FRICKIN' SHOOT!
WHAT IF THE CAPTAIN IS STILL ALIVE UNDER THERE?!
DON'T WORRY...

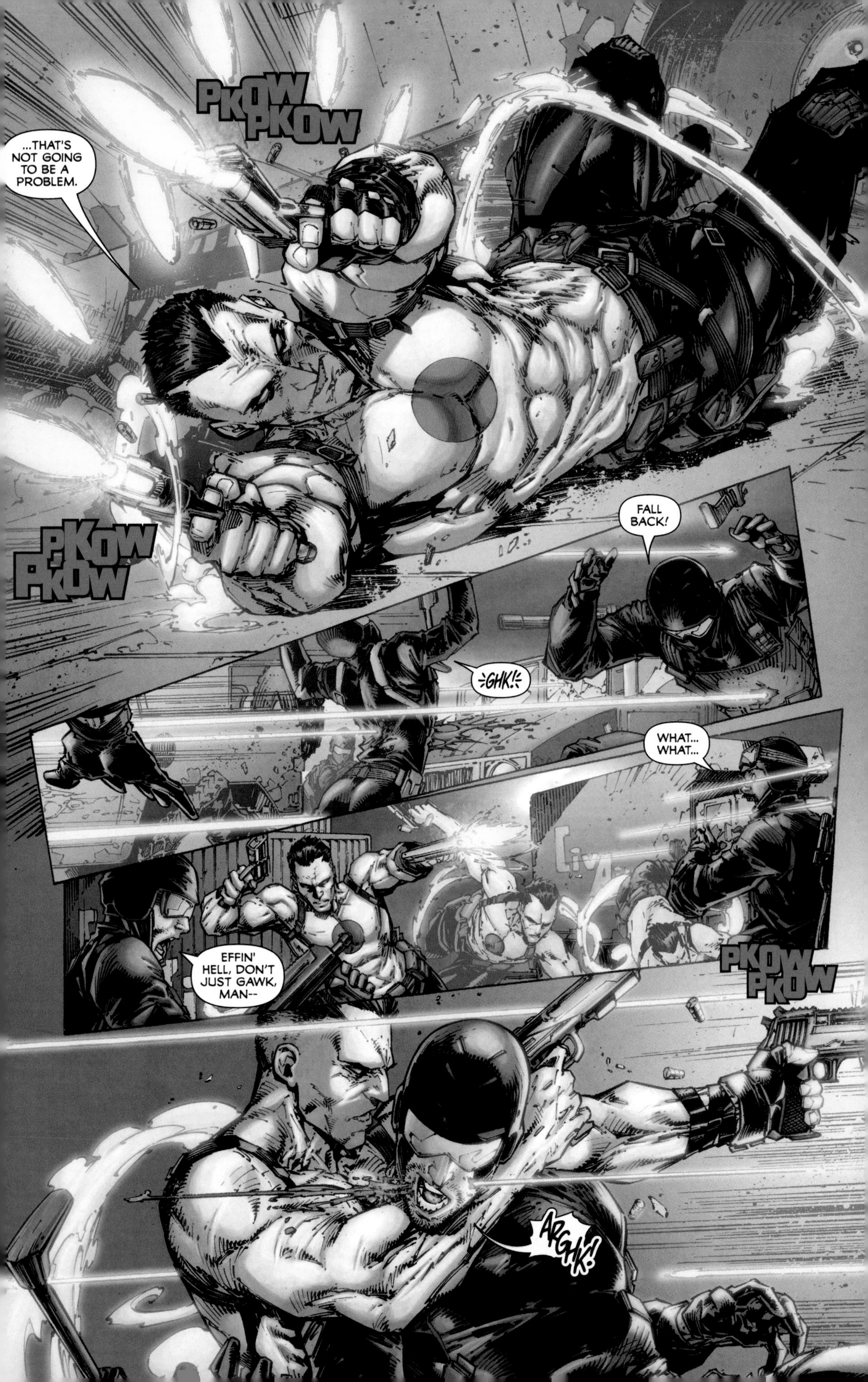
PKOW PKOW
...THAT'S NOT GOING TO BE A PROBLEM.
PKOW PKOW
FALL BACK!
GHK!
WHAT... WHAT...
EFFIN' HELL, DON'T JUST GAWK, MAN--
PKOW PKOW
ARGHK!

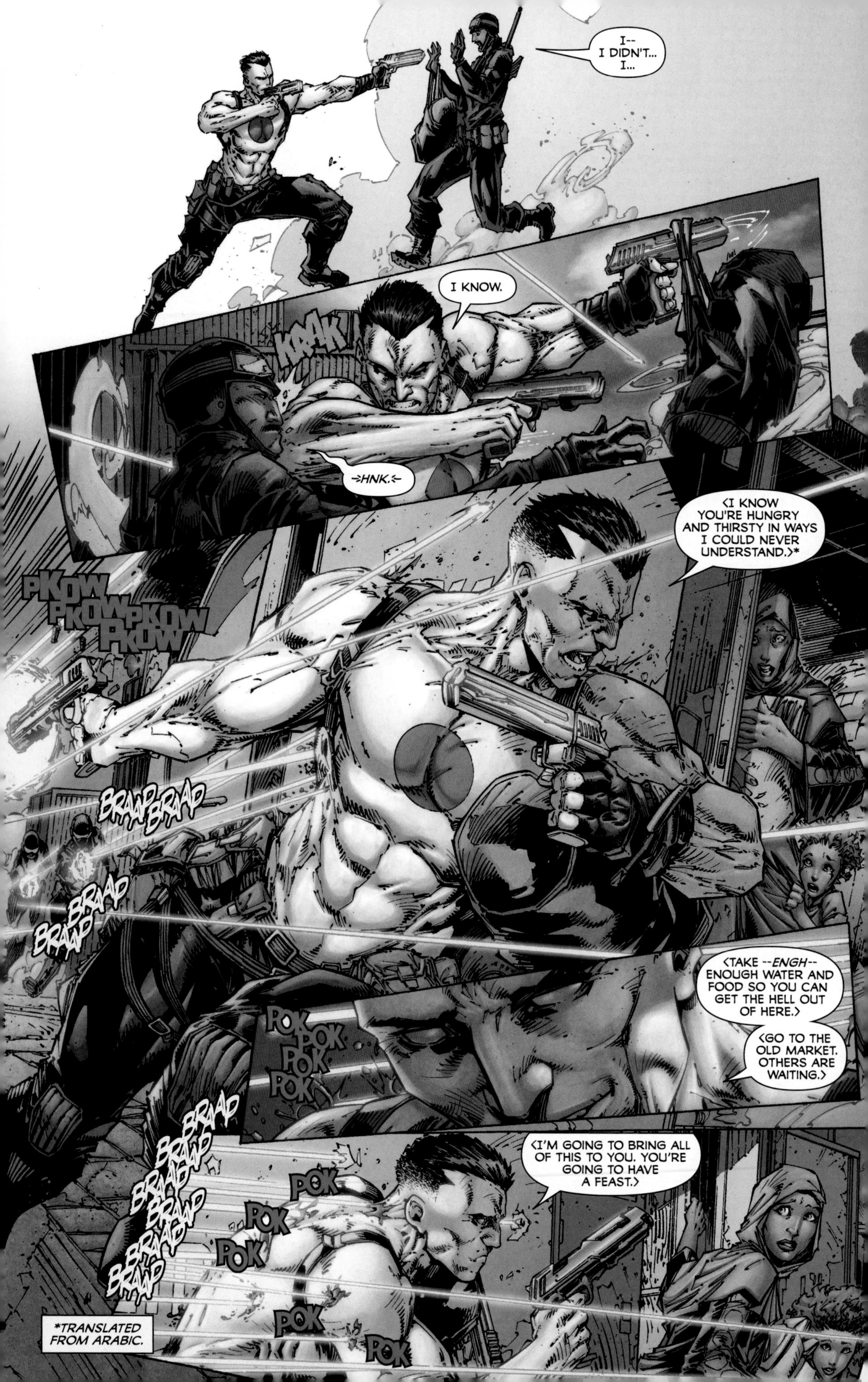

I-- I DIDN'T... I...
I KNOW.
KRAK
HNK.
<I KNOW YOU'RE HUNGRY AND THIRSTY IN WAYS I COULD NEVER UNDERSTAND.>*
PKOW PKOW PKOW PKOW
BRAAP BRAAP
BRAAP BRAAP
<TAKE --ENGH-- ENOUGH WATER AND FOOD SO YOU CAN GET THE HELL OUT OF HERE.>
<GO TO THE OLD MARKET. OTHERS ARE WAITING.>
POK POK POK POK
<I'M GOING TO BRING ALL OF THIS TO YOU. YOU'RE GOING TO HAVE A FEAST.>
BRAAP BRAAP BRAAP BRAAP BRAAP BRAAP
POK POK POK POK POK
*TRANSLATED FROM ARABIC.

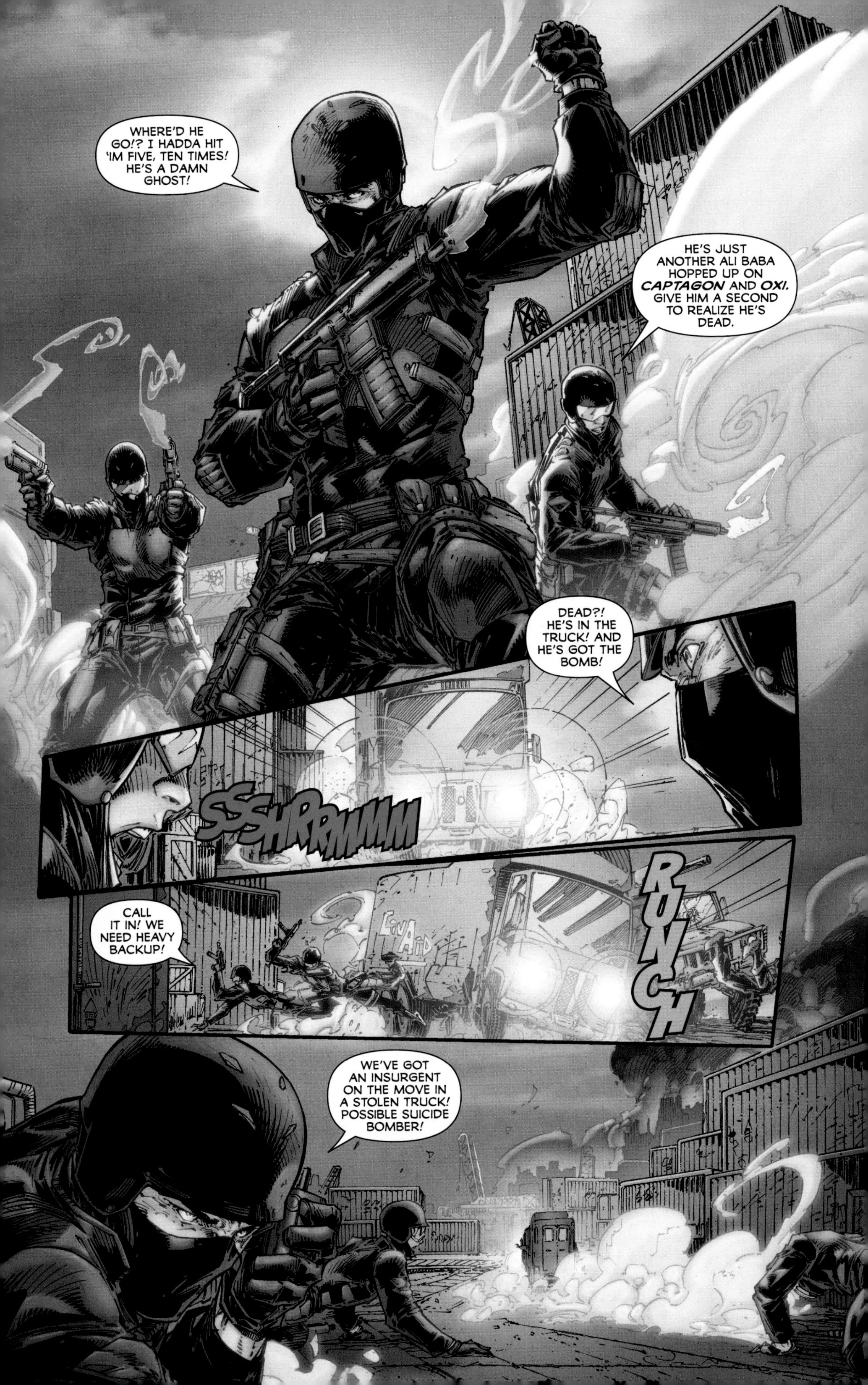
WHERE'D HE GO!? I HADDA HIT 'IM FIVE, TEN TIMES! HE'S A DAMN GHOST!
HE'S JUST ANOTHER ALI BABA HOPPED UP ON CAPTAGON AND OXI. GIVE HIM A SECOND TO REALIZE HE'S DEAD.
DEAD?! HE'S IN THE TRUCK! AND HE'S GOT THE BOMB!
SSSHRRMMMM
CALL IT IN! WE NEED HEAVY BACKUP!
RUNCH
WE'VE GOT AN INSURGENT ON THE MOVE IN A STOLEN TRUCK! POSSIBLE SUICIDE BOMBER!

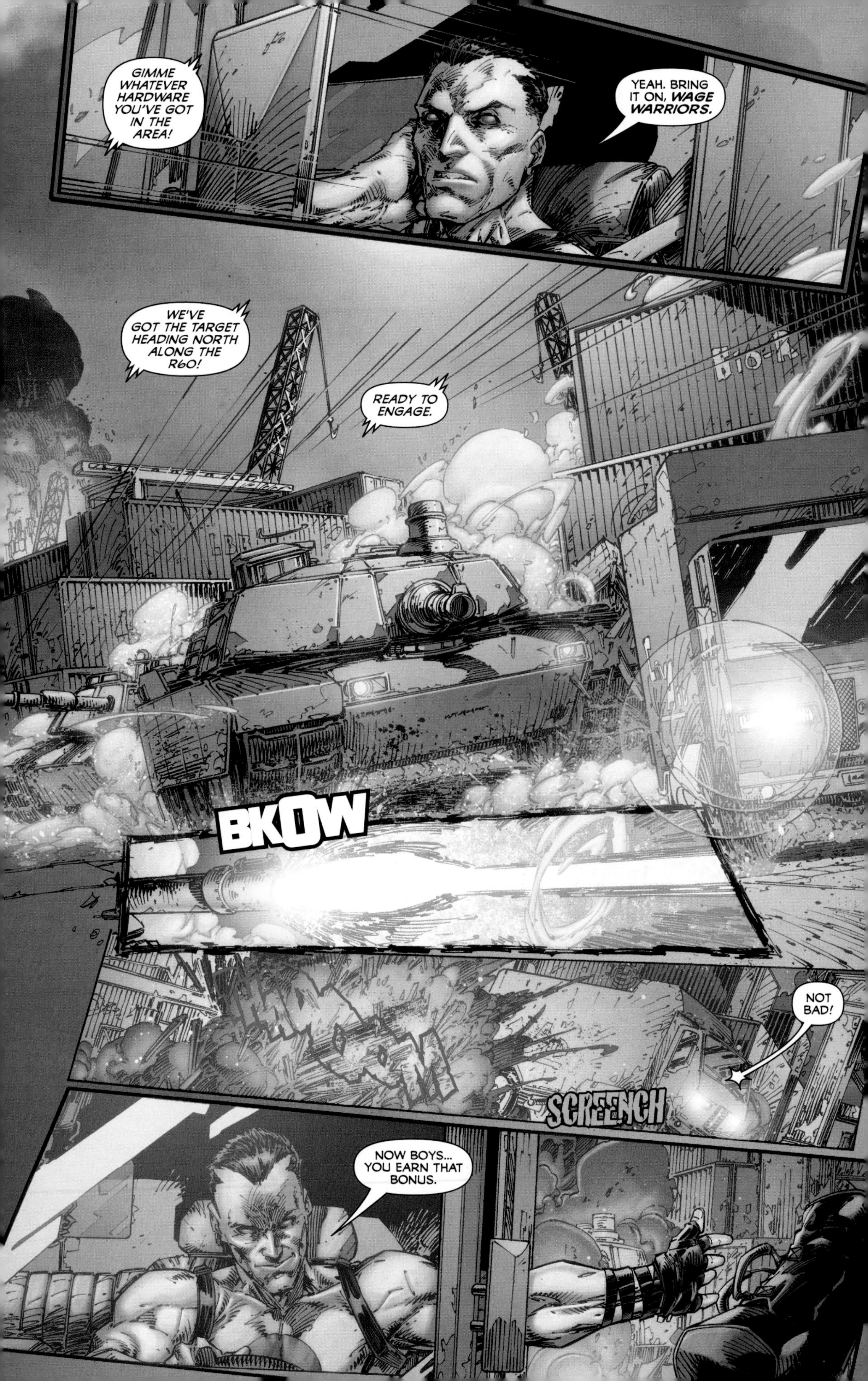

GIMME WHATEVER HARDWARE YOU'VE GOT IN THE AREA!
YEAH. BRING IT ON, *WAGE WARRIORS.*
WE'VE GOT THE TARGET HEADING NORTH ALONG THE R60!
READY TO ENGAGE.
BKOW
NOT BAD!
SCREENCH
NOW BOYS... YOU EARN THAT BONUS.

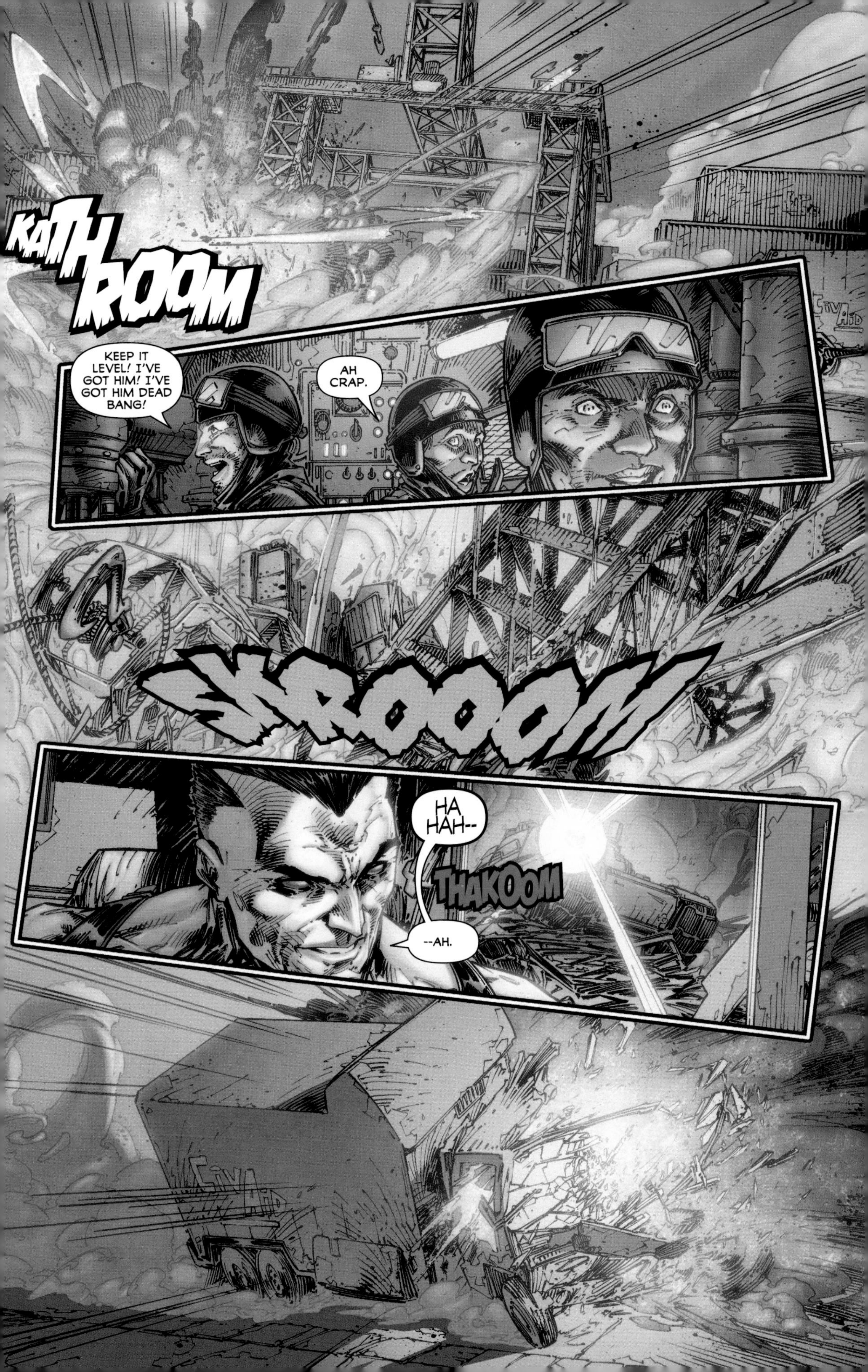
KATH
ROOM
KEEP IT LEVEL! I'VE GOT HIM! I'VE GOT HIM DEAD BANG!
AH CRAP.
SKROOOM
HA HAH--
THAKOOM
--AH.

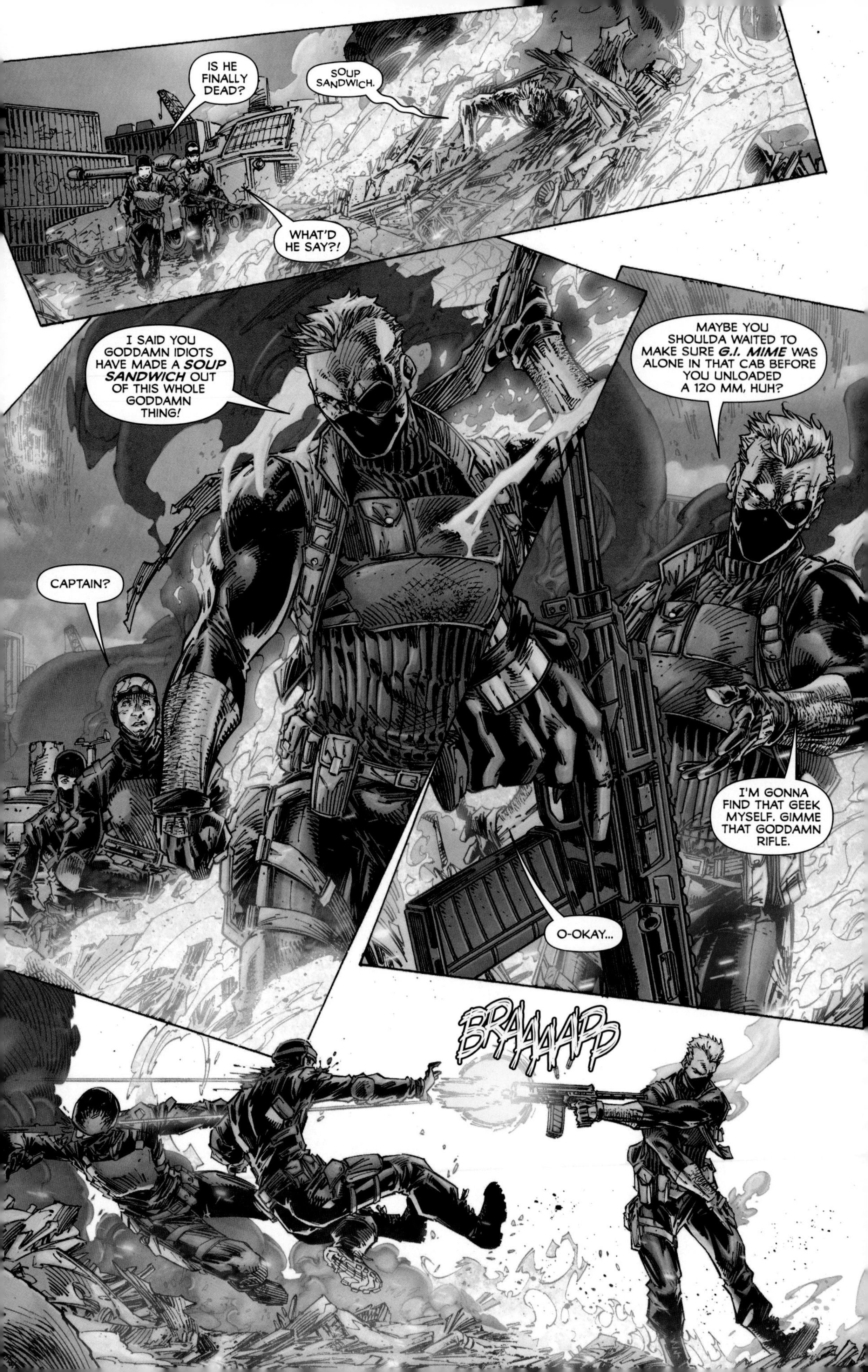
IS HE FINALLY DEAD?
SOUP SANDWICH.
WHAT'D HE SAY?!
I SAID YOU GODDAMN IDIOTS HAVE MADE A *SOUP SANDWICH* OUT OF THIS WHOLE GODDAMN THING!
MAYBE YOU SHOULDA WAITED TO MAKE SURE *G.I. MIME* WAS ALONE IN THAT CAB BEFORE YOU UNLOADED A 120 MM, HUH?
CAPTAIN?
I'M GONNA FIND THAT GEEK MYSELF. GIMME THAT GODDAMN RIFLE.
O-OKAY...
BRAAAAAPP

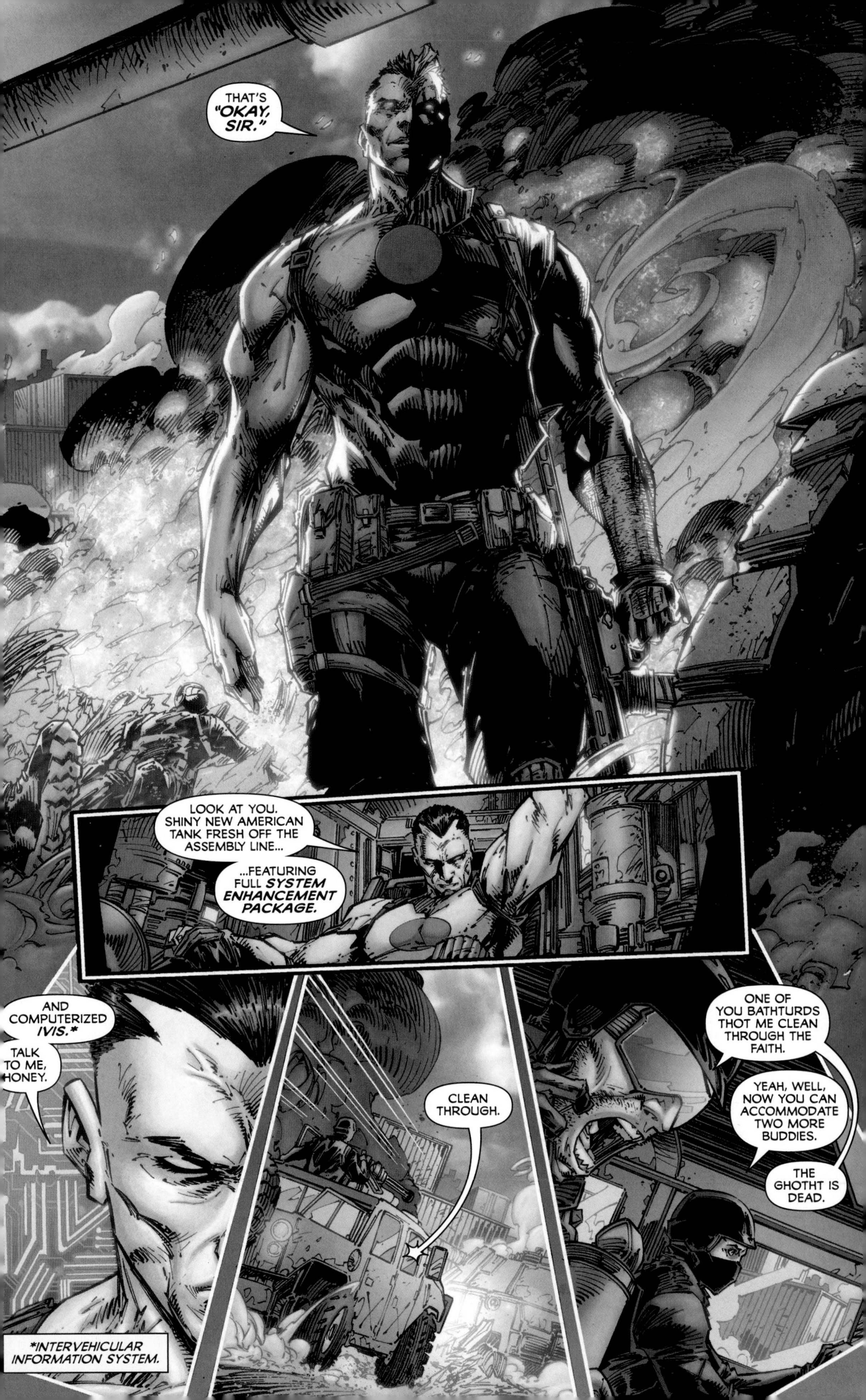
THAT'S "OKAY, SIR."
LOOK AT YOU. SHINY NEW AMERICAN TANK FRESH OFF THE ASSEMBLY LINE...
...FEATURING FULL SYSTEM ENHANCEMENT PACKAGE.
AND COMPUTERIZED IVIS.*
TALK TO ME, HONEY.
CLEAN THROUGH.
ONE OF YOU BATHTURDS THOT ME CLEAN THROUGH THE FAITH.
YEAH, WELL, NOW YOU CAN ACCOMMODATE TWO MORE BUDDIES.
THE GHOTHT IS DEAD.
*INTERVEHICULAR INFORMATION SYSTEM.

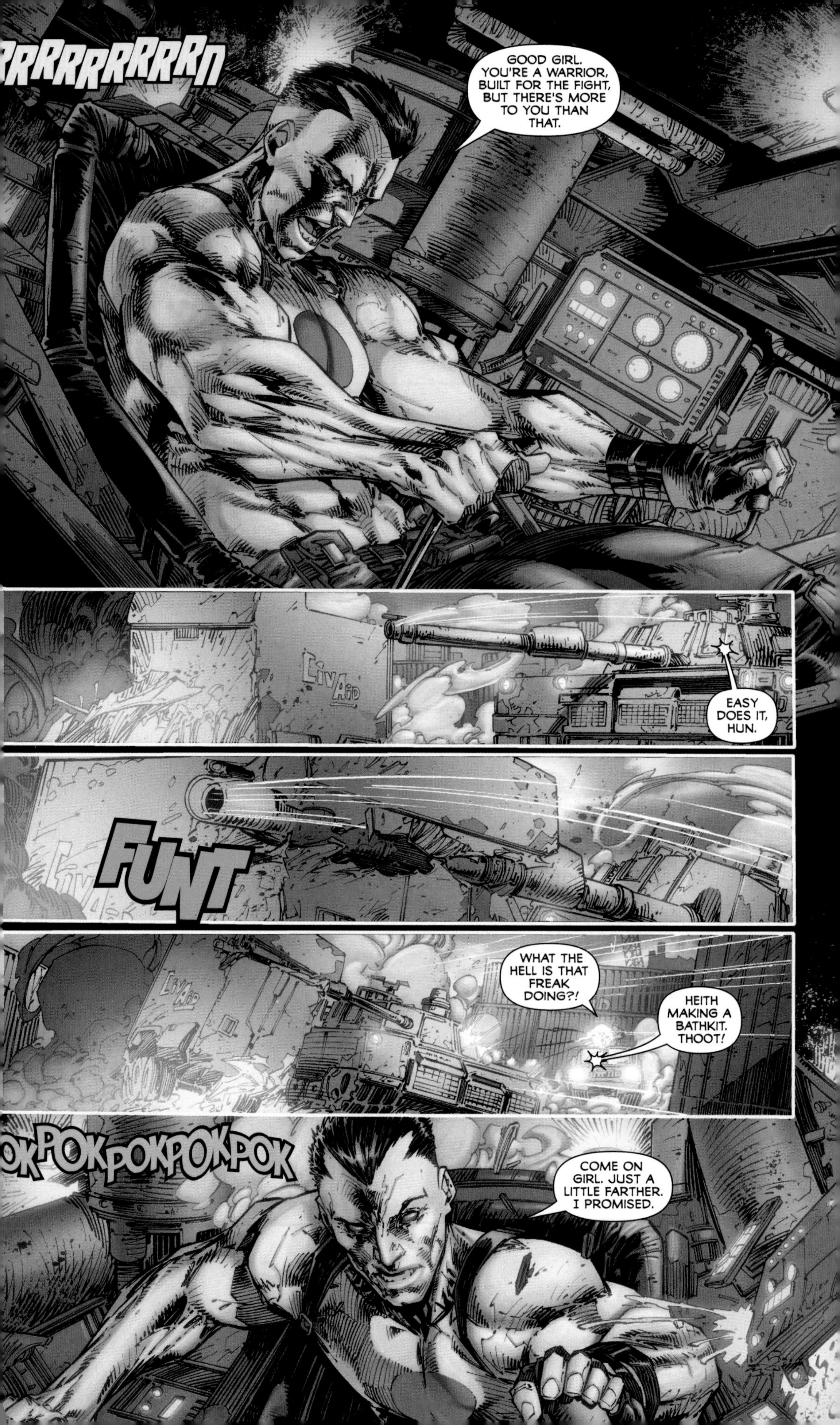
RRRRRRRRRRn
GOOD GIRL. YOU'RE A WARRIOR, BUILT FOR THE FIGHT, BUT THERE'S MORE TO YOU THAN THAT.
CIV AID
EASY DOES IT, HUN.
FUNT
WHAT THE HELL IS THAT FREAK DOING?!
HEITH MAKING A BATHKIT. THOOT!
OKPOKPOKPOKPOK
COME ON GIRL. JUST A LITTLE FARTHER. I PROMISED.

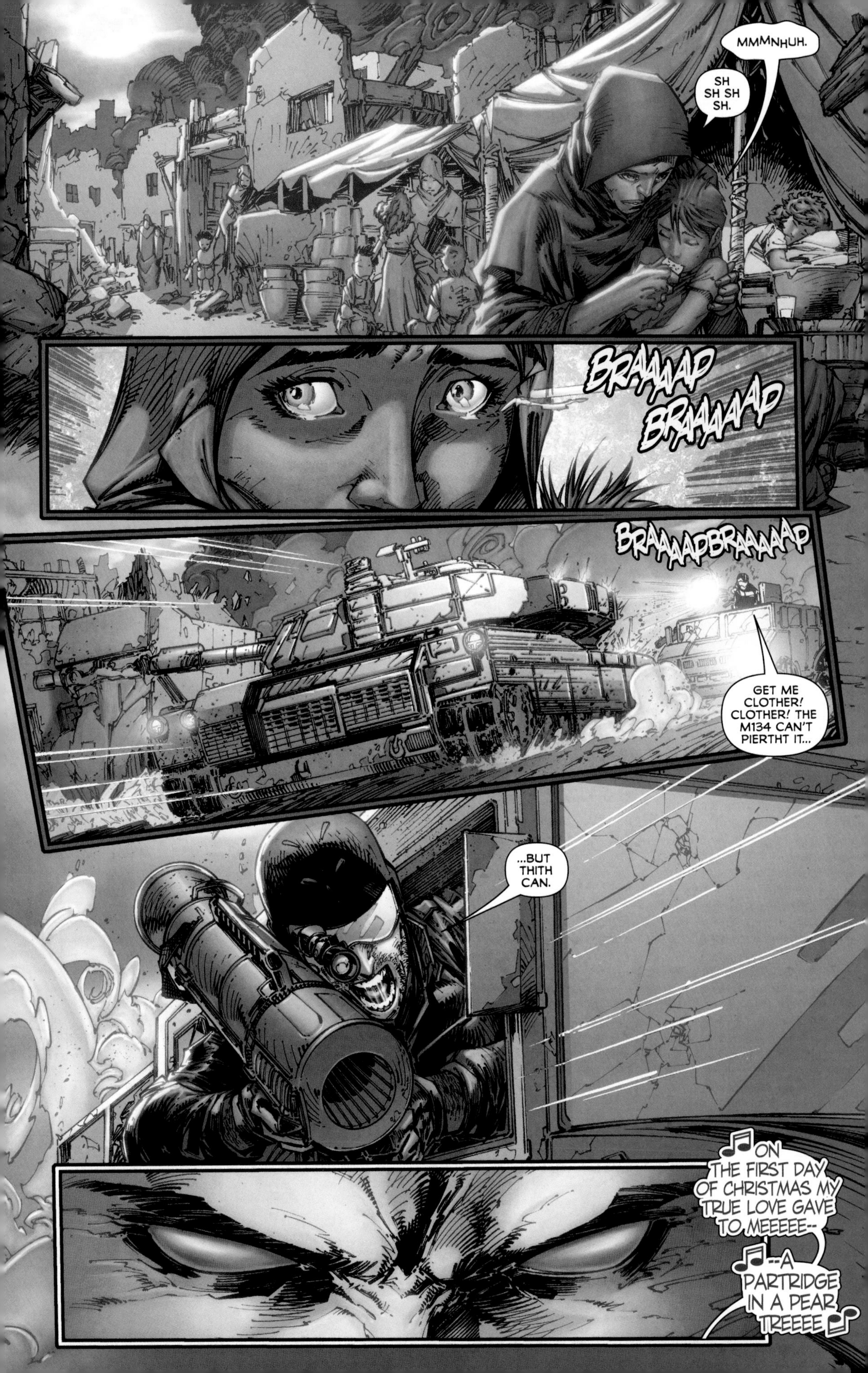

SH SH SH SH.
MMMNHUH.
BRAAAAP
BRAAAAAAP
BRAAAAPBRAAAAAP
GET ME CLOTHER! CLOTHER! THE M134 CAN'T PIERTHT IT...
...BUT THITH CAN.
ON THE FIRST DAY OF CHRISTMAS MY TRUE LOVE GAVE TO MEEEEE--
--A PARTRIDGE IN A PEAR TREEEE

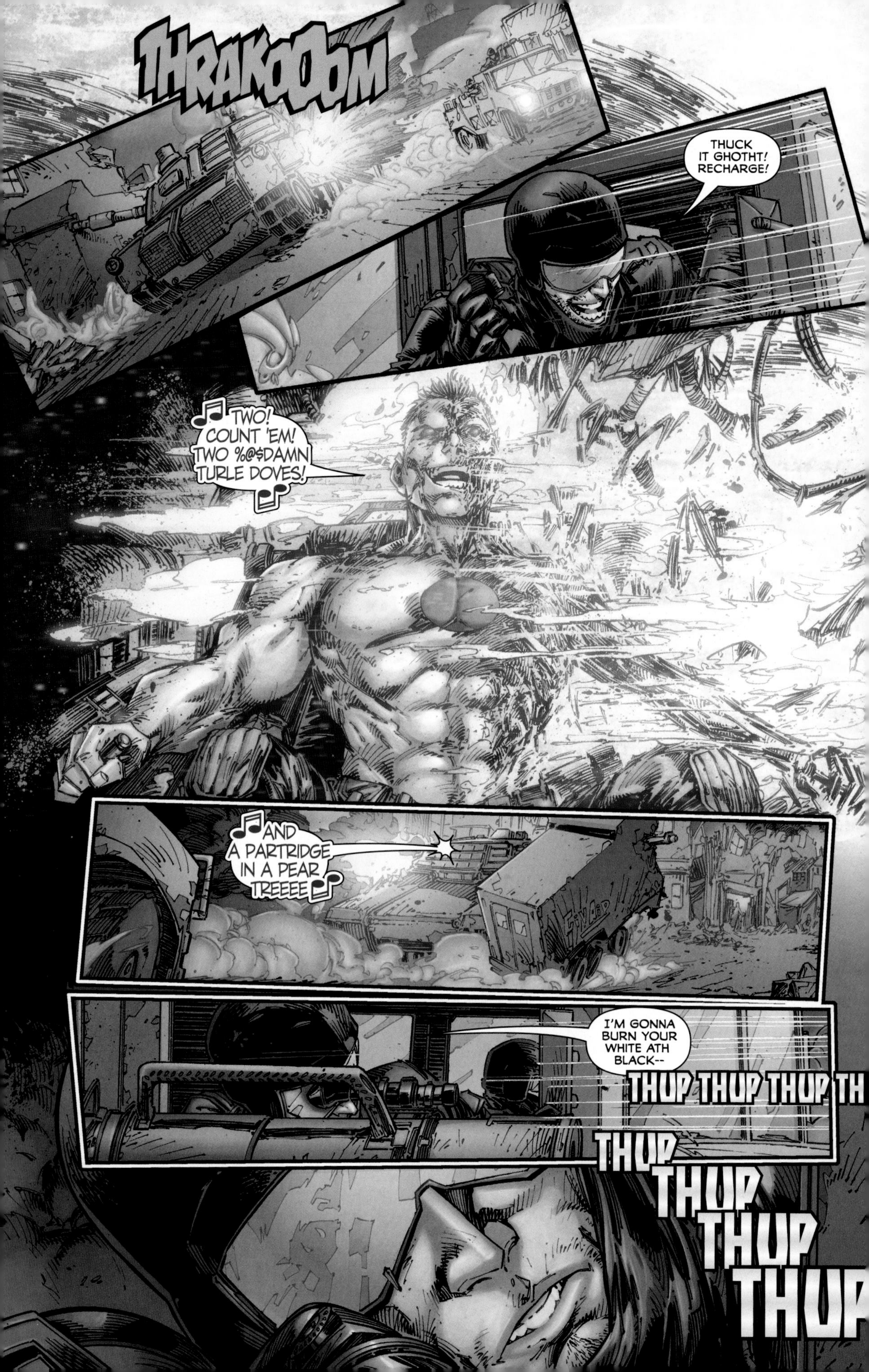
THRAKOOOM
THUCK IT GHOTHT! RECHARGE!
TWO! COUNT 'EM! TWO %@$DAMN TURLE DOVES!
AND A PARTRIDGE IN A PEAR TREEEE
I'M GONNA BURN YOUR WHITE ATH BLACK--
THUP THUP THUP TH
THUP
THUP
THUP
THUP

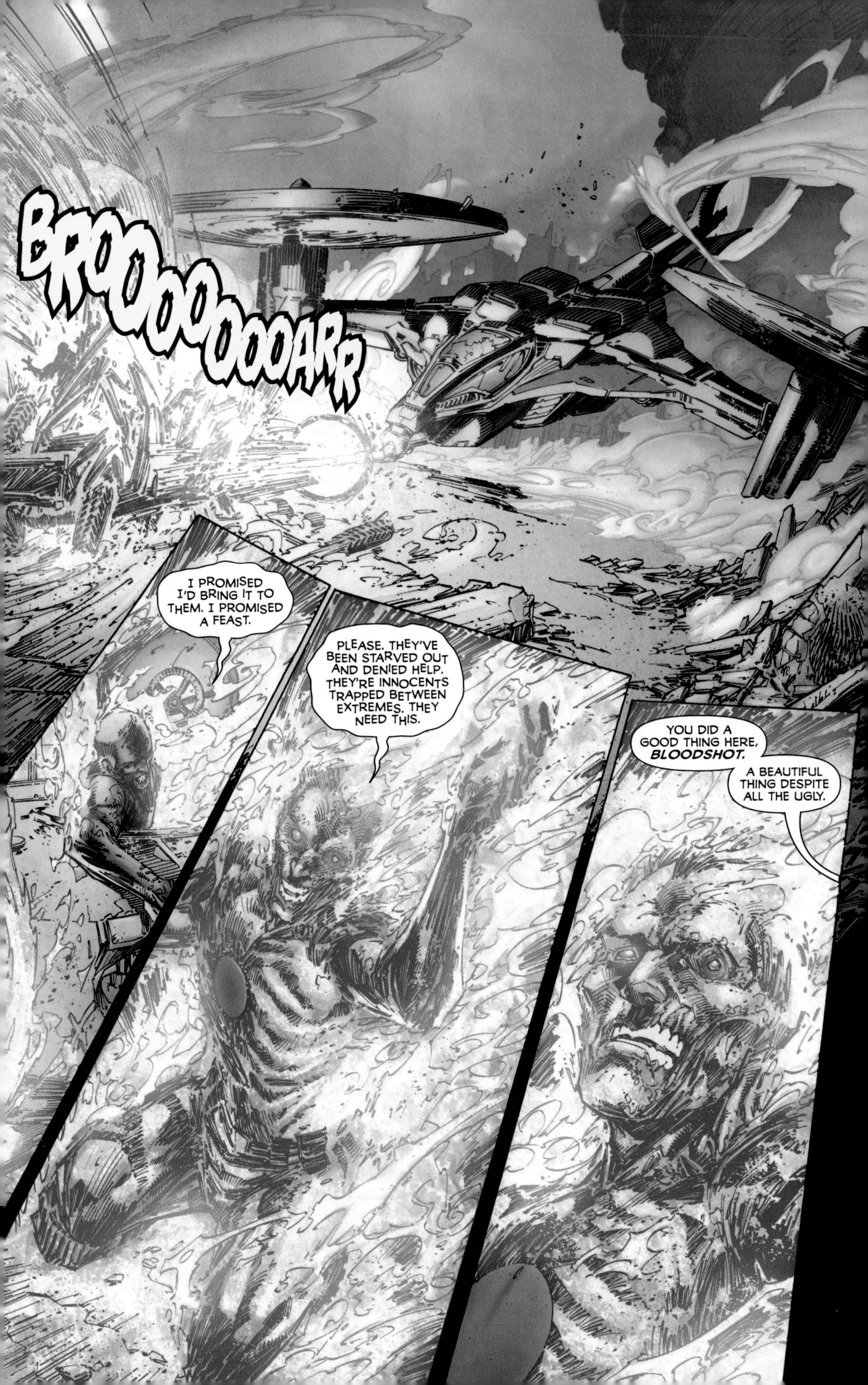
BROOOOOOOOARR
I PROMISED I'D BRING IT TO THEM. I PROMISED A FEAST.
PLEASE. THEY'VE BEEN STARVED OUT AND DENIED HELP. THEY'RE INNOCENTS TRAPPED BETWEEN EXTREMES. THEY NEED THIS.
YOU DID A GOOD THING HERE, *BLOODSHOT.*
A BEAUTIFUL THING DESPITE ALL THE UGLY.

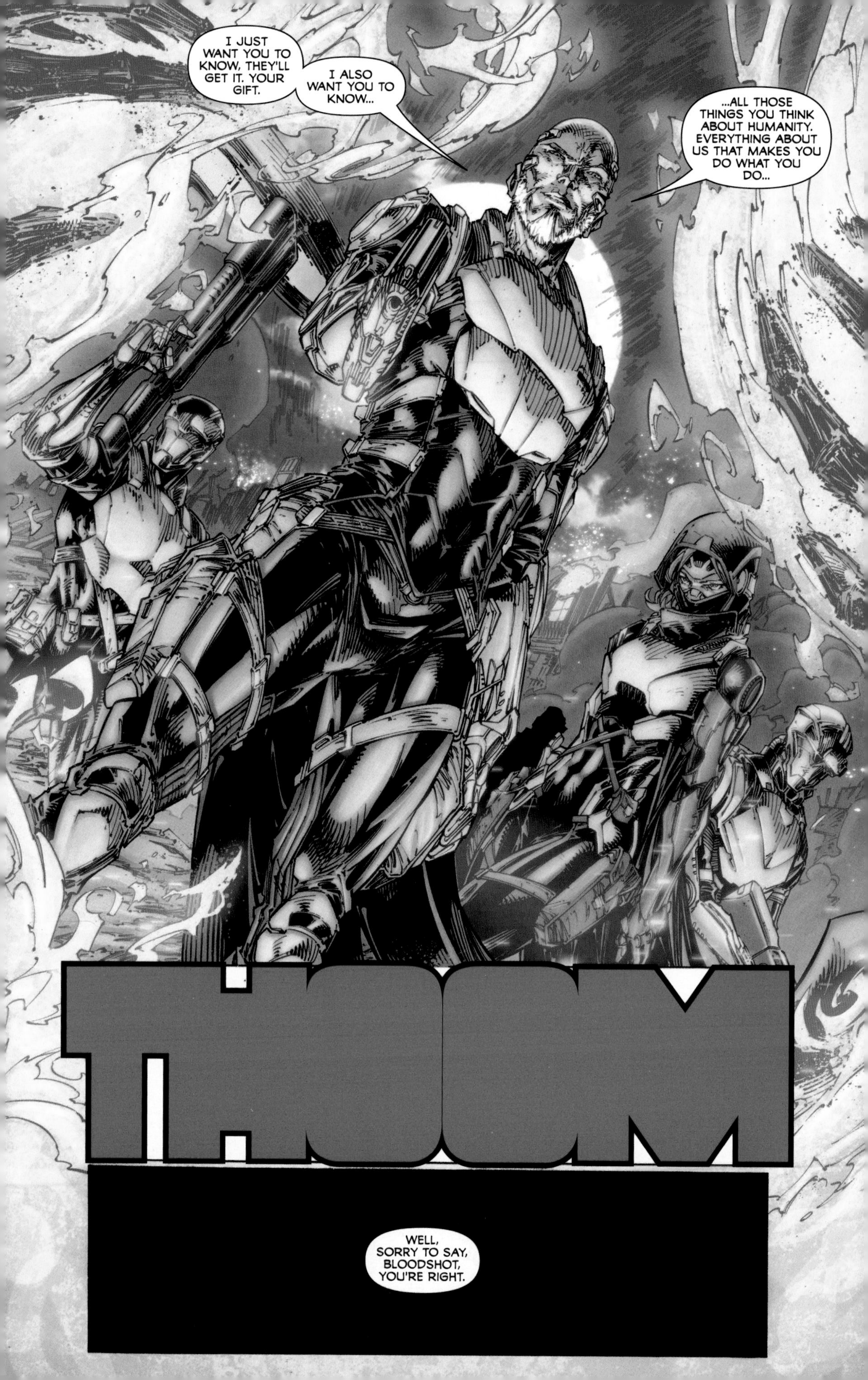
I JUST WANT YOU TO KNOW, THEY'LL GET IT. YOUR GIFT.
I ALSO WANT YOU TO KNOW...
...ALL THOSE THINGS YOU THINK ABOUT HUMANITY. EVERYTHING ABOUT US THAT MAKES YOU DO WHAT YOU DO...
THOOM
WELL, SORRY TO SAY, BLOODSHOT, YOU'RE RIGHT.

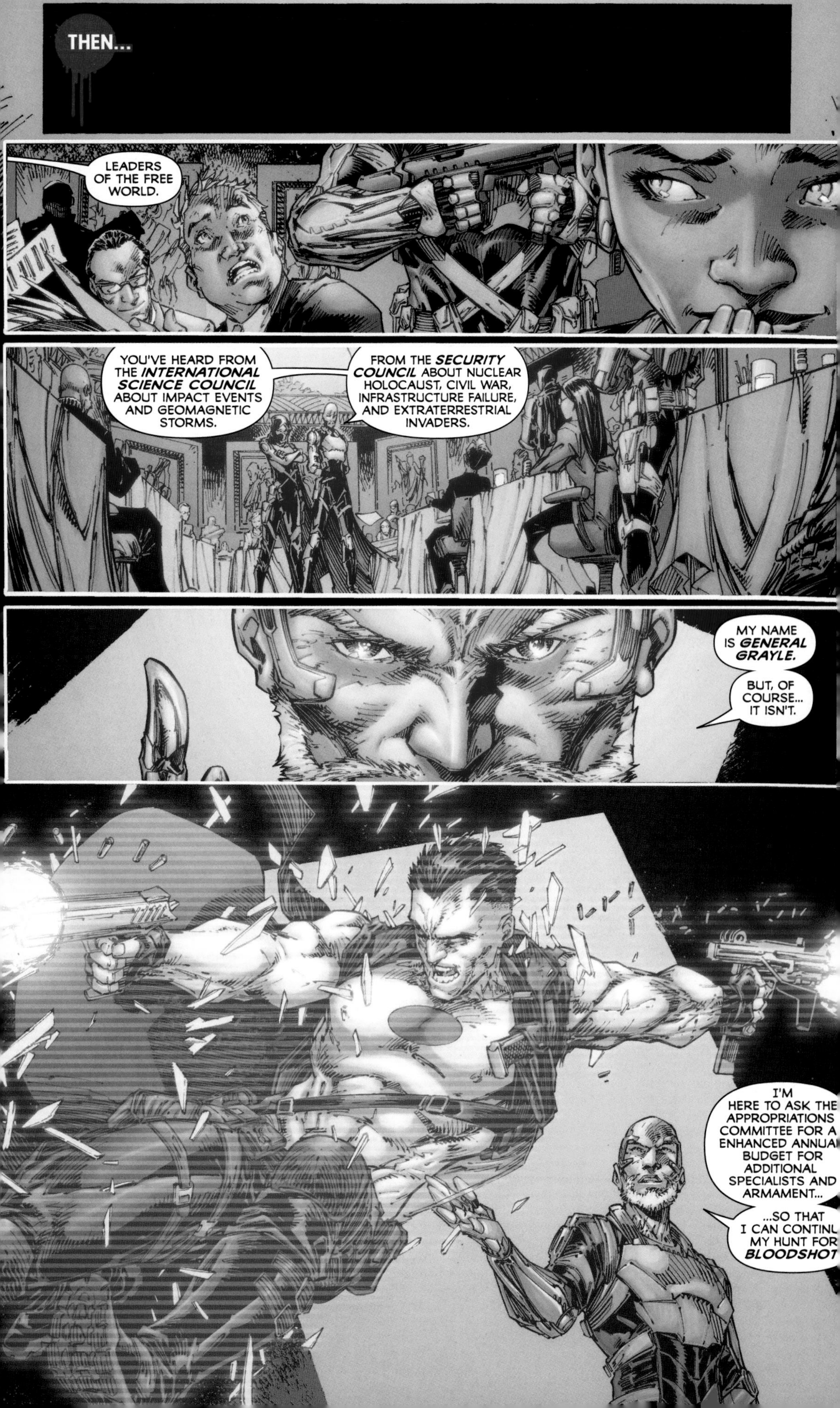
THEN...
LEADERS OF THE FREE WORLD.
YOU'VE HEARD FROM THE INTERNATIONAL SCIENCE COUNCIL ABOUT IMPACT EVENTS AND GEOMAGNETIC STORMS.
FROM THE SECURITY COUNCIL ABOUT NUCLEAR HOLOCAUST, CIVIL WAR, INFRASTRUCTURE FAILURE, AND EXTRATERRESTRIAL INVADERS.
MY NAME IS GENERAL GRAYLE.
BUT, OF COURSE... IT ISN'T.
I'M HERE TO ASK THE APPROPRIATIONS COMMITTEE FOR A ENHANCED ANNUA BUDGET FOR ADDITIONAL SPECIALISTS AND ARMAMENT...
...SO THAT I CAN CONTINU MY HUNT FOR BLOODSHOT

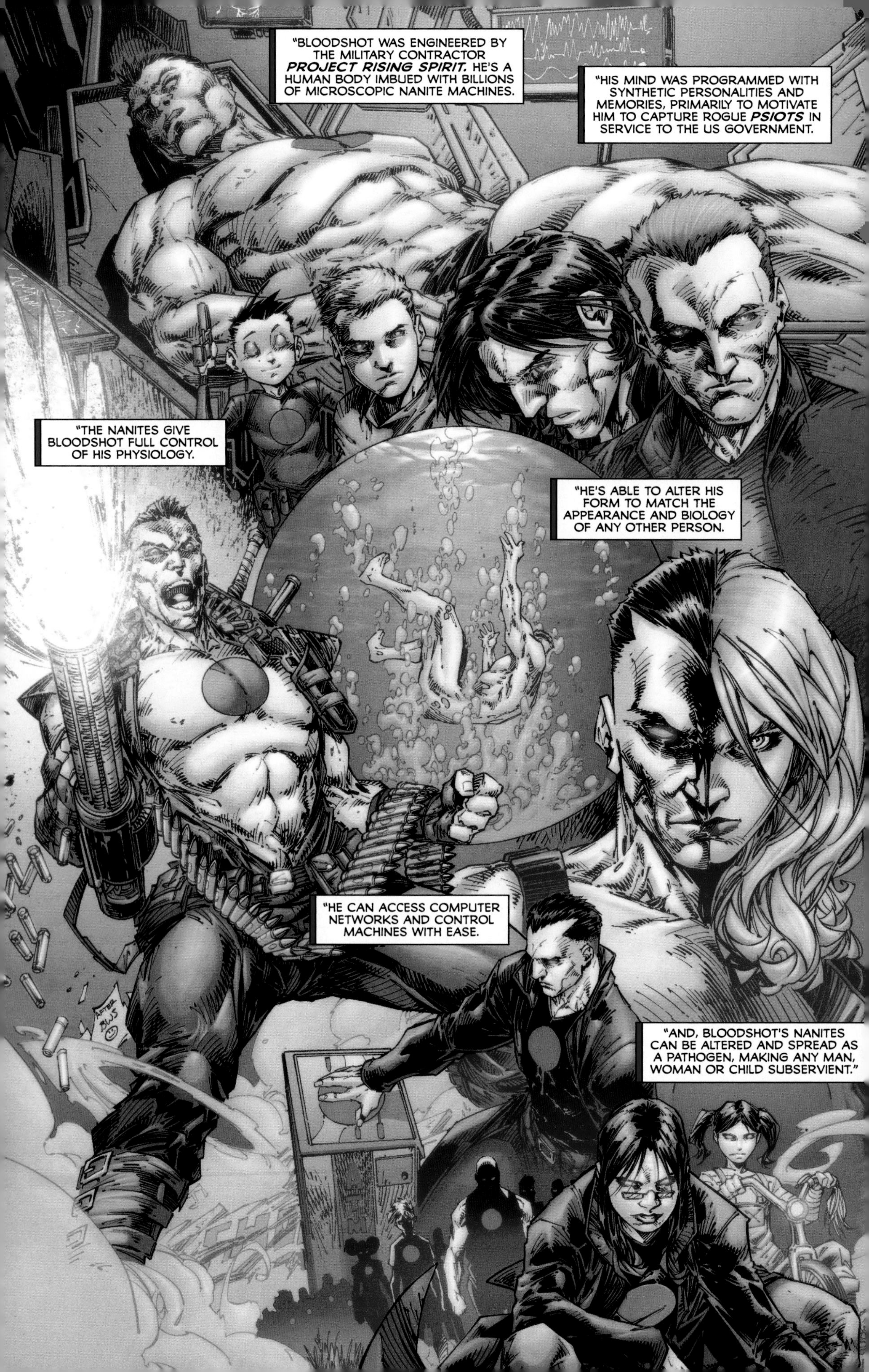
"BLOODSHOT WAS ENGINEERED BY THE MILITARY CONTRACTOR PROJECT RISING SPIRIT. HE'S A HUMAN BODY IMBUED WITH BILLIONS OF MICROSCOPIC NANITE MACHINES.
"HIS MIND WAS PROGRAMMED WITH SYNTHETIC PERSONALITIES AND MEMORIES, PRIMARILY TO MOTIVATE HIM TO CAPTURE ROGUE PSIOTS IN SERVICE TO THE US GOVERNMENT.
"THE NANITES GIVE BLOODSHOT FULL CONTROL OF HIS PHYSIOLOGY.
"HE'S ABLE TO ALTER HIS FORM TO MATCH THE APPEARANCE AND BIOLOGY OF ANY OTHER PERSON.
"HE CAN ACCESS COMPUTER NETWORKS AND CONTROL MACHINES WITH EASE.
"AND, BLOODSHOT'S NANITES CAN BE ALTERED AND SPREAD AS A PATHOGEN, MAKING ANY MAN, WOMAN OR CHILD SUBSERVIENT."

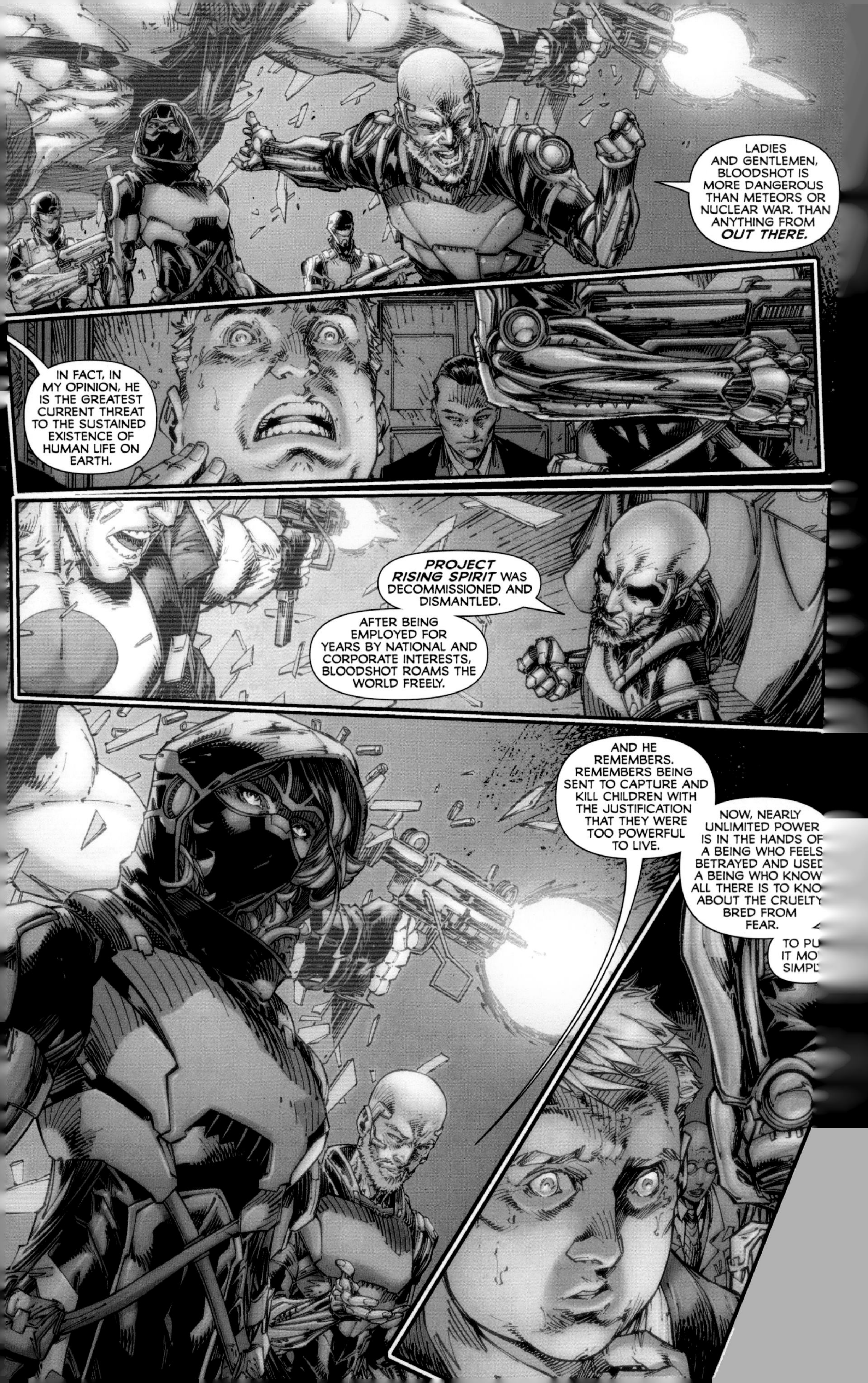

LADIES AND GENTLEMEN, BLOODSHOT IS MORE DANGEROUS THAN METEORS OR NUCLEAR WAR. THAN ANYTHING FROM *OUT THERE.*
IN FACT, IN MY OPINION, HE IS THE GREATEST CURRENT THREAT TO THE SUSTAINED EXISTENCE OF HUMAN LIFE ON EARTH.
PROJECT RISING SPIRIT WAS DECOMMISSIONED AND DISMANTLED.
AFTER BEING EMPLOYED FOR YEARS BY NATIONAL AND CORPORATE INTERESTS, BLOODSHOT ROAMS THE WORLD FREELY.
AND HE REMEMBERS. REMEMBERS BEING SENT TO CAPTURE AND KILL CHILDREN WITH THE JUSTIFICATION THAT THEY WERE TOO POWERFUL TO LIVE.
NOW, NEARLY UNLIMITED POWER IS IN THE HANDS OF A BEING WHO FEELS BETRAYED AND USED A BEING WHO KNOW ALL THERE IS TO KNO ABOUT THE CRUELTY BRED FROM FEAR.
TO PU IT MO SIMPL

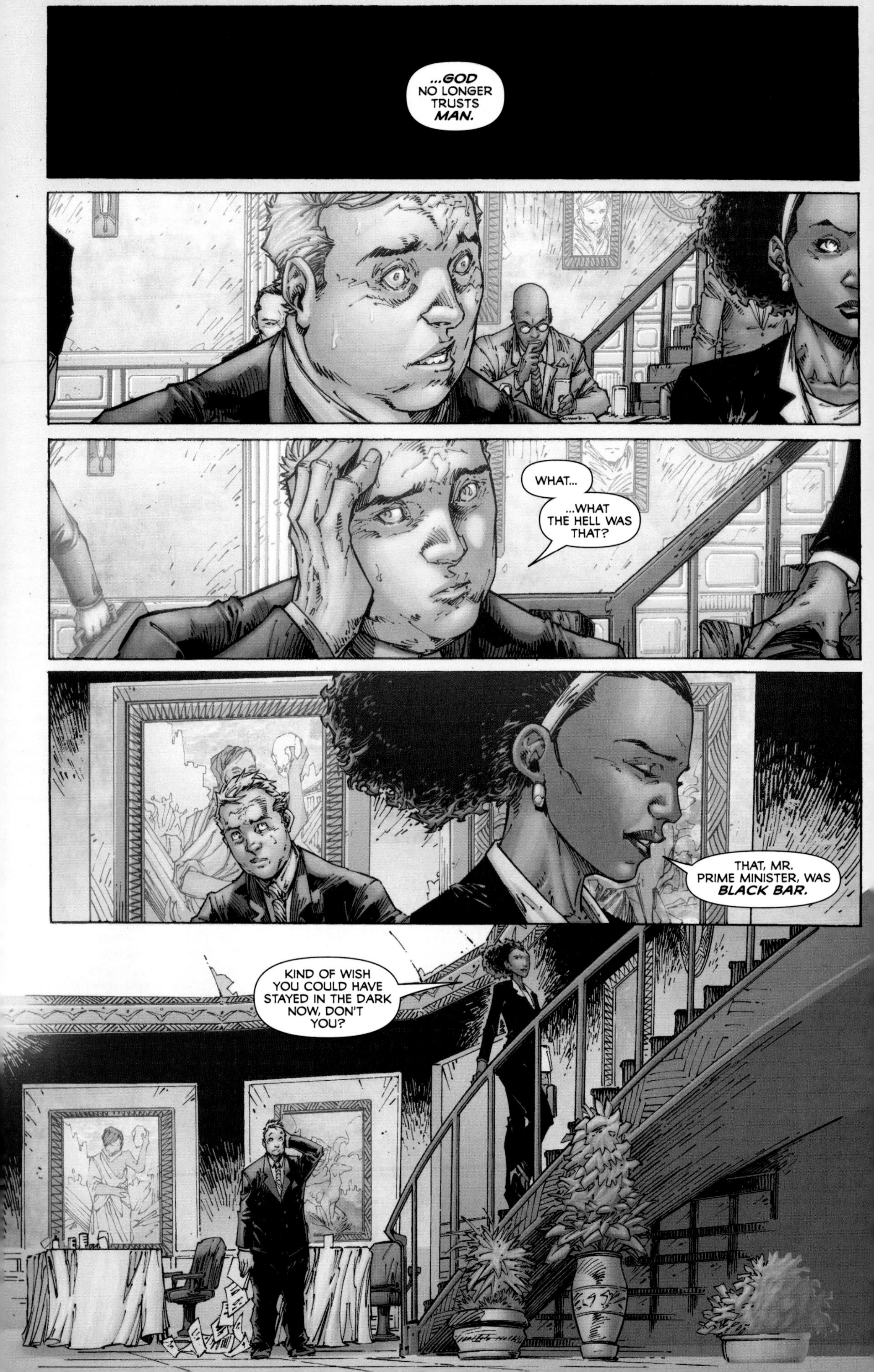
...GOD NO LONGER TRUSTS MAN.
WHAT...
...WHAT THE HELL WAS THAT?
THAT, MR. PRIME MINISTER, WAS BLACK BAR.
KIND OF WISH YOU COULD HAVE STAYED IN THE DARK NOW, DON'T YOU?

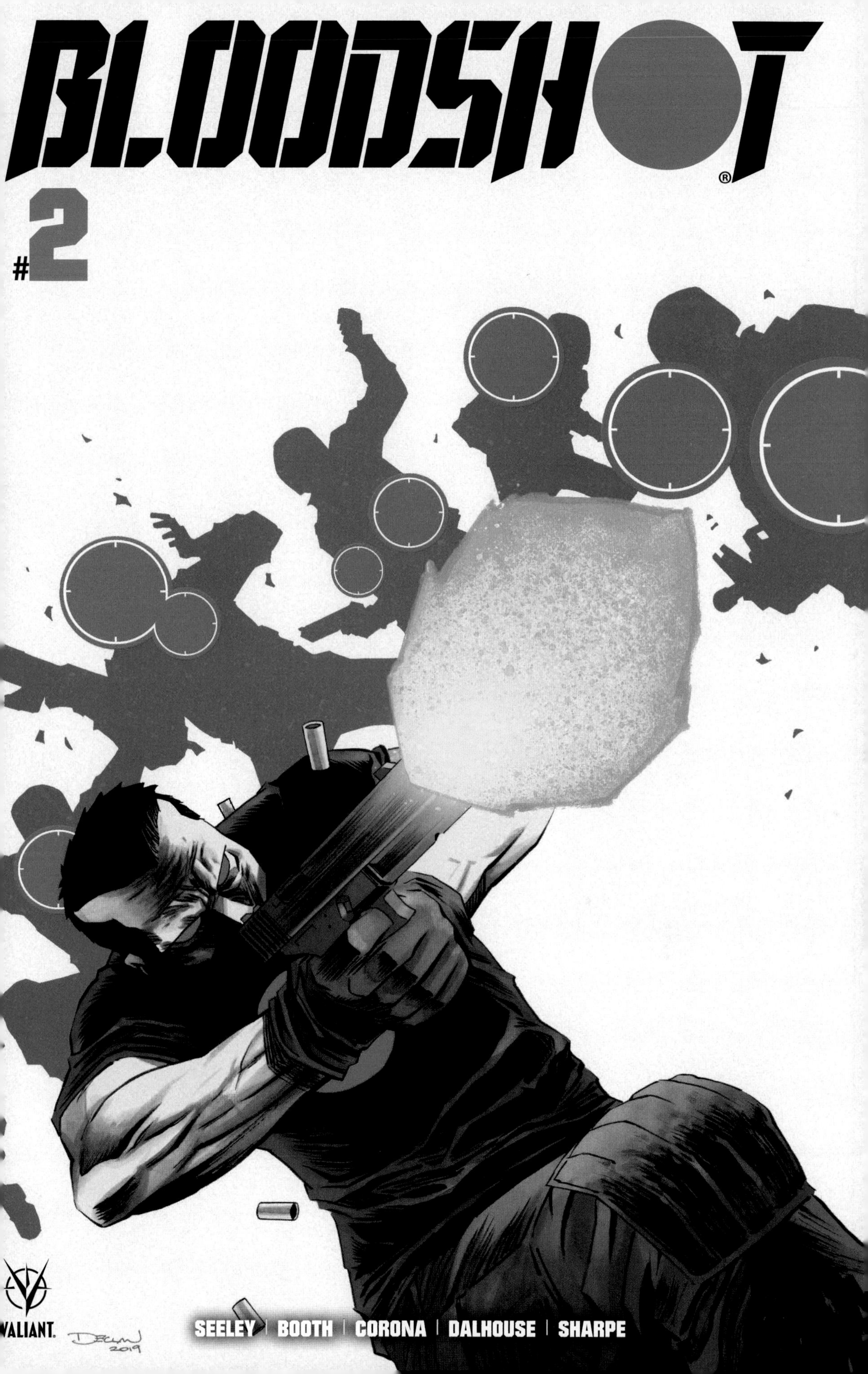

BLOODSHOT®
#2
VALIANT
DECLAN 2019
SEELEY | BOOTH | CORONA | DALHOUSE | SHARPE

BLOODSHOT #2

WRITER: Tim Seeley
ARTIST: Brett Booth
INKER: Adelso Corona
COLORS: Andrew Dalhouse
LETTERS: Dave Sharpe
COVER ARTIST: Declan Shalvey
ASSISTANT EDITOR: Drew Baumgartner
EDITOR: Lysa Hawkins

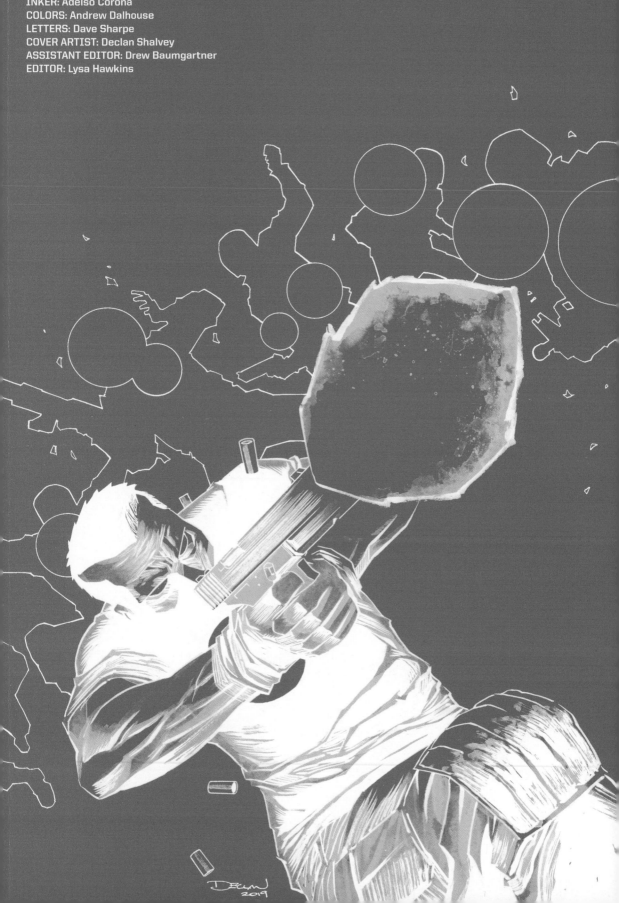

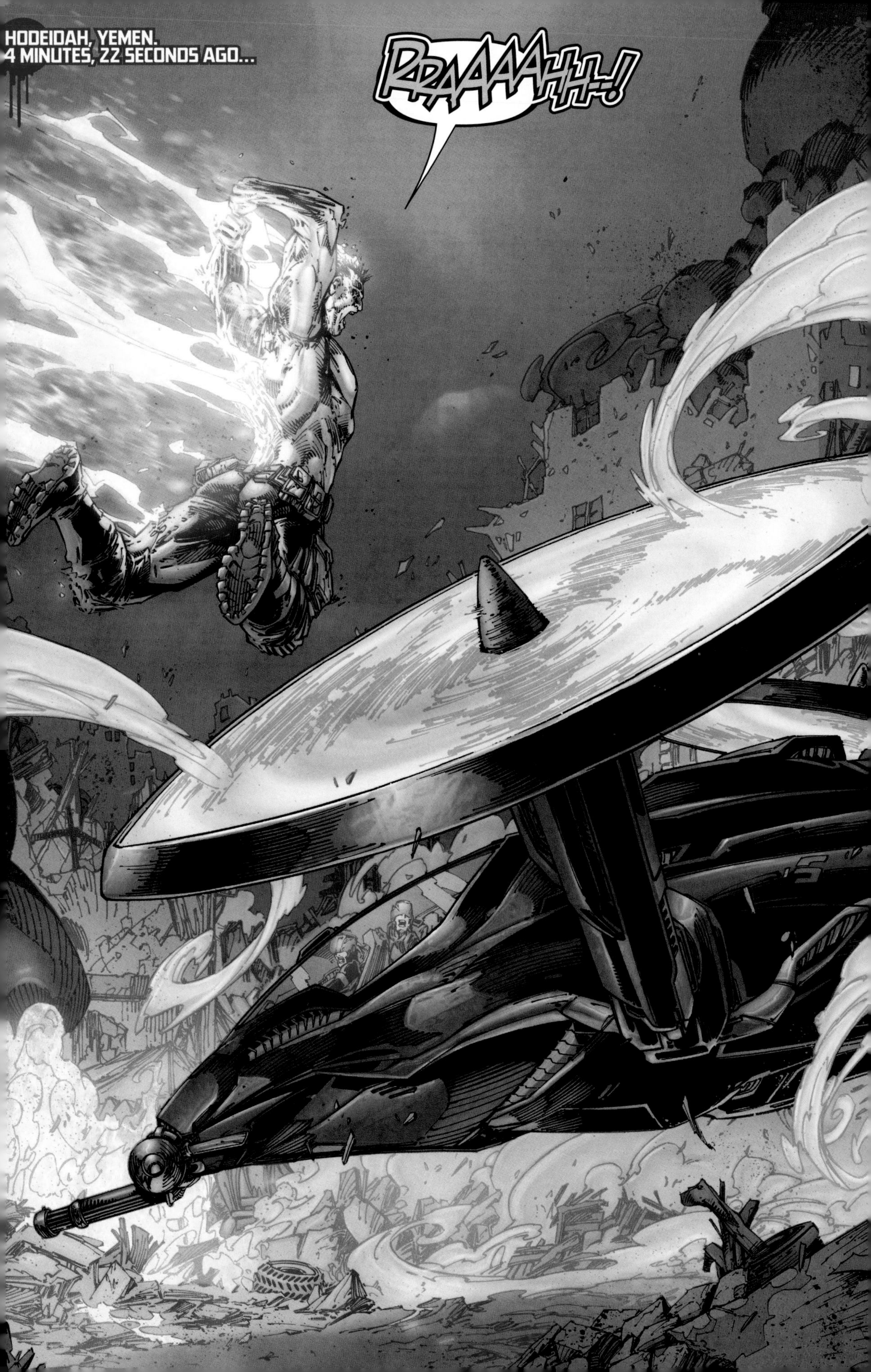
HODEIDAH, YEMEN.
4 MINUTES, 22 SECONDS AGO...
RRRAAAAAHHH-!

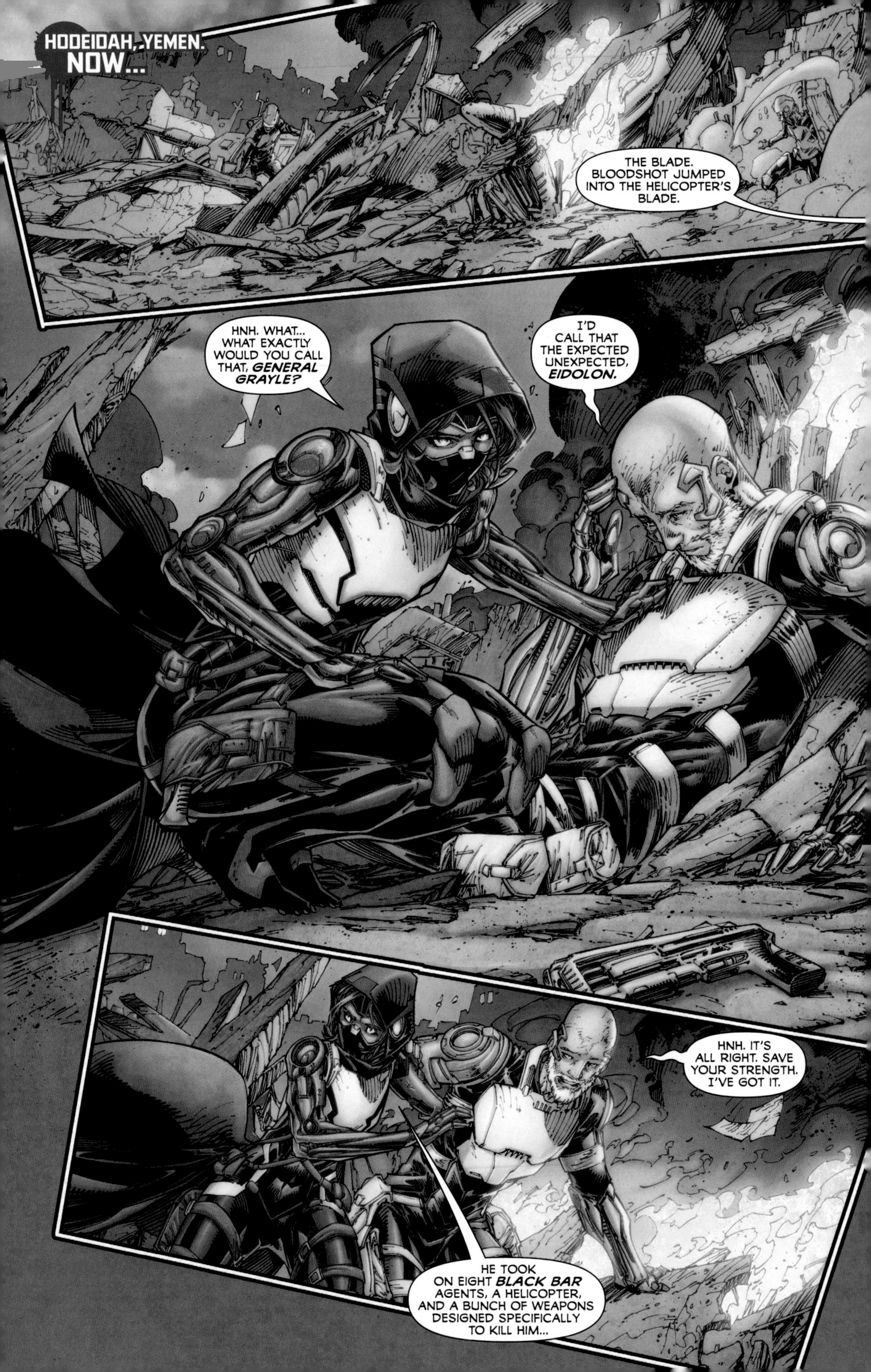
HODEIDAH, YEMEN. NOW...
THE BLADE. BLOODSHOT JUMPED INTO THE HELICOPTER'S BLADE.
HNH. WHAT... WHAT EXACTLY WOULD YOU CALL THAT, GENERAL GRAYLE?
I'D CALL THAT THE EXPECTED UNEXPECTED, EIDOLON.
HNH. IT'S ALL RIGHT. SAVE YOUR STRENGTH. I'VE GOT IT.
HE TOOK ON EIGHT BLACK BAR AGENTS, A HELICOPTER, AND A BUNCH OF WEAPONS DESIGNED SPECIFICALLY TO KILL HIM...

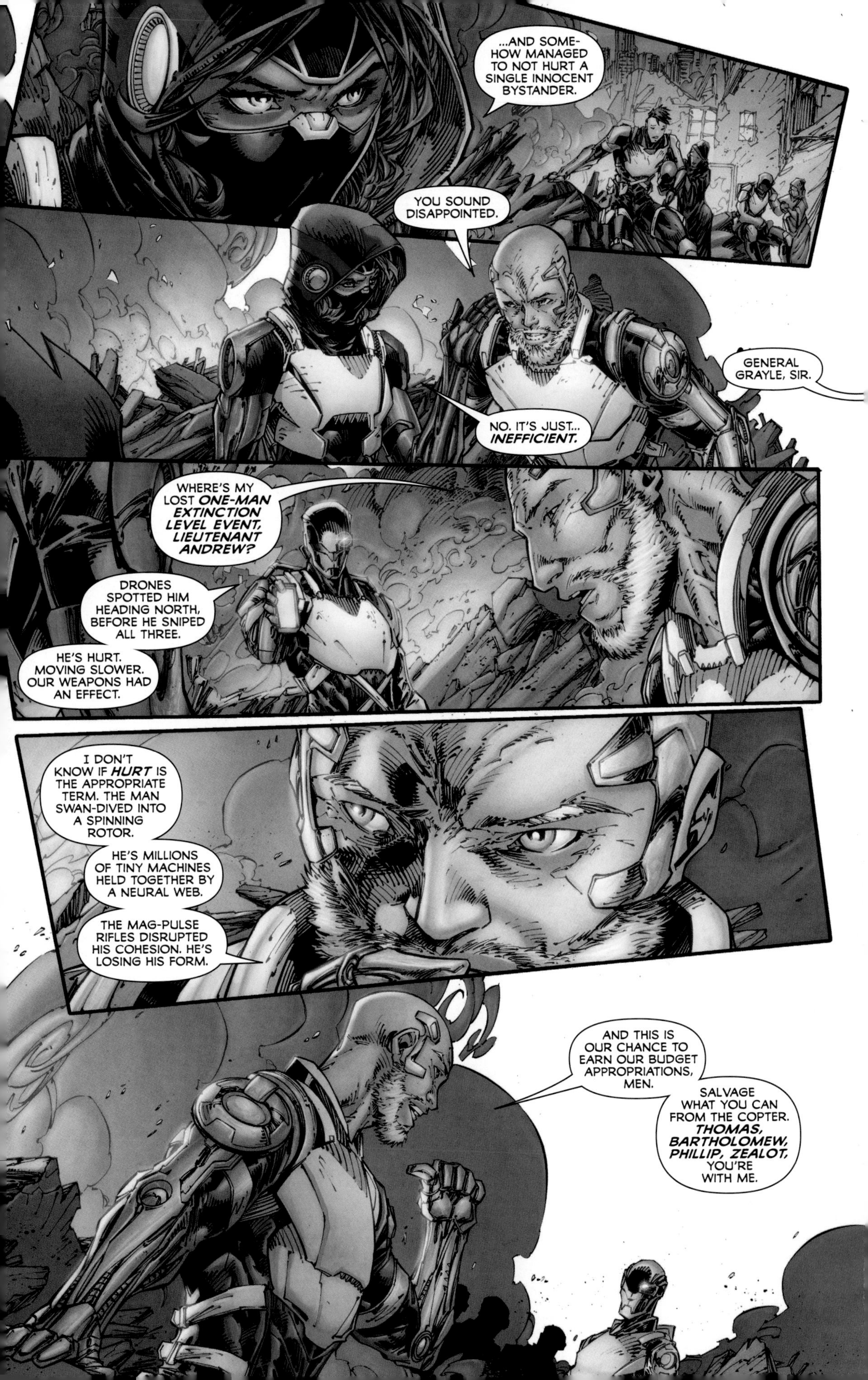
...AND SOME-HOW MANAGED TO NOT HURT A SINGLE INNOCENT BYSTANDER.
YOU SOUND DISAPPOINTED.
NO. IT'S JUST... INEFFICIENT.
GENERAL GRAYLE, SIR.
WHERE'S MY LOST ONE-MAN EXTINCTION LEVEL EVENT, LIEUTENANT ANDREW?
DRONES SPOTTED HIM HEADING NORTH, BEFORE HE SNIPED ALL THREE.
HE'S HURT. MOVING SLOWER. OUR WEAPONS HAD AN EFFECT.
I DON'T KNOW IF HURT IS THE APPROPRIATE TERM. THE MAN SWAN-DIVED INTO A SPINNING ROTOR.
HE'S MILLIONS OF TINY MACHINES HELD TOGETHER BY A NEURAL WEB.
THE MAG-PULSE RIFLES DISRUPTED HIS COHESION. HE'S LOSING HIS FORM.
AND THIS IS OUR CHANCE TO EARN OUR BUDGET APPROPRIATIONS, MEN.
SALVAGE WHAT YOU CAN FROM THE COPTER. THOMAS, BARTHOLOMEW, PHILLIP, ZEALOT, YOU'RE WITH ME.

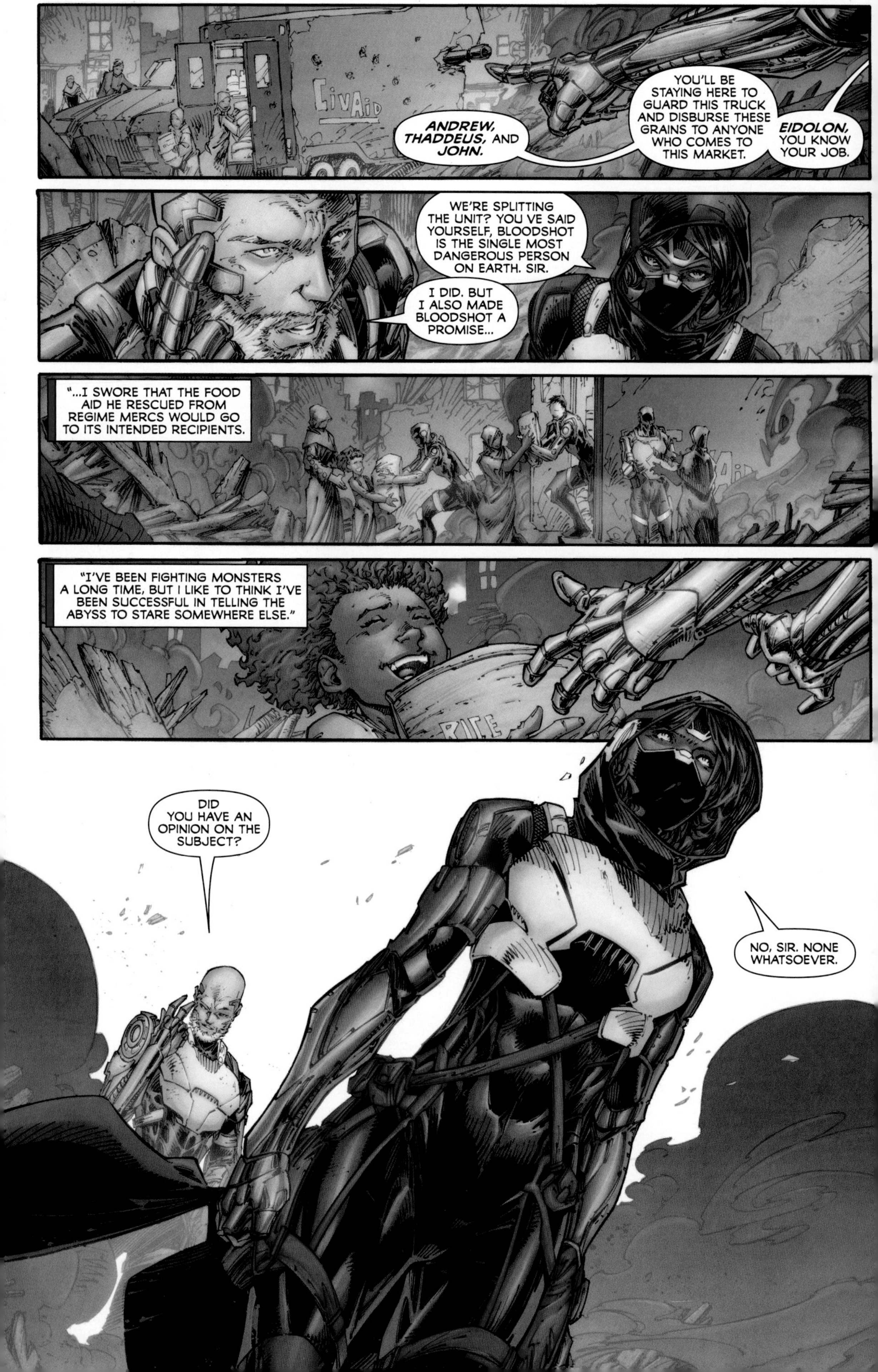

ANDREW, THADDEUS, AND ***JOHN.***
YOU'LL BE STAYING HERE TO GUARD THIS TRUCK AND DISBURSE THESE GRAINS TO ANYONE WHO COMES TO THIS MARKET.
EIDOLON, YOU KNOW YOUR JOB.
CIVAID
WE'RE SPLITTING THE UNIT? YOU VE SAID YOURSELF, BLOODSHOT IS THE SINGLE MOST DANGEROUS PERSON ON EARTH. SIR.
I DID. BUT I ALSO MADE BLOODSHOT A PROMISE...
"...I SWORE THAT THE FOOD AID HE RESCUED FROM REGIME MERCS WOULD GO TO ITS INTENDED RECIPIENTS.
"I'VE BEEN FIGHTING MONSTERS A LONG TIME, BUT I LIKE TO THINK I'VE BEEN SUCCESSFUL IN TELLING THE ABYSS TO STARE SOMEWHERE ELSE."
RICE
DID YOU HAVE AN OPINION ON THE SUBJECT?
NO, SIR. NONE WHATSOEVER.

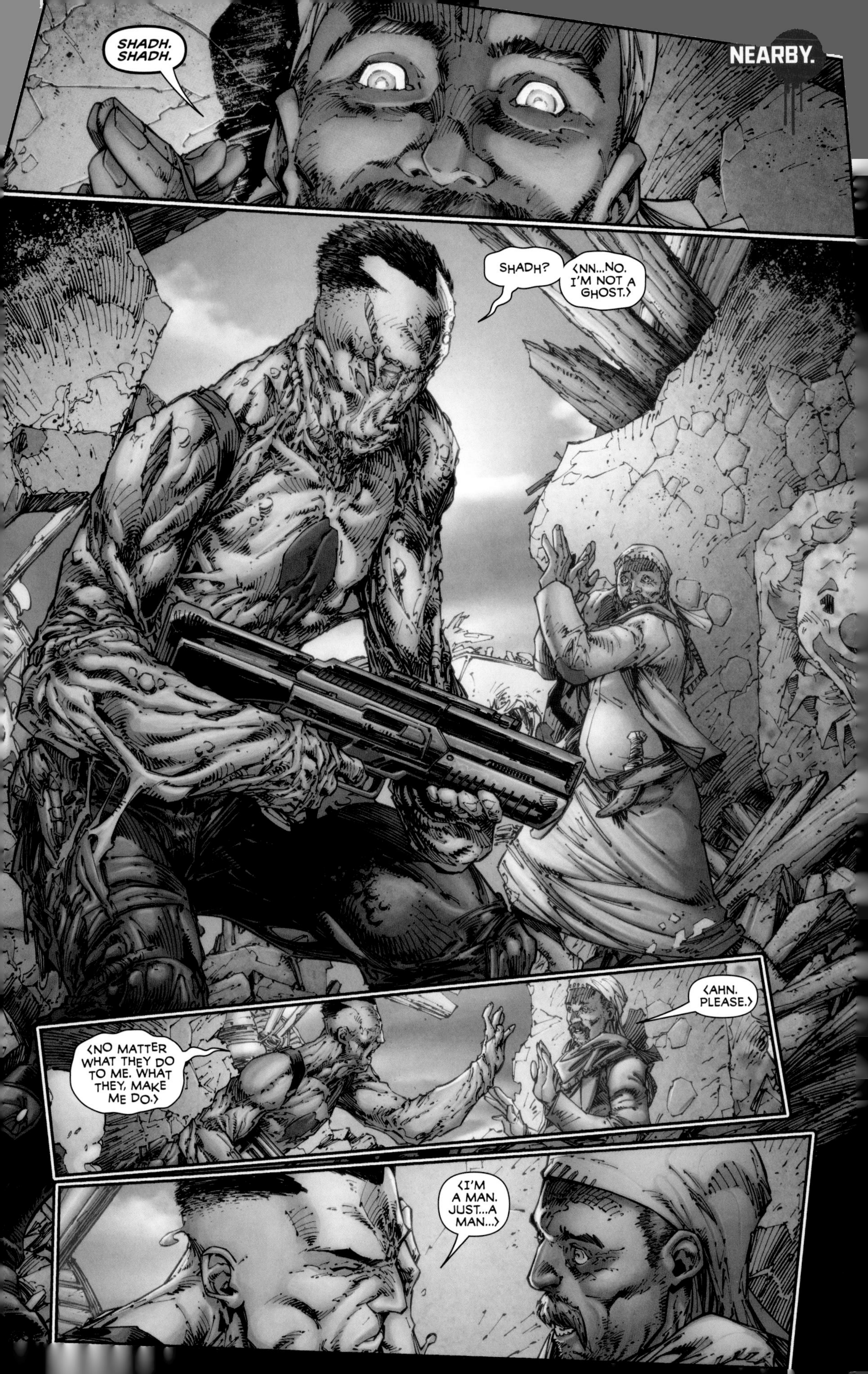
NEARBY.
SHADH. SHADH.
SHADH?
‹NN...NO. I'M NOT A GHOST.›
‹AHN. PLEASE.›
‹NO MATTER WHAT THEY DO TO ME. WHAT THEY, MAKE ME DO.›
‹I'M A MAN. JUST...A MAN...›

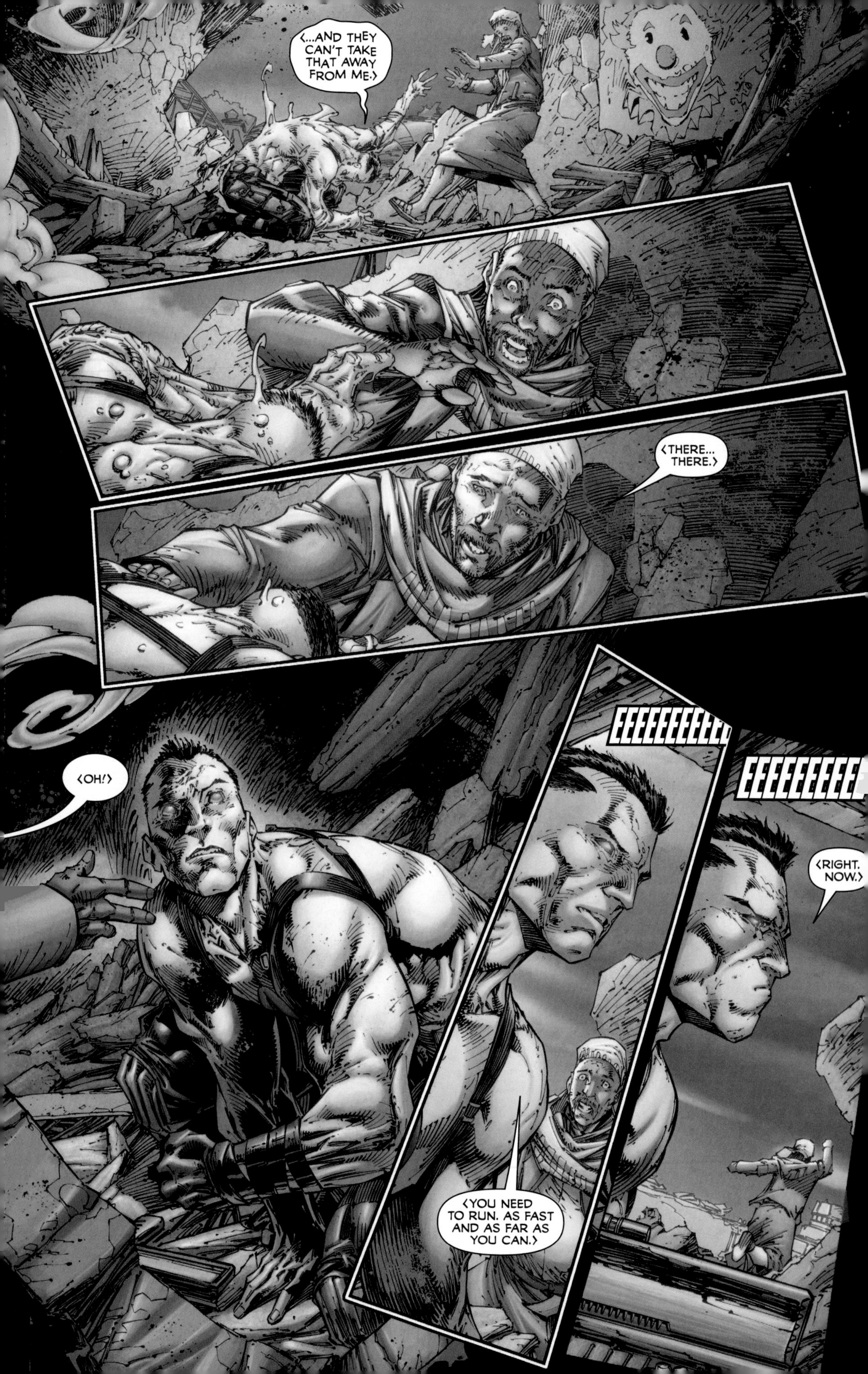

‹...AND THEY CAN'T TAKE THAT AWAY FROM ME.›
‹THERE... THERE.›
‹OH!›
EEEEEEEEEEE
EEEEEEEEE
‹YOU NEED TO RUN. AS FAST AND AS FAR AS YOU CAN.›
‹RIGHT. NOW.›

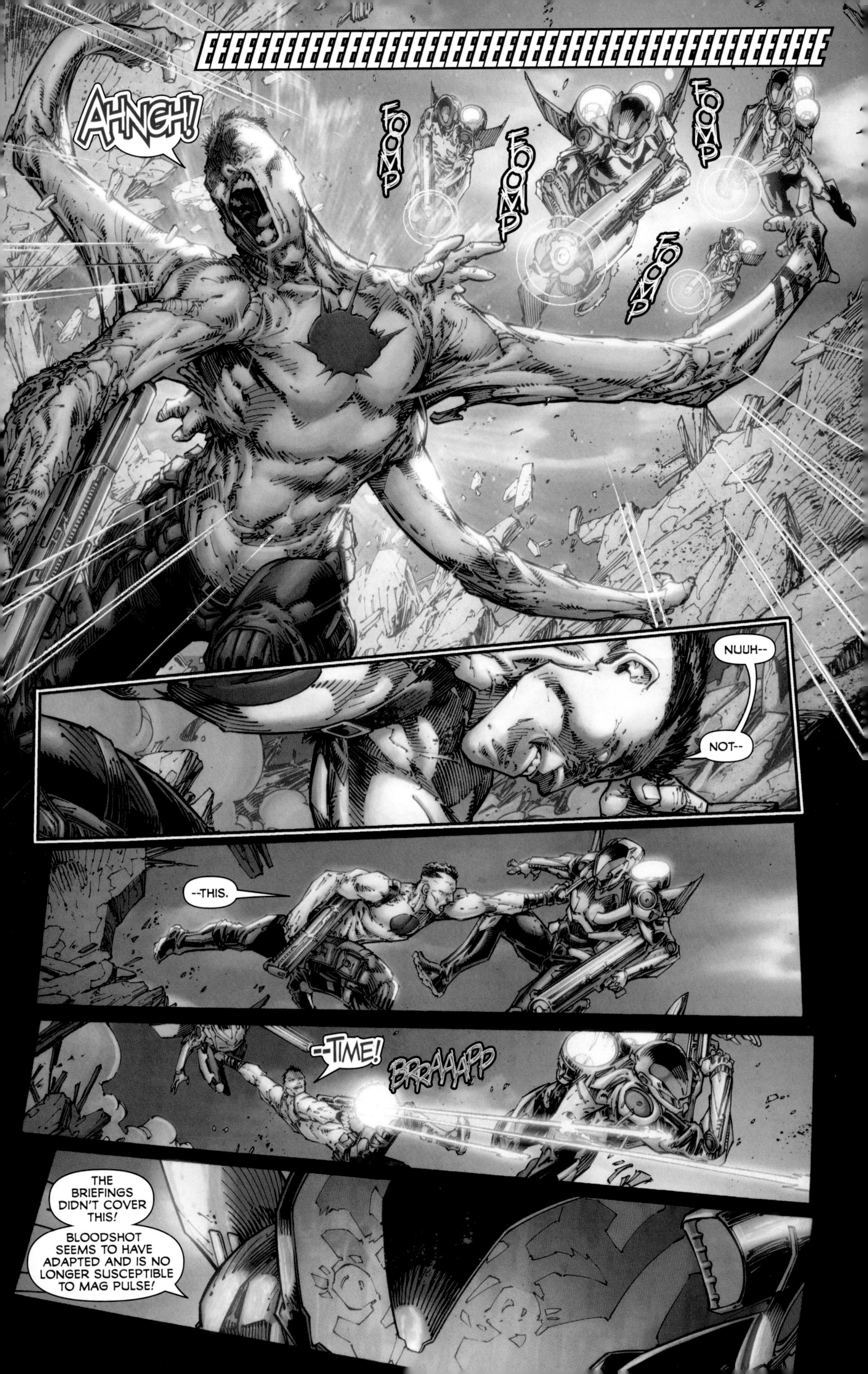
EEEEEEEEEEEEEEEEEEEEEEEEEEEEEEEEEEEEEEEEE
AHNGH!
FOOMP
FOOMP
FOOMP
FOOMP
NUUH--
NOT--
--THIS.
--TIME!
BRRAAAPP
THE BRIEFINGS DIDN'T COVER THIS!
BLOODSHOT SEEMS TO HAVE ADAPTED AND IS NO LONGER SUSCEPTIBLE TO MAG PULSE!

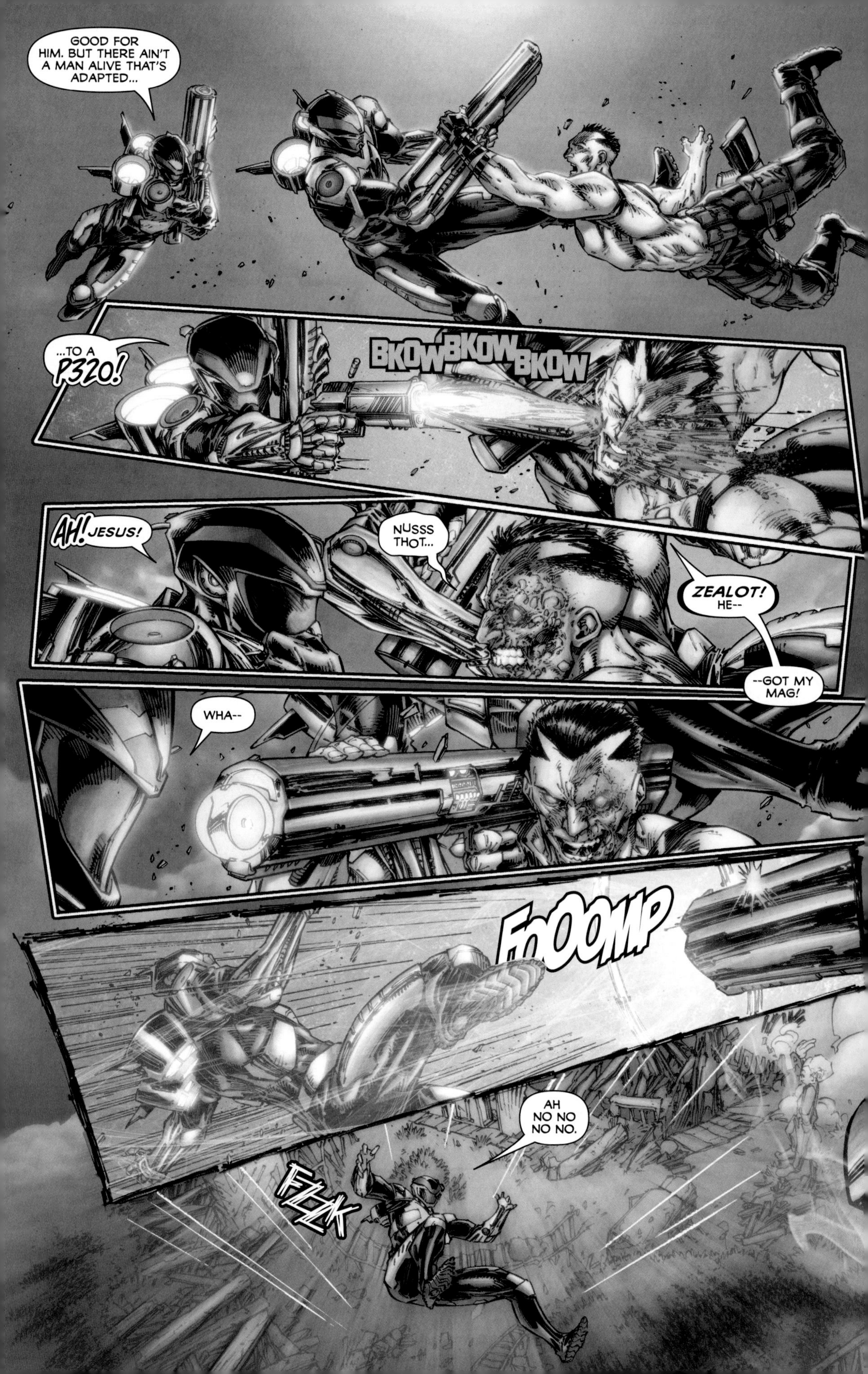
GOOD FOR HIM. BUT THERE AIN'T A MAN ALIVE THAT'S ADAPTED...
...TO A P320!
BKOWBKOWBKOW
AH! JESUS!
NUSSS THOT...
ZEALOT! HE--
--GOT MY MAG!
WHA--
FOOOMP
AH NO NO NO NO.
FZZK

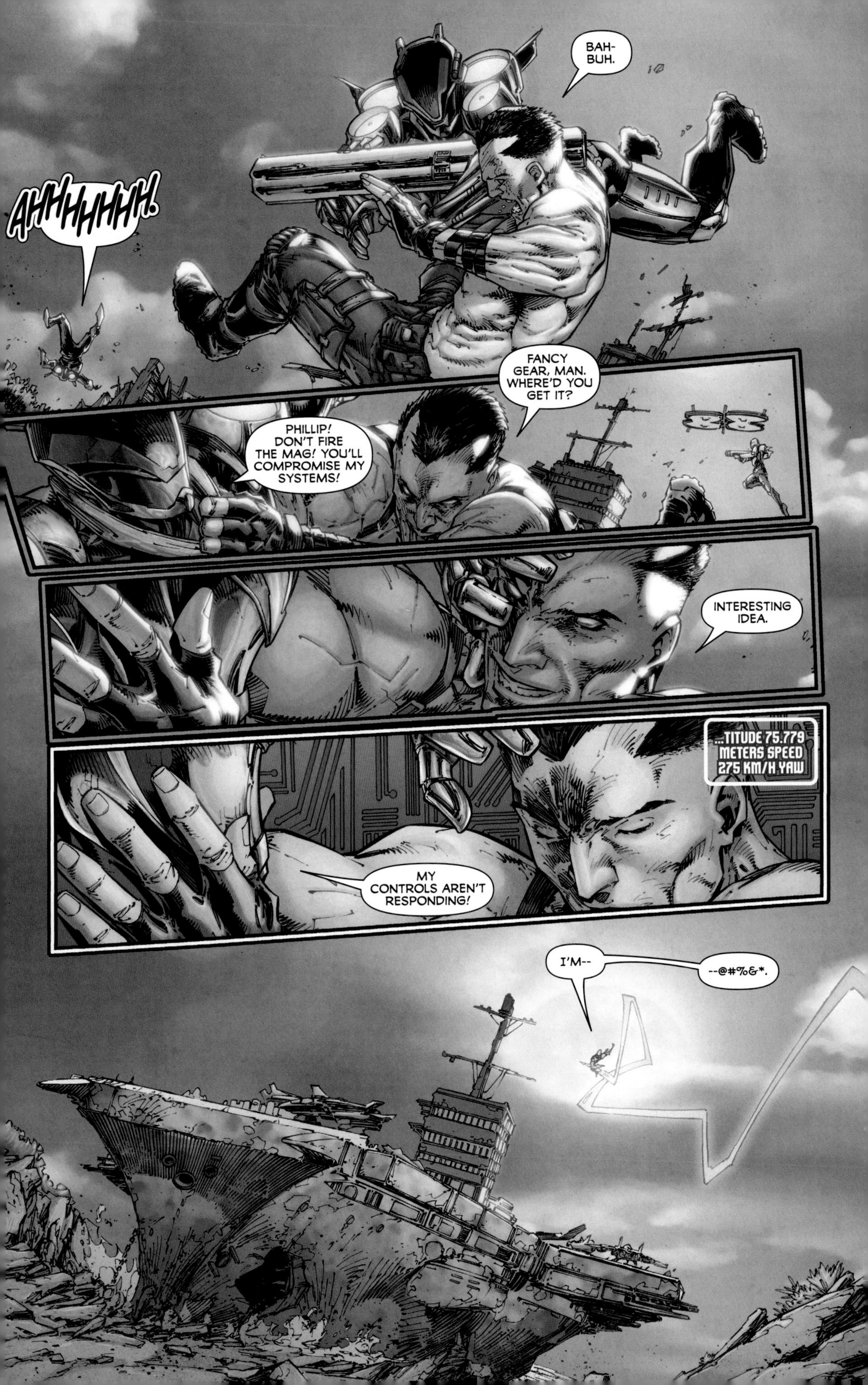
BAH-BUH.
AHHHHHHH!
FANCY GEAR, MAN. WHERE'D YOU GET IT?
PHILLIP! DON'T FIRE THE MAG! YOU'LL COMPROMISE MY SYSTEMS!
INTERESTING IDEA.
...TITUDE 75.779 METERS SPEED 275 KM/H YAW
MY CONTROLS AREN'T RESPONDING!
I'M--
--@#%&*.

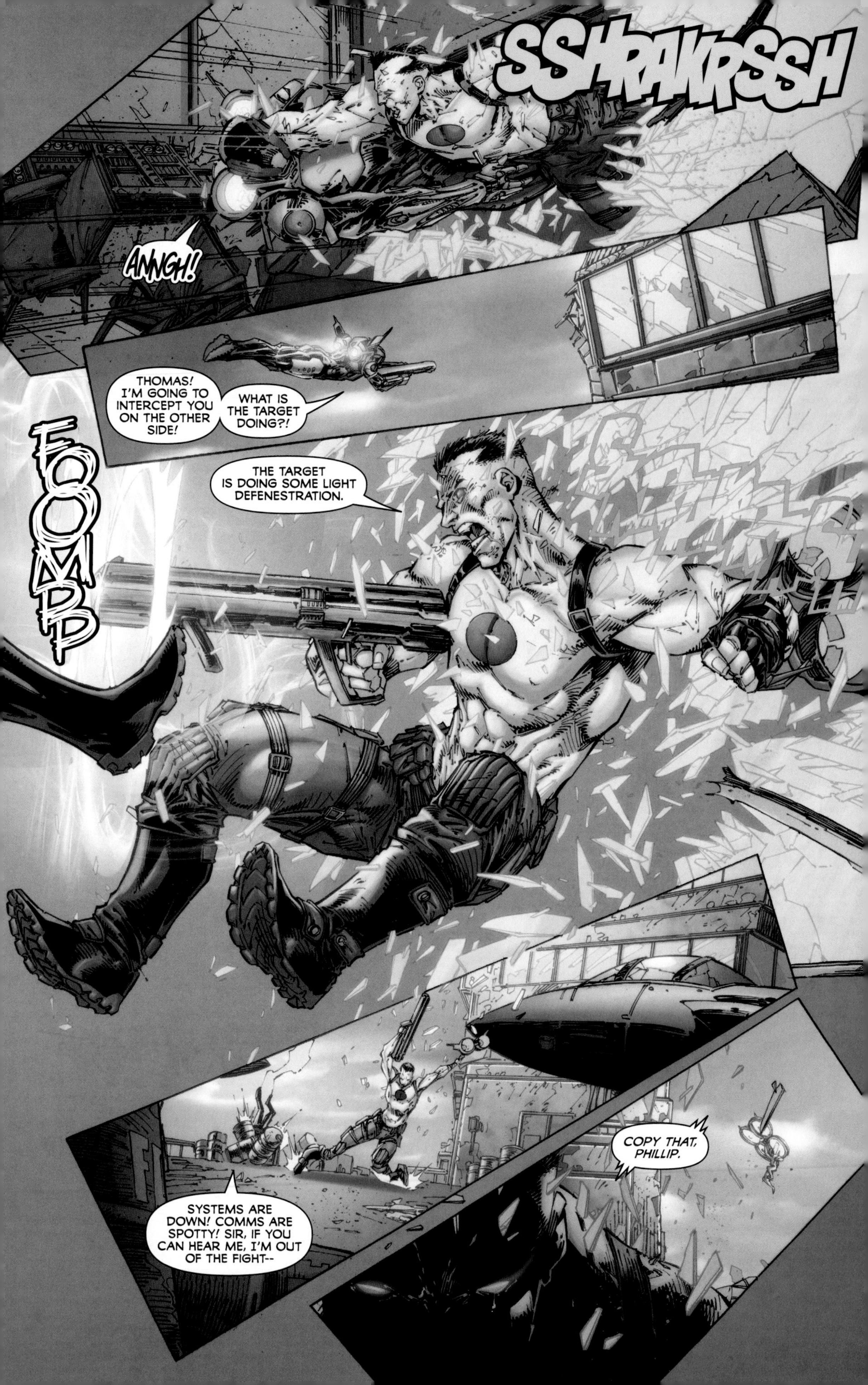
SSHRAKRSSH
ANNGH!
THOMAS! I'M GOING TO INTERCEPT YOU ON THE OTHER SIDE!
WHAT IS THE TARGET DOING?!
FOOMP
THE TARGET IS DOING SOME LIGHT DEFENESTRATION.
SYSTEMS ARE DOWN! COMMS ARE SPOTTY! SIR, IF YOU CAN HEAR ME, I'M OUT OF THE FIGHT--
COPY THAT, PHILLIP.

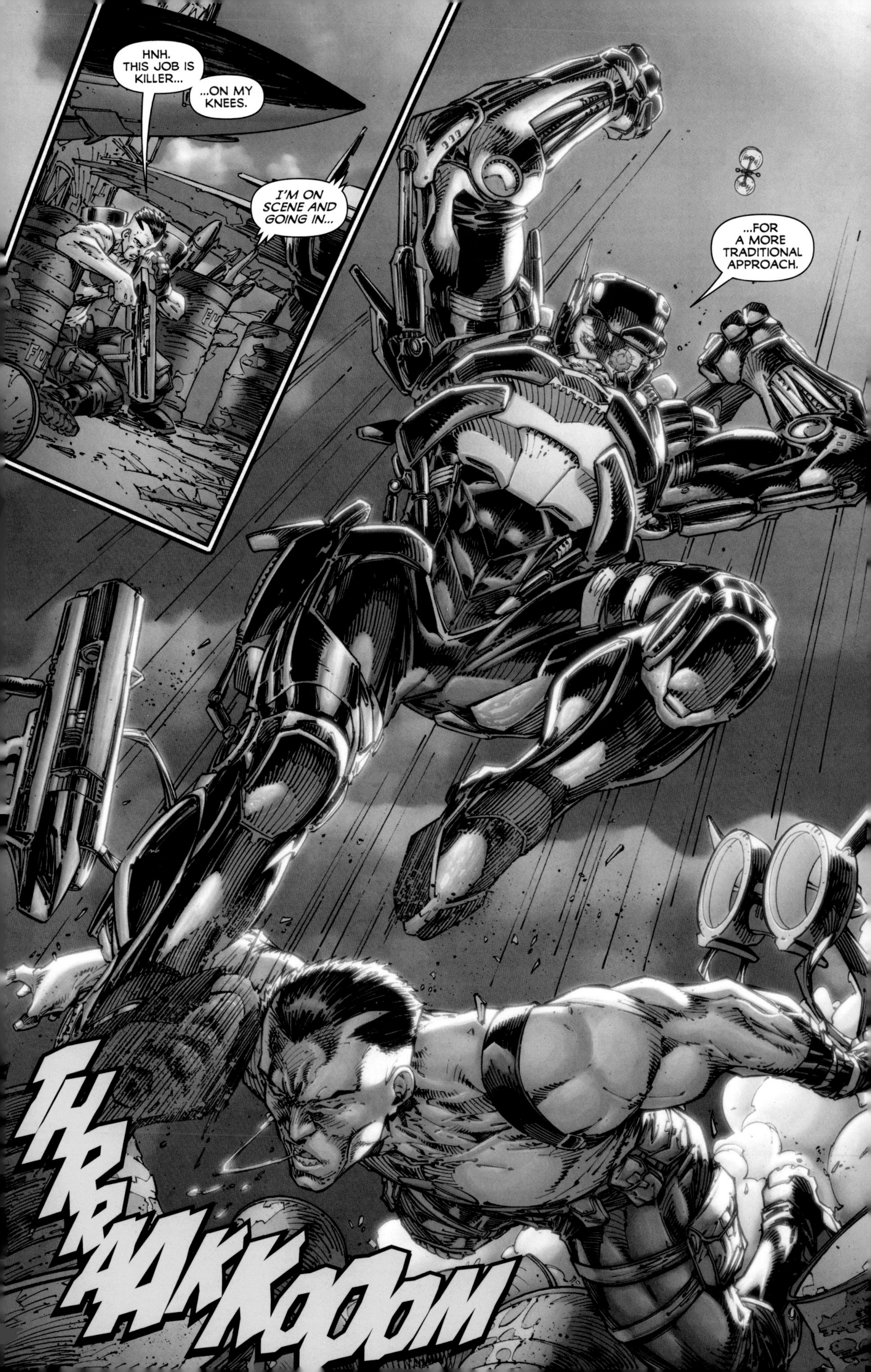
HNH. THIS JOB IS KILLER...
...ON MY KNEES.
I'M ON SCENE AND GOING IN...
...FOR A MORE TRADITIONAL APPROACH.
THRAKKOOOM

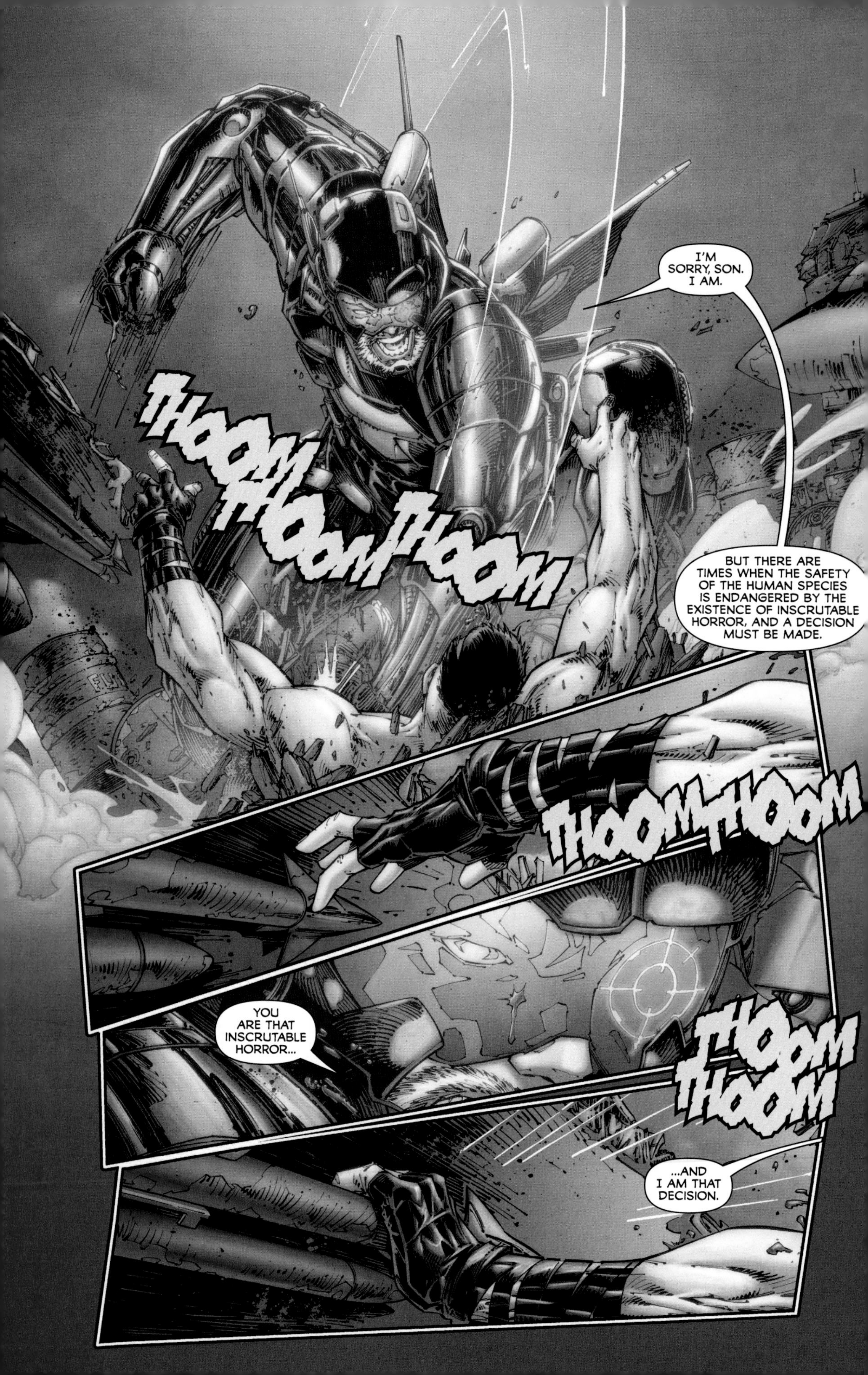
I'M SORRY, SON. I AM.
THOOM THOOM THOOM THOOM
BUT THERE ARE TIMES WHEN THE SAFETY OF THE HUMAN SPECIES IS ENDANGERED BY THE EXISTENCE OF INSCRUTABLE HORROR, AND A DECISION MUST BE MADE.
THOOM THOOM
YOU ARE THAT INSCRUTABLE HORROR...
THOOM THOOM
...AND I AM THAT DECISION.

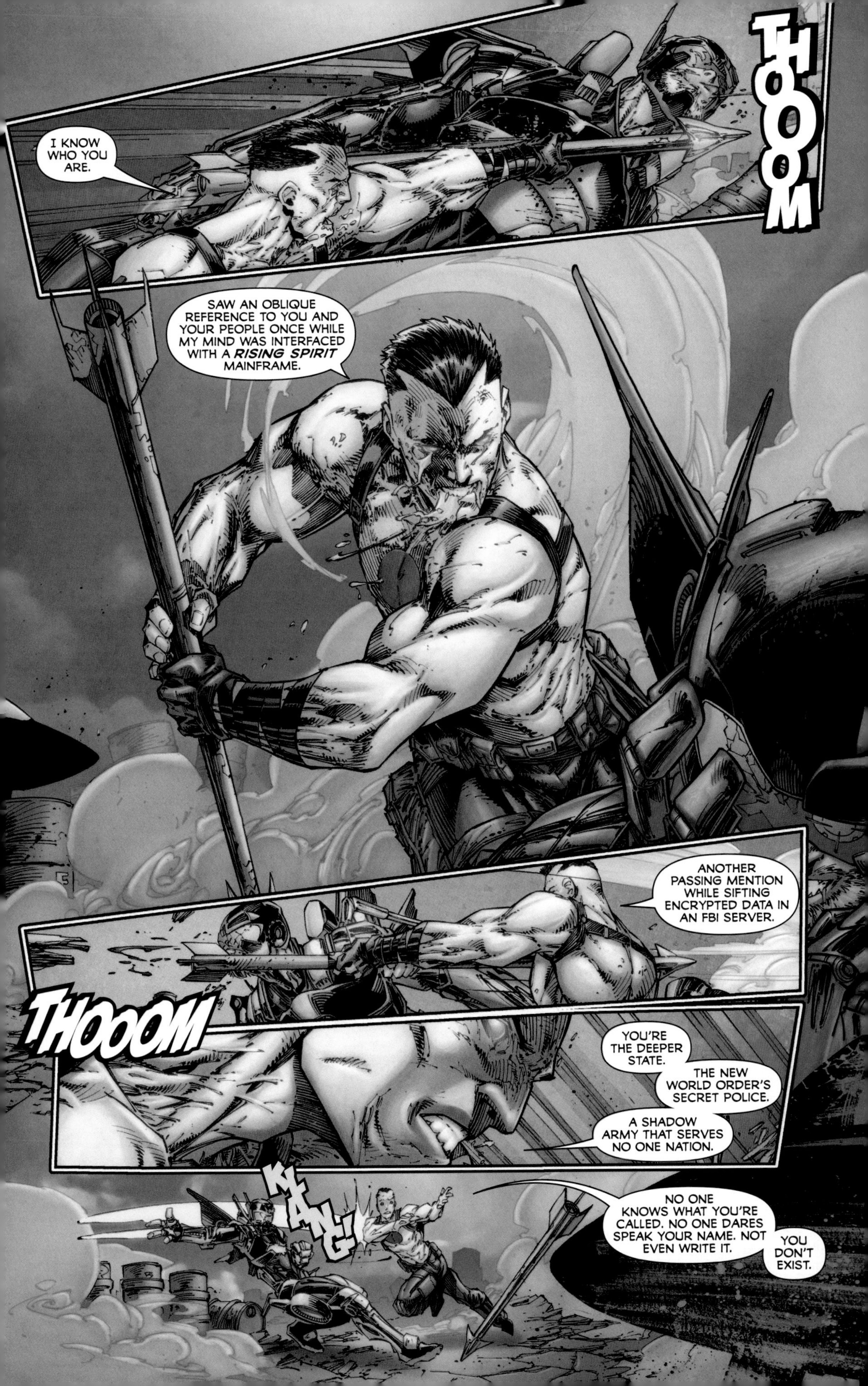

I KNOW WHO YOU ARE.
THOOOM
SAW AN OBLIQUE REFERENCE TO YOU AND YOUR PEOPLE ONCE WHILE MY MIND WAS INTERFACED WITH A *RISING SPIRIT* MAINFRAME.
ANOTHER PASSING MENTION WHILE SIFTING ENCRYPTED DATA IN AN FBI SERVER.
THOOOM
YOU'RE THE DEEPER STATE.
THE NEW WORLD ORDER'S SECRET POLICE.
A SHADOW ARMY THAT SERVES NO ONE NATION.
KLANG!
NO ONE KNOWS WHAT YOU'RE CALLED. NO ONE DARES SPEAK YOUR NAME. NOT EVEN WRITE IT.
YOU DON'T EXIST.

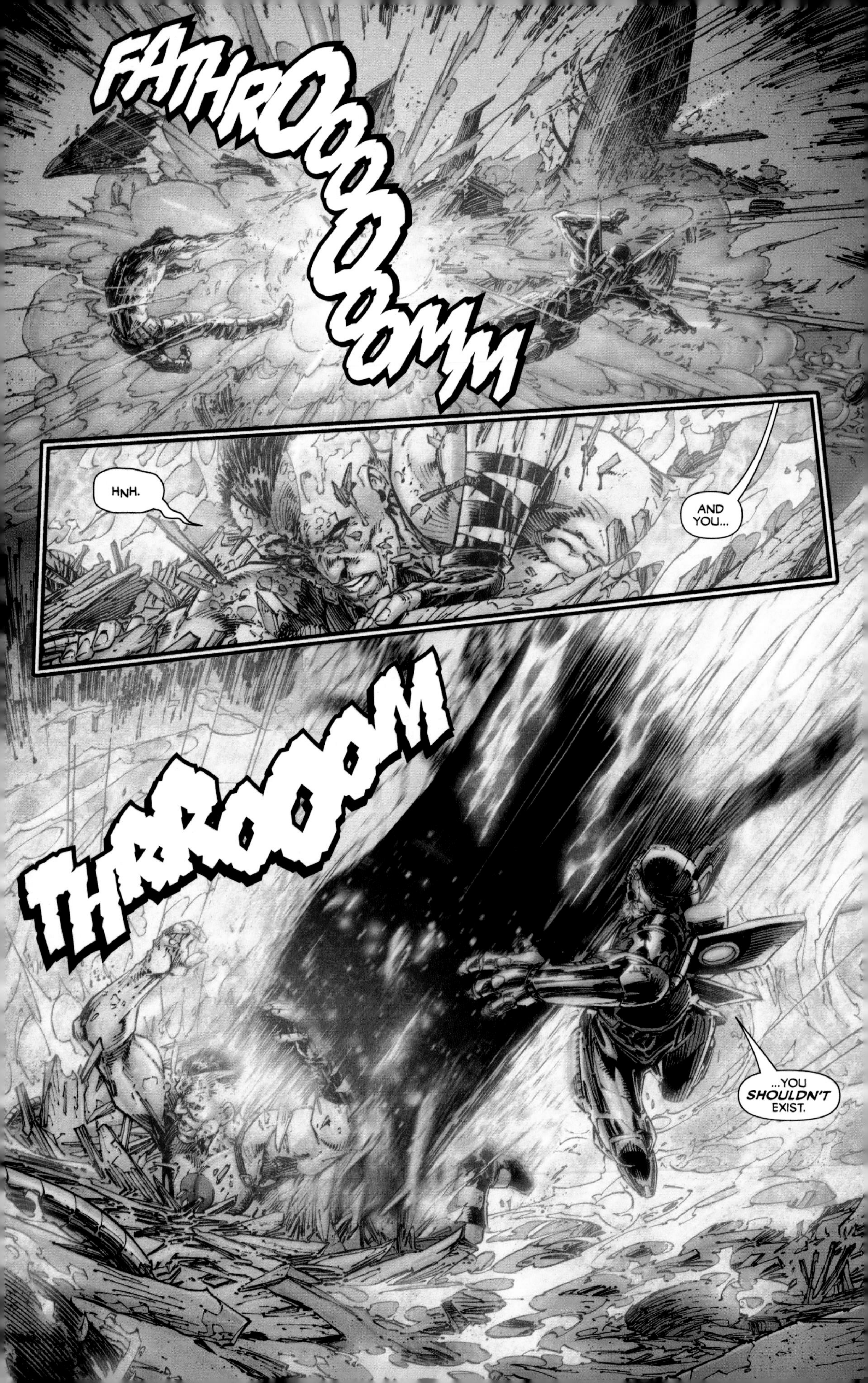
FATHROOOOOOOOOM
HNH.
AND YOU...
THROOOOOM
...YOU *SHOULDN'T* EXIST.

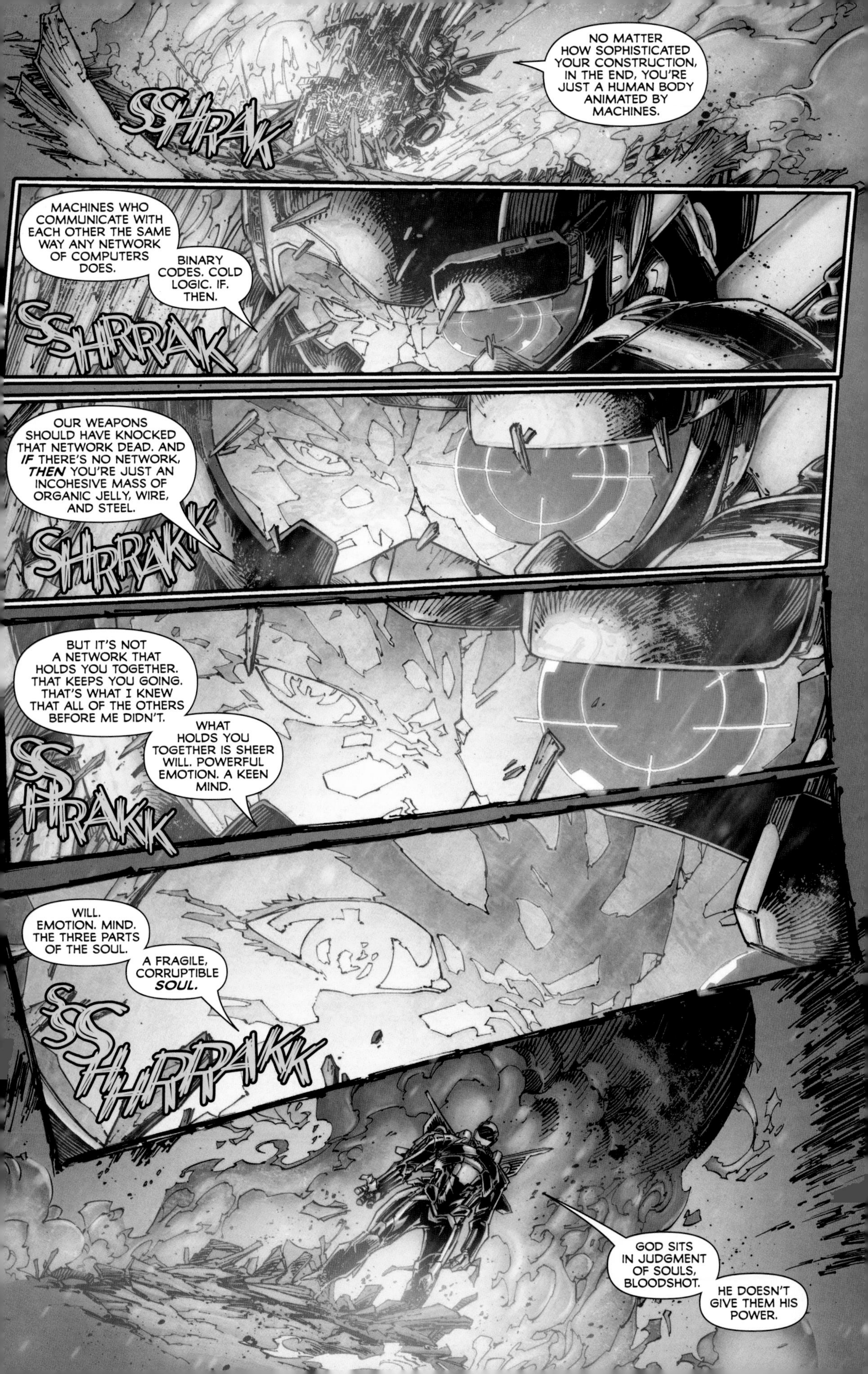
NO MATTER HOW SOPHISTICATED YOUR CONSTRUCTION, IN THE END, YOU'RE JUST A HUMAN BODY ANIMATED BY MACHINES.
SSHRAK
MACHINES WHO COMMUNICATE WITH EACH OTHER THE SAME WAY ANY NETWORK OF COMPUTERS DOES.
BINARY CODES. COLD LOGIC. IF. THEN.
SSHRRAK
OUR WEAPONS SHOULD HAVE KNOCKED THAT NETWORK DEAD. AND *IF* THERE'S NO NETWORK, ***THEN*** YOU'RE JUST AN INCOHESIVE MASS OF ORGANIC JELLY, WIRE, AND STEEL.
SHRRAKK
BUT IT'S NOT A NETWORK THAT HOLDS YOU TOGETHER. THAT KEEPS YOU GOING. THAT'S WHAT I KNEW THAT ALL OF THE OTHERS BEFORE ME DIDN'T.
WHAT HOLDS YOU TOGETHER IS SHEER WILL. POWERFUL EMOTION. A KEEN MIND.
SSHRAKK
WILL. EMOTION. MIND. THE THREE PARTS OF THE SOUL.
A FRAGILE, CORRUPTIBLE ***SOUL.***
SSSHHRRAKK
GOD SITS IN JUDGMENT OF SOULS, BLOODSHOT.
HE DOESN'T GIVE THEM HIS POWER.

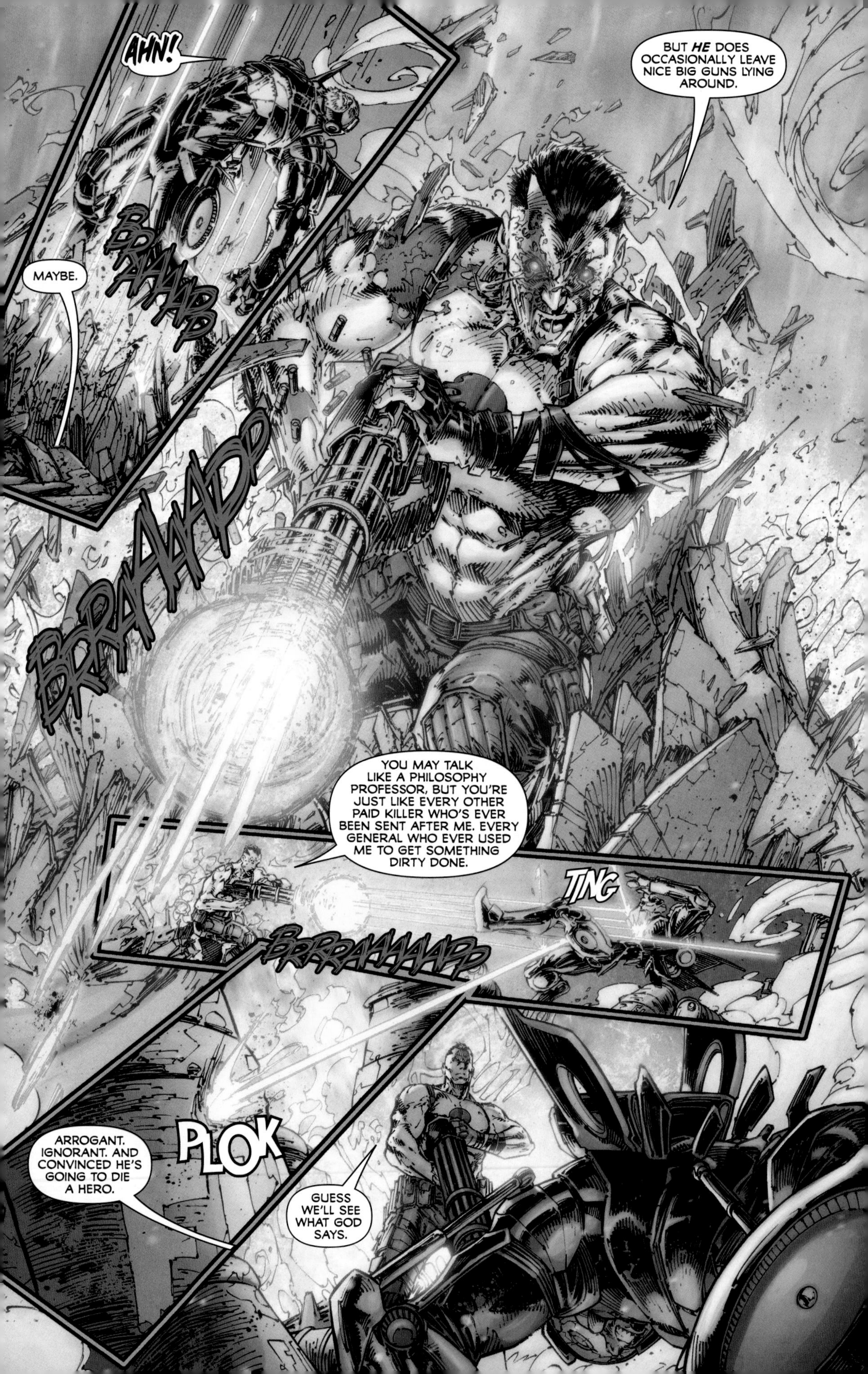
AHN!
BUT HE DOES OCCASIONALLY LEAVE NICE BIG GUNS LYING AROUND.
BRRAAAAPP
MAYBE.
BRRAAAAPP
YOU MAY TALK LIKE A PHILOSOPHY PROFESSOR, BUT YOU'RE JUST LIKE EVERY OTHER PAID KILLER WHO'S EVER BEEN SENT AFTER ME. EVERY GENERAL WHO EVER USED ME TO GET SOMETHING DIRTY DONE.
TING
BRRRAAAAAPP
PLOK
ARROGANT. IGNORANT. AND CONVINCED HE'S GOING TO DIE A HERO.
GUESS WE'LL SEE WHAT GOD SAYS.

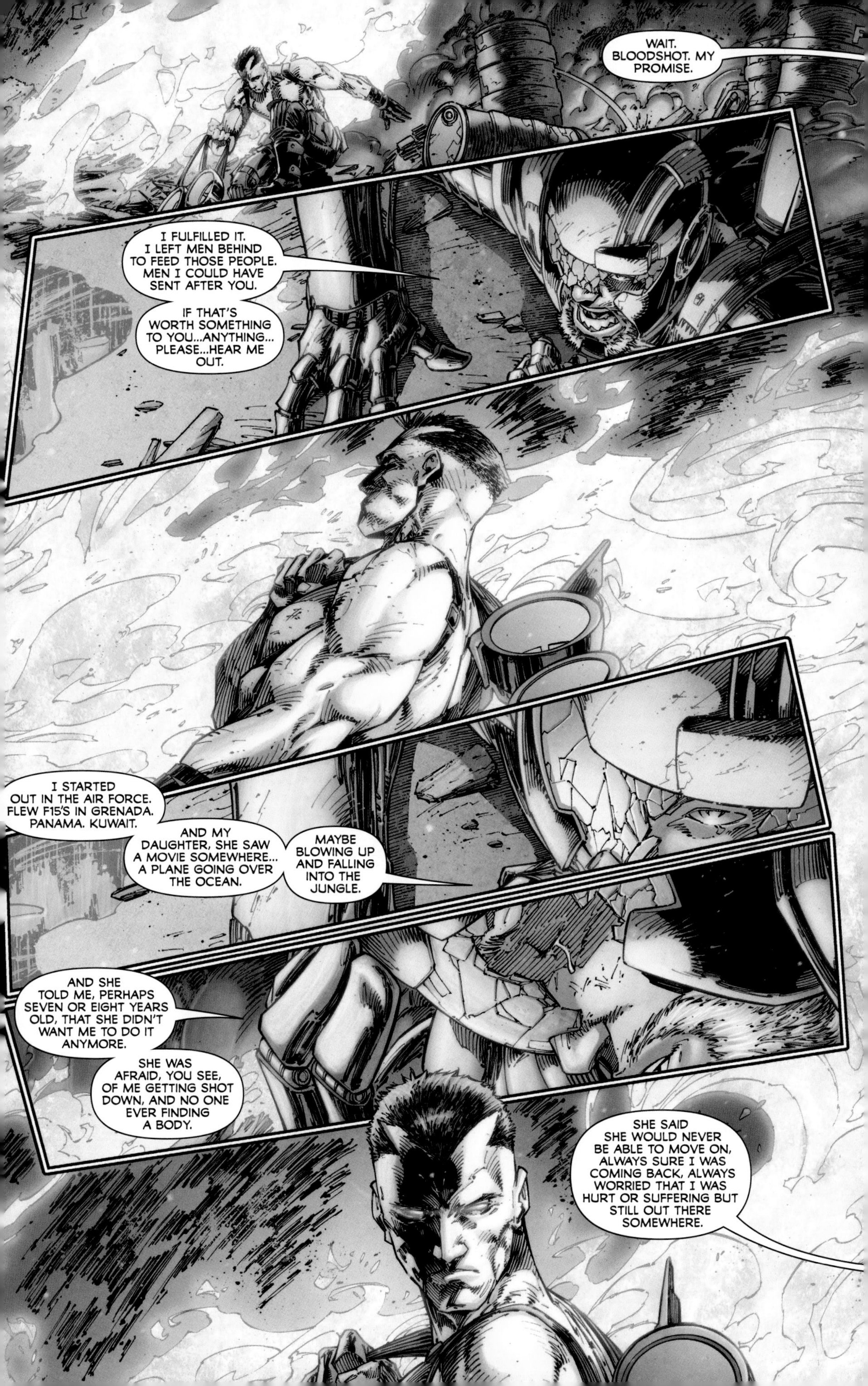
WAIT. BLOODSHOT. MY PROMISE.
I FULFILLED IT. I LEFT MEN BEHIND TO FEED THOSE PEOPLE. MEN I COULD HAVE SENT AFTER YOU.
IF THAT'S WORTH SOMETHING TO YOU...ANYTHING... PLEASE...HEAR ME OUT.
I STARTED OUT IN THE AIR FORCE. FLEW F15'S IN GRENADA. PANAMA. KUWAIT.
AND MY DAUGHTER, SHE SAW A MOVIE SOMEWHERE... A PLANE GOING OVER THE OCEAN.
MAYBE BLOWING UP AND FALLING INTO THE JUNGLE.
AND SHE TOLD ME, PERHAPS SEVEN OR EIGHT YEARS OLD, THAT SHE DIDN'T WANT ME TO DO IT ANYMORE.
SHE WAS AFRAID, YOU SEE, OF ME GETTING SHOT DOWN, AND NO ONE EVER FINDING A BODY.
SHE SAID SHE WOULD NEVER BE ABLE TO MOVE ON, ALWAYS SURE I WAS COMING BACK, ALWAYS WORRIED THAT I WAS HURT OR SUFFERING BUT STILL OUT THERE SOMEWHERE.

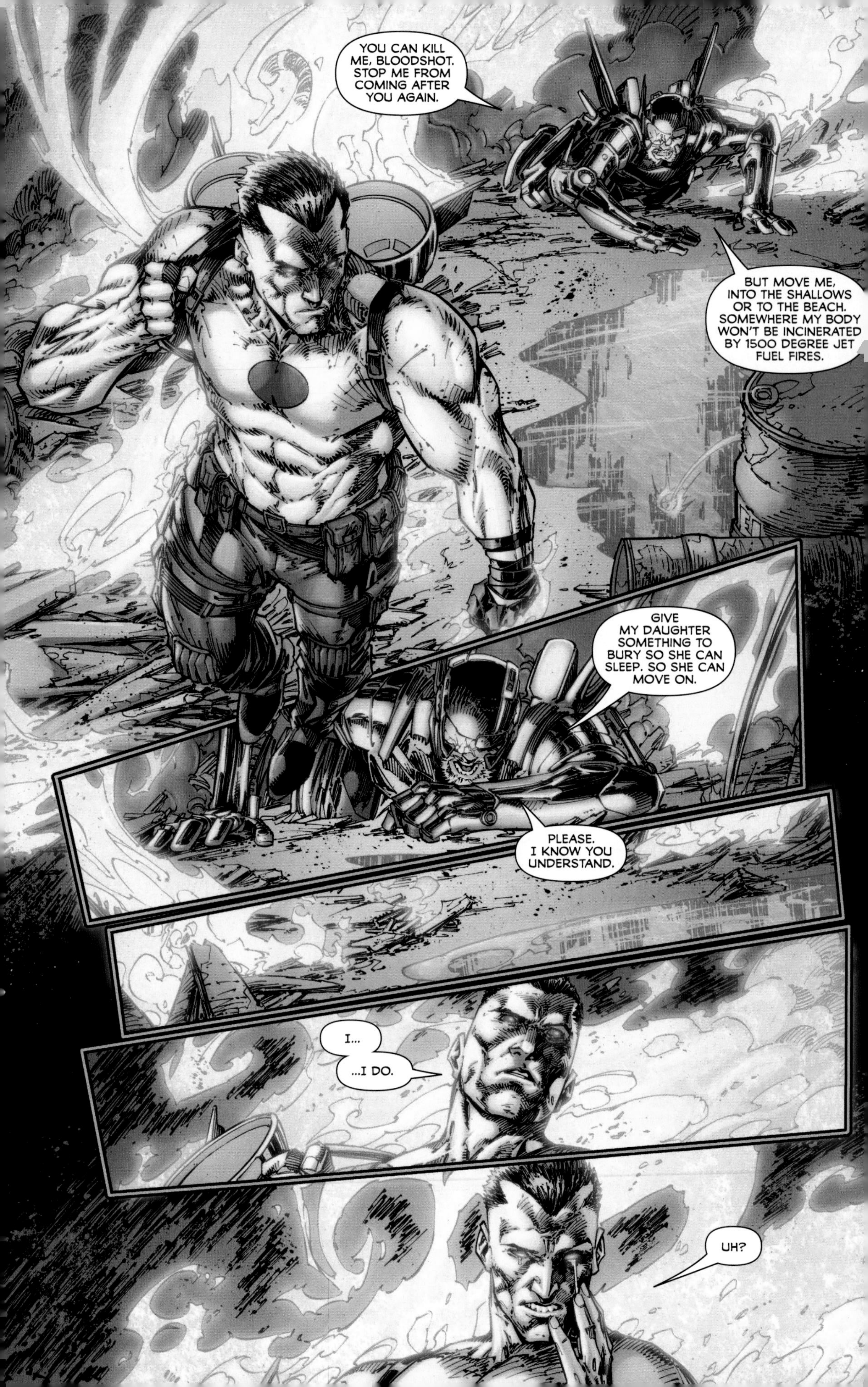
YOU CAN KILL ME, BLOODSHOT. STOP ME FROM COMING AFTER YOU AGAIN.
BUT MOVE ME, INTO THE SHALLOWS OR TO THE BEACH. SOMEWHERE MY BODY WON'T BE INCINERATED BY 1500 DEGREE JET FUEL FIRES.
GIVE MY DAUGHTER SOMETHING TO BURY SO SHE CAN SLEEP. SO SHE CAN MOVE ON.
PLEASE. I KNOW YOU UNDERSTAND.
I...
...I DO.
UH?

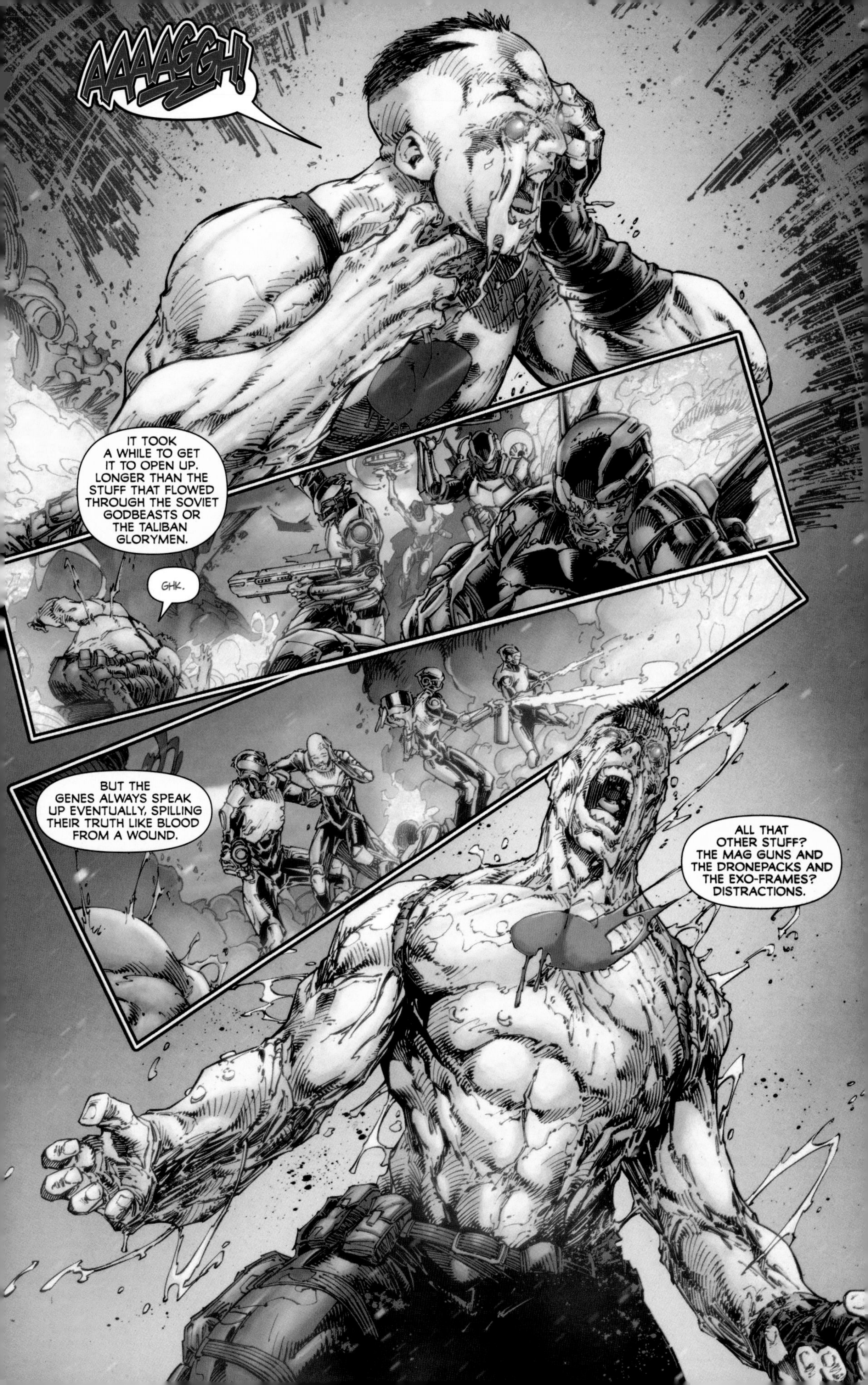
AAAAGGH!
IT TOOK A WHILE TO GET IT TO OPEN UP. LONGER THAN THE STUFF THAT FLOWED THROUGH THE SOVIET GODBEASTS OR THE TALIBAN GLORYMEN.
GHK.
BUT THE GENES ALWAYS SPEAK UP EVENTUALLY, SPILLING THEIR TRUTH LIKE BLOOD FROM A WOUND.
ALL THAT OTHER STUFF? THE MAG GUNS AND THE DRONEPACKS AND THE EXO-FRAMES? DISTRACTIONS.

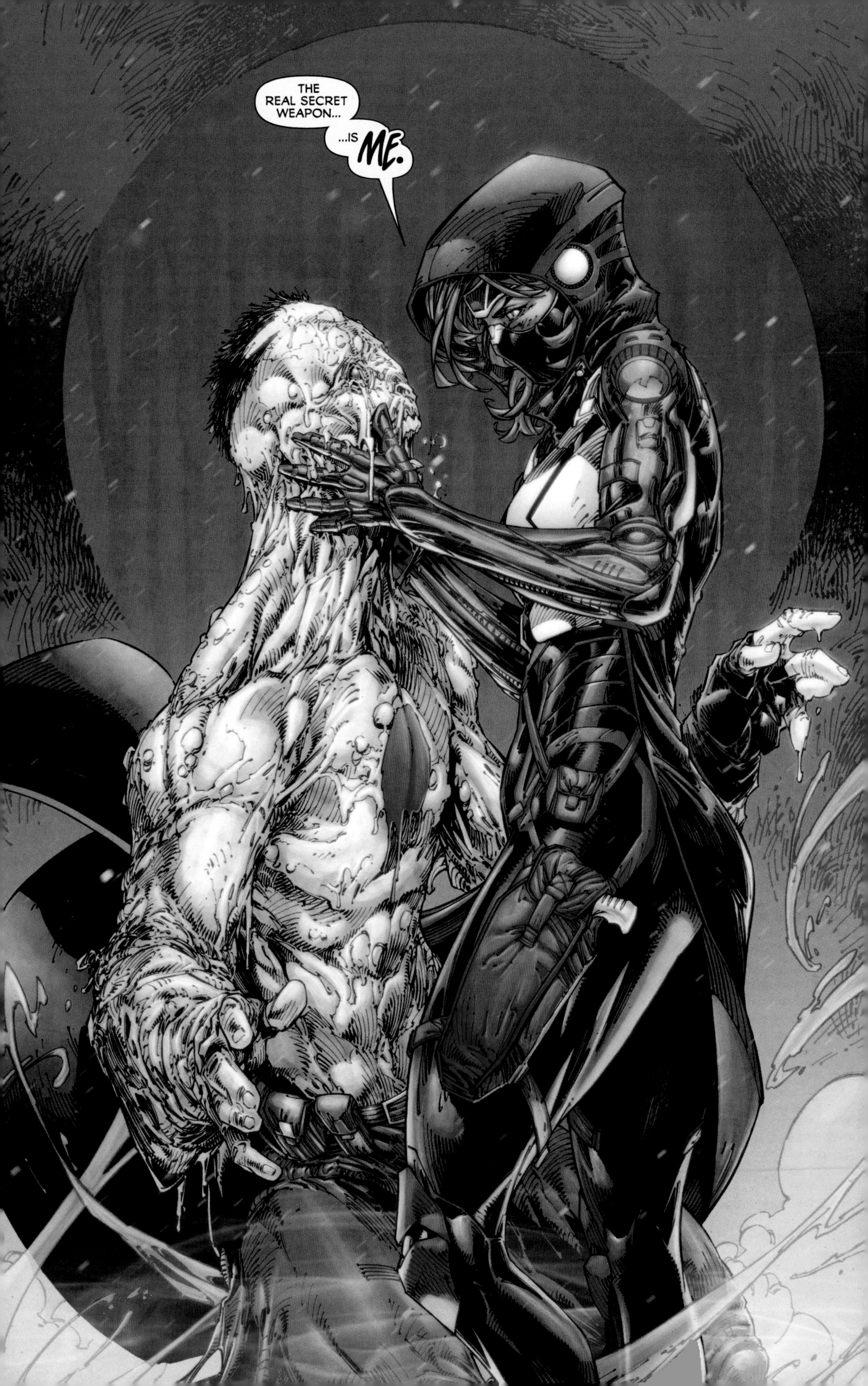
THE REAL SECRET WEAPON...
...IS ME.

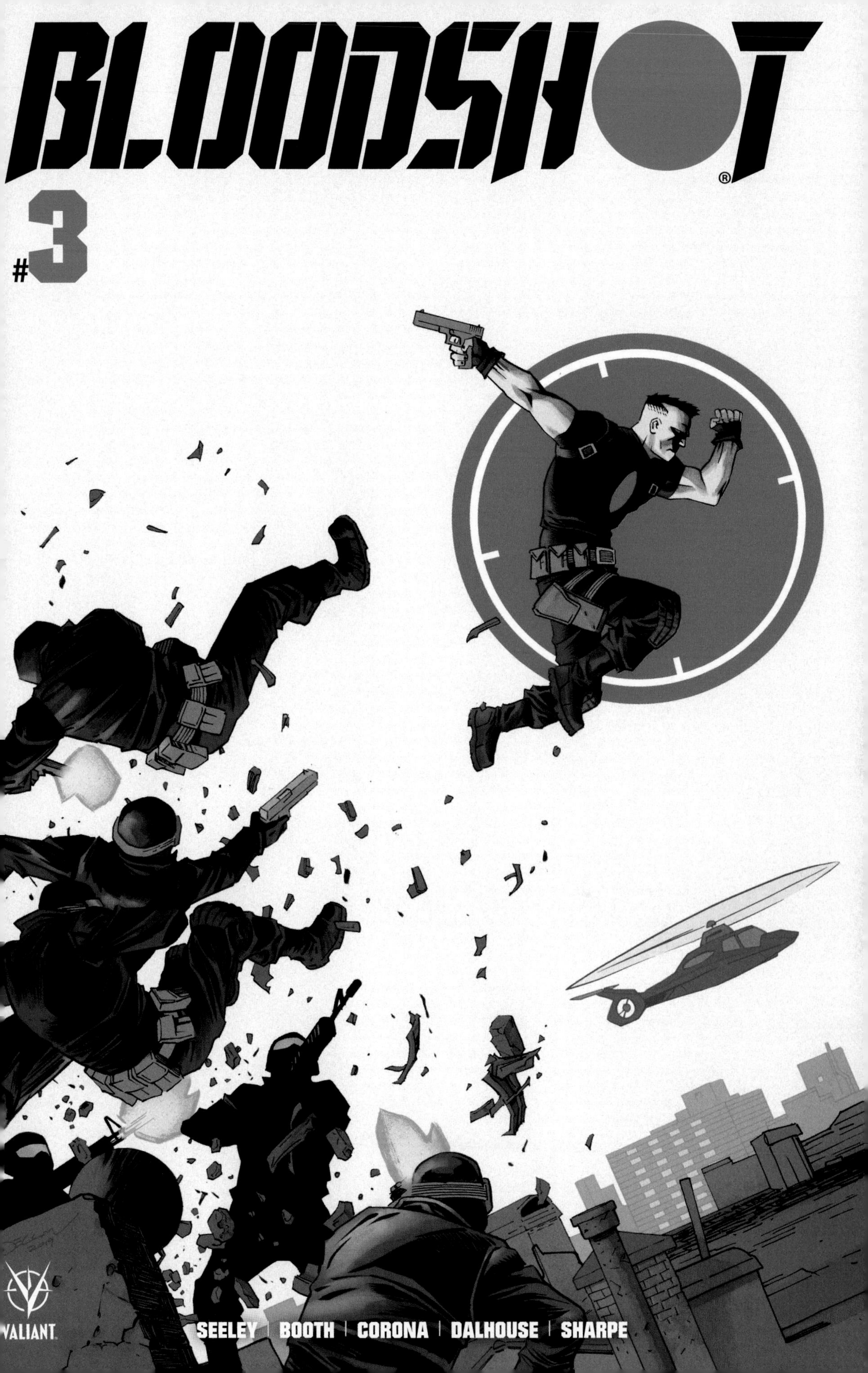
BLOODSHOT®
#3
VALIANT
SEELEY | BOOTH | CORONA | DALHOUSE | SHARPE

BLOODSHOT #3

WRITER: Tim Seeley
ARTIST: Brett Booth
INKER: Adelso Corona
COLORS: Andrew Dalhouse
LETTERS: Dave Sharpe
COVER ARTIST: Declan Shalvey
ASSISTANT EDITOR: Drew Baumgartner
EDITOR: Lysa Hawkins

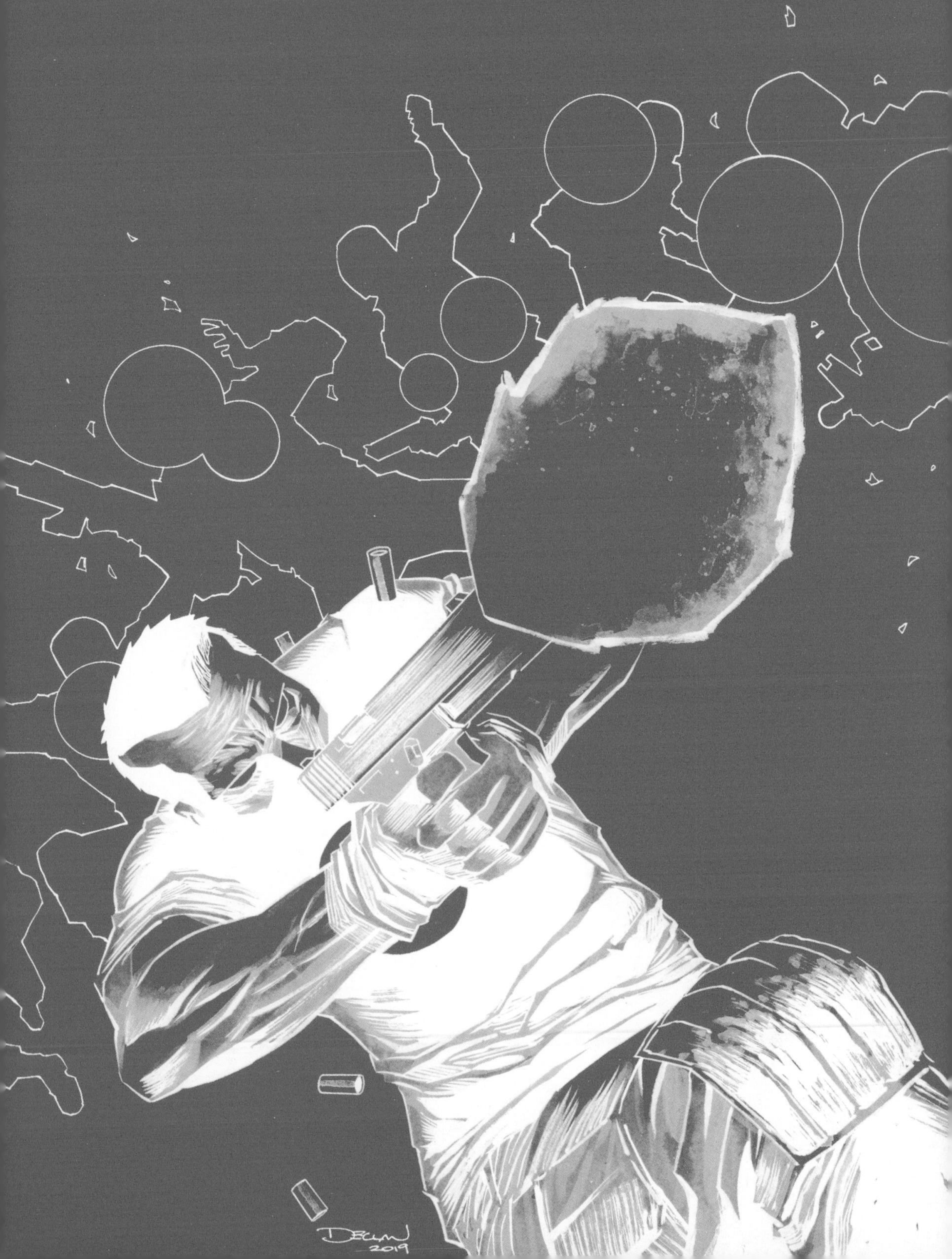
DECLAN
2019

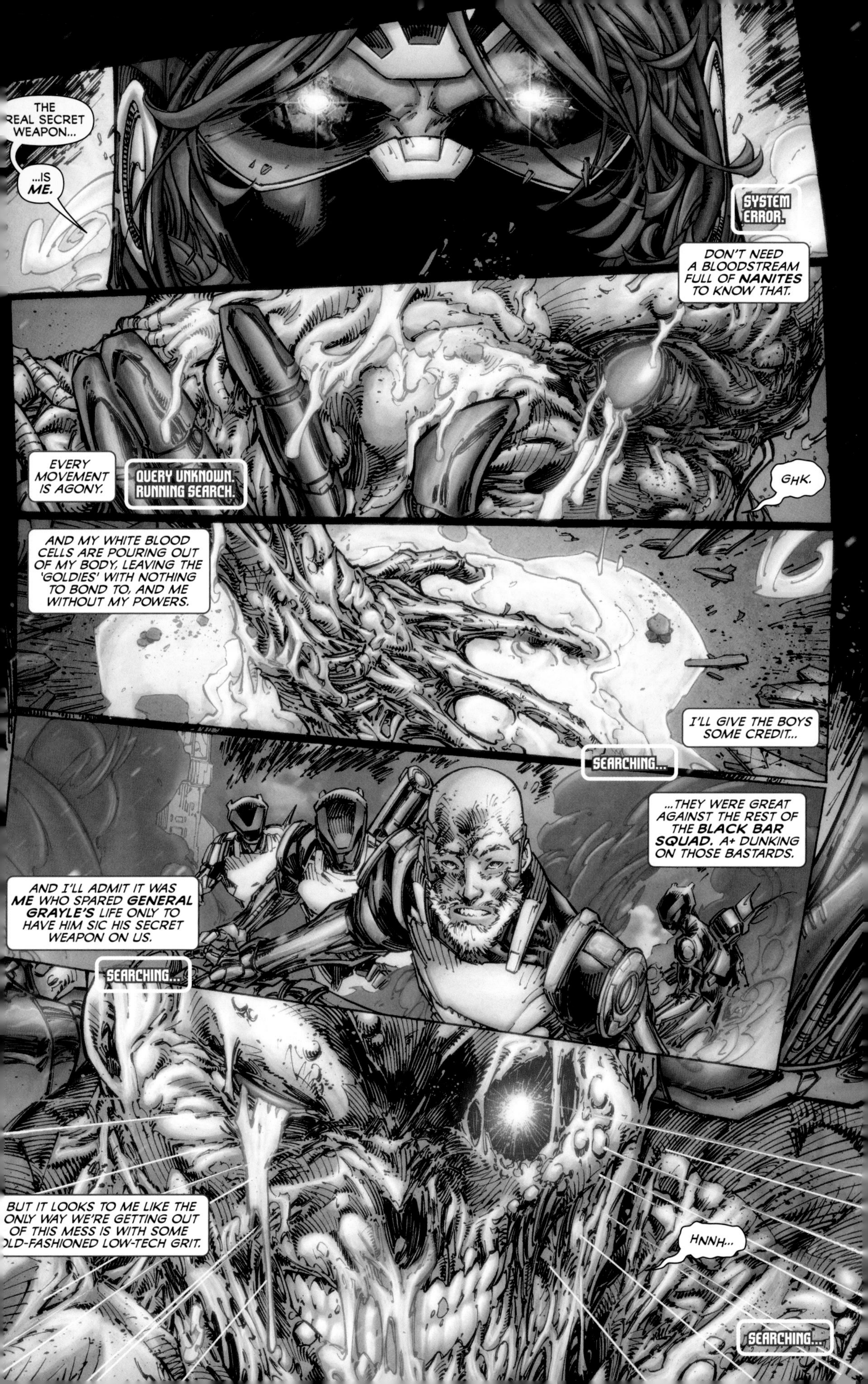
THE REAL SECRET WEAPON...
...IS ME.
SYSTEM ERROR.
DON'T NEED A BLOODSTREAM FULL OF NANITES TO KNOW THAT.
EVERY MOVEMENT IS AGONY.
QUERY UNKNOWN. RUNNING SEARCH.
GHK.
AND MY WHITE BLOOD CELLS ARE POURING OUT OF MY BODY, LEAVING THE 'GOLDIES' WITH NOTHING TO BOND TO, AND ME WITHOUT MY POWERS.
I'LL GIVE THE BOYS SOME CREDIT...
SEARCHING...
...THEY WERE GREAT AGAINST THE REST OF THE BLACK BAR SQUAD. A+ DUNKING ON THOSE BASTARDS.
AND I'LL ADMIT IT WAS ME WHO SPARED GENERAL GRAYLE'S LIFE ONLY TO HAVE HIM SIC HIS SECRET WEAPON ON US.
SEARCHING...
BUT IT LOOKS TO ME LIKE THE ONLY WAY WE'RE GETTING OUT OF THIS MESS IS WITH SOME OLD-FASHIONED LOW-TECH GRIT.
HNNH...
SEARCHING...

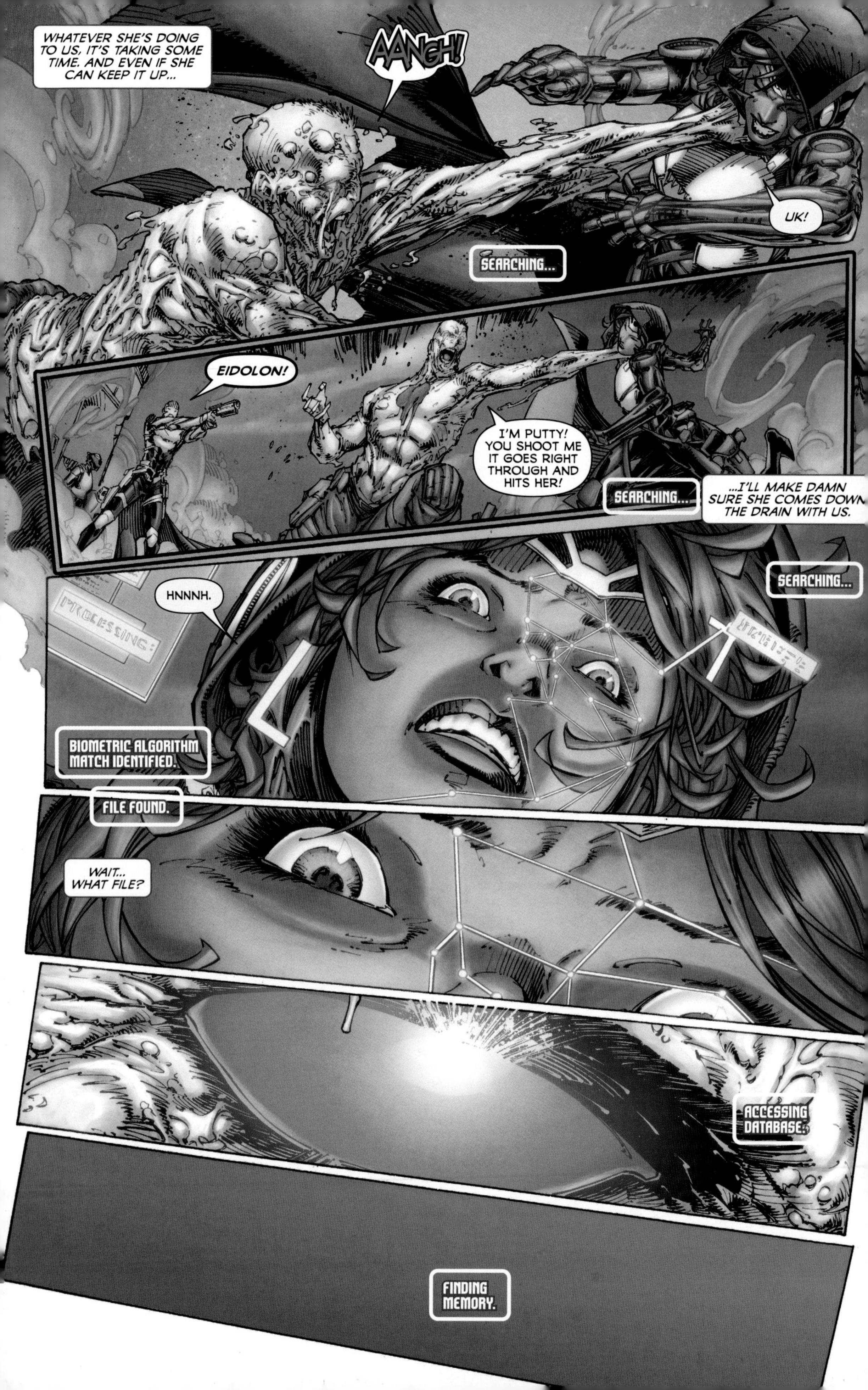

WHATEVER SHE'S DOING TO US, IT'S TAKING SOME TIME. AND EVEN IF SHE CAN KEEP IT UP...
AANGH!
UK!
SEARCHING...
EIDOLON!
I'M PUTTY! YOU SHOOT ME IT GOES RIGHT THROUGH AND HITS HER!
SEARCHING...
...I'LL MAKE DAMN SURE SHE COMES DOWN THE DRAIN WITH US.
SEARCHING...
HNNNH.
PROCESSING:
BIOMETRIC ALGORITHM MATCH IDENTIFIED.
FILE FOUND.
WAIT... WHAT FILE?
ACCESSING DATABASE.
FINDING MEMORY.

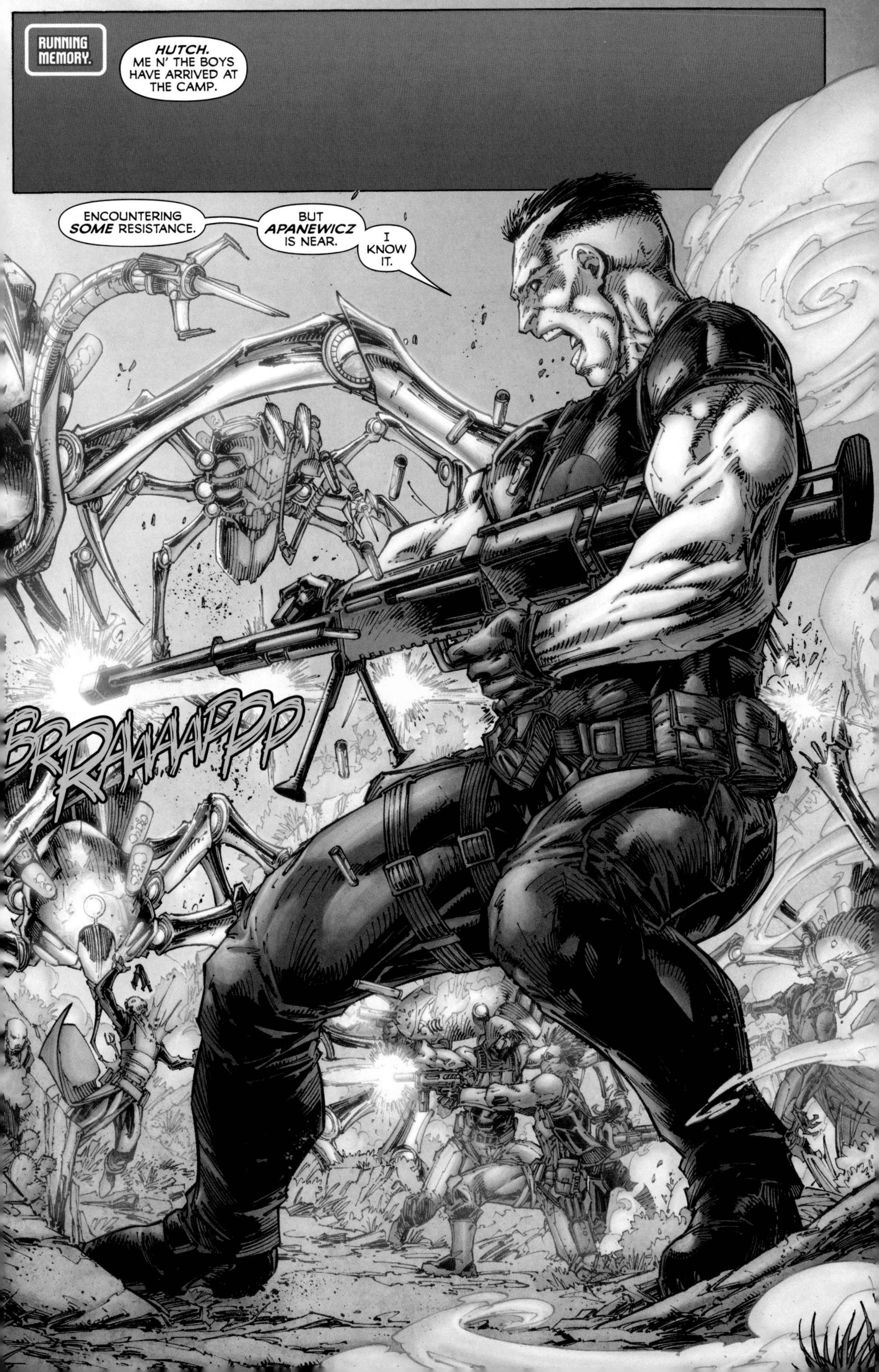
RUNNING MEMORY.
HUTCH. ME N' THE BOYS HAVE ARRIVED AT THE CAMP.
ENCOUNTERING SOME RESISTANCE.
BUT APANEWICZ IS NEAR.
I KNOW IT.
BRRAAAAPPPP

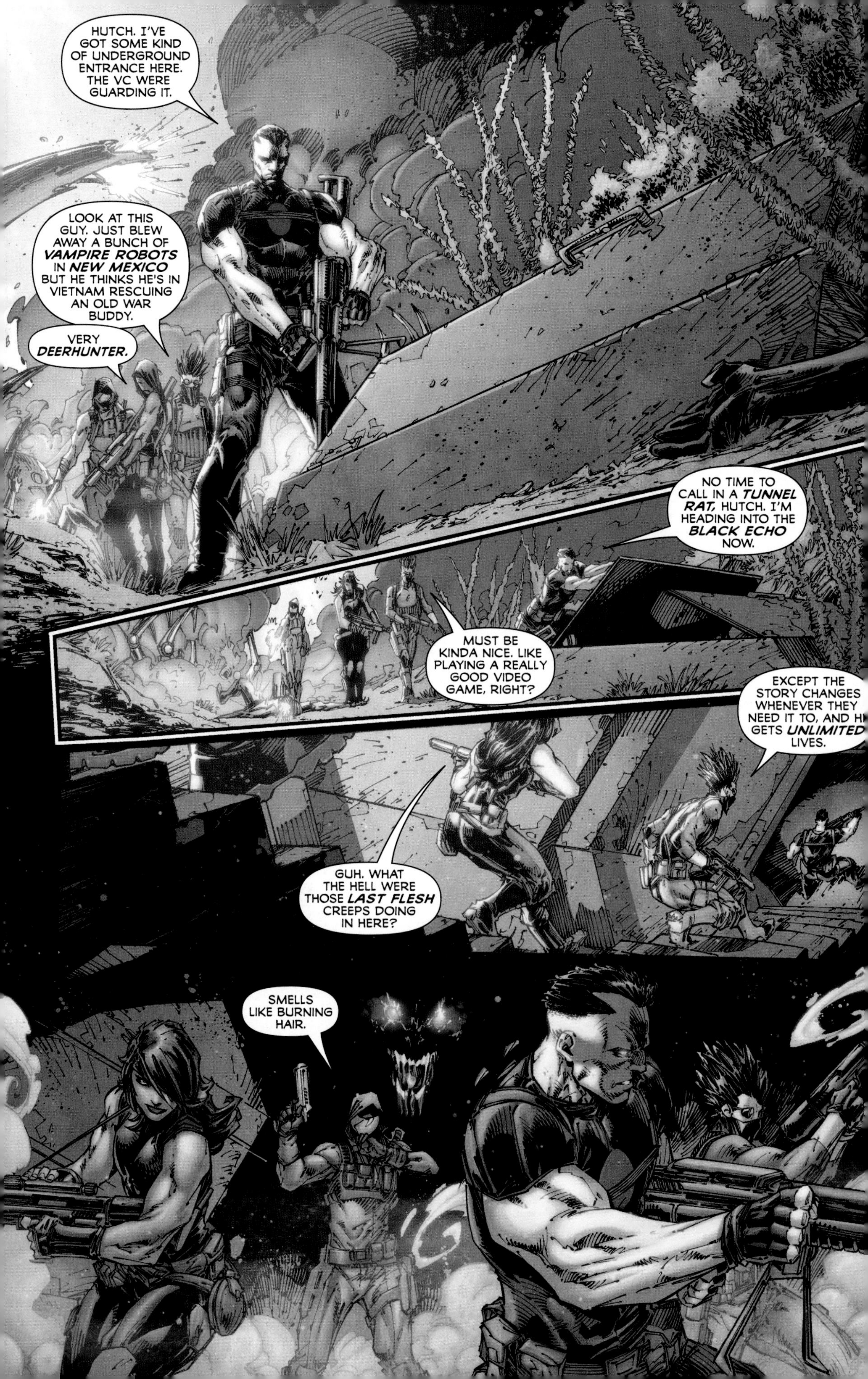
HUTCH. I'VE GOT SOME KIND OF UNDERGROUND ENTRANCE HERE. THE VC WERE GUARDING IT.
LOOK AT THIS GUY. JUST BLEW AWAY A BUNCH OF *VAMPIRE ROBOTS* IN *NEW MEXICO* BUT HE THINKS HE'S IN VIETNAM RESCUING AN OLD WAR BUDDY.
VERY *DEERHUNTER.*
NO TIME TO CALL IN A *TUNNEL RAT,* HUTCH. I'M HEADING INTO THE *BLACK ECHO* NOW.
MUST BE KINDA NICE. LIKE PLAYING A REALLY GOOD VIDEO GAME, RIGHT?
EXCEPT THE STORY CHANGES WHENEVER THEY NEED IT TO, AND H GETS *UNLIMITED* LIVES.
GUH. WHAT THE HELL WERE THOSE *LAST FLESH* CREEPS DOING IN HERE?
SMELLS LIKE BURNING HAIR.

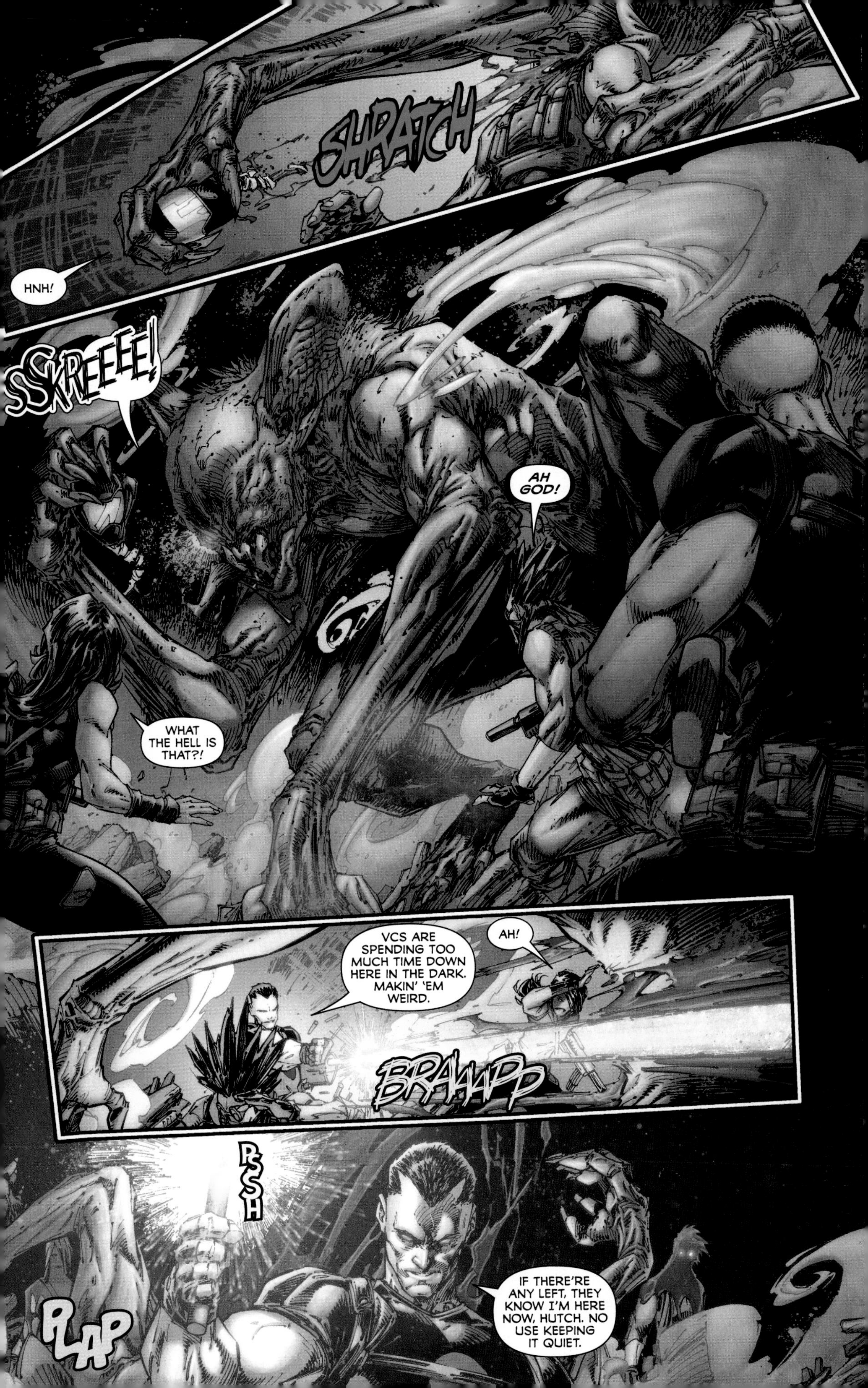
SHRATCH
HNH!
SSKREEEEE!
AH GOD!
WHAT THE HELL IS THAT?!
VCS ARE SPENDING TOO MUCH TIME DOWN HERE IN THE DARK. MAKIN' 'EM WEIRD.
AH!
BRAKAPP
PSSH
PLAP
IF THERE'RE ANY LEFT, THEY KNOW I'M HERE NOW, HUTCH. NO USE KEEPING IT QUIET.

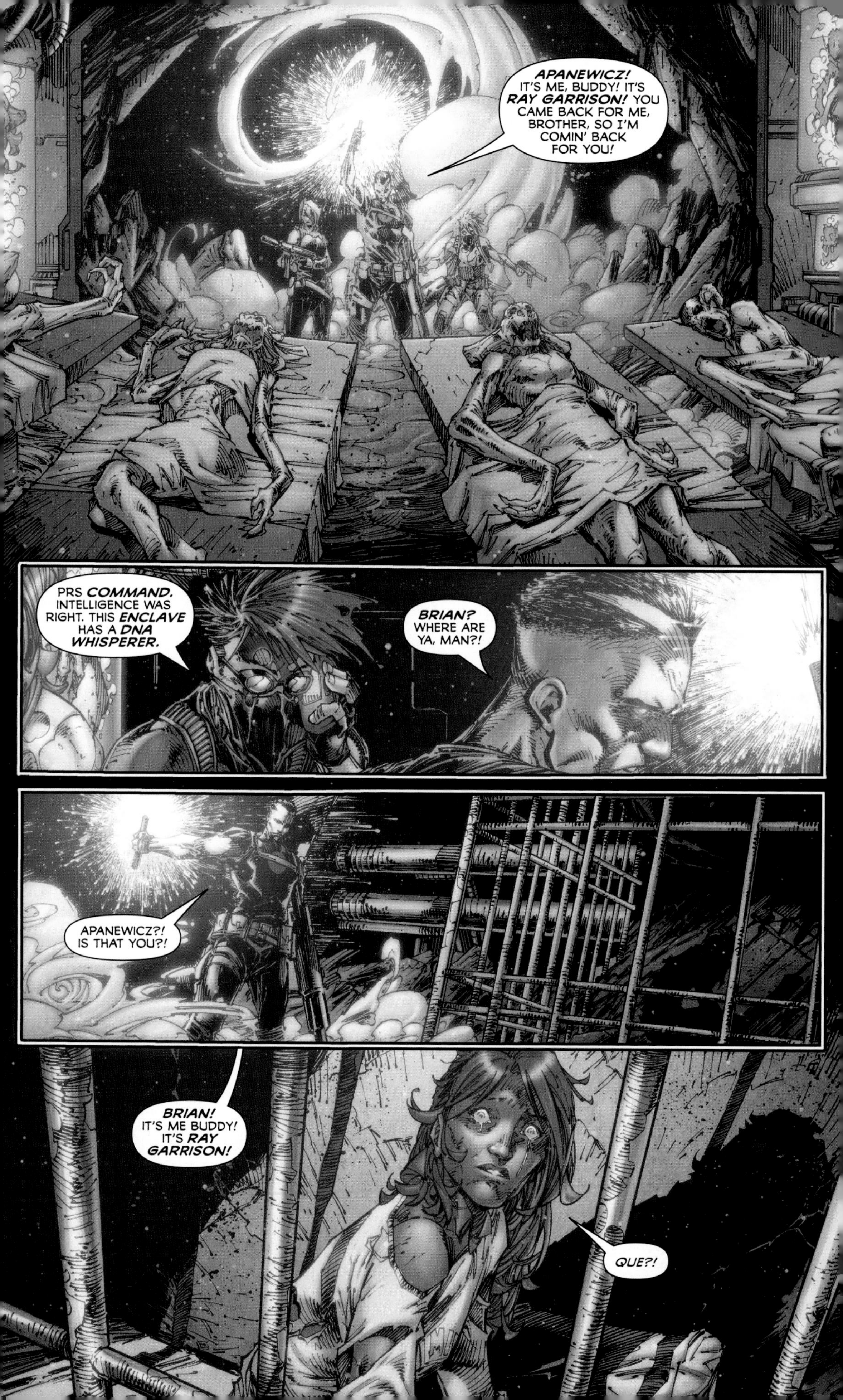
APANEWICZ! IT'S ME, BUDDY! IT'S RAY GARRISON! YOU CAME BACK FOR ME, BROTHER, SO I'M COMIN' BACK FOR YOU!
PRS COMMAND. INTELLIGENCE WAS RIGHT. THIS ENCLAVE HAS A DNA WHISPERER.
BRIAN? WHERE ARE YA, MAN?!
APANEWICZ?! IS THAT YOU?!
BRIAN! IT'S ME BUDDY! IT'S RAY GARRISON!
QUE?!

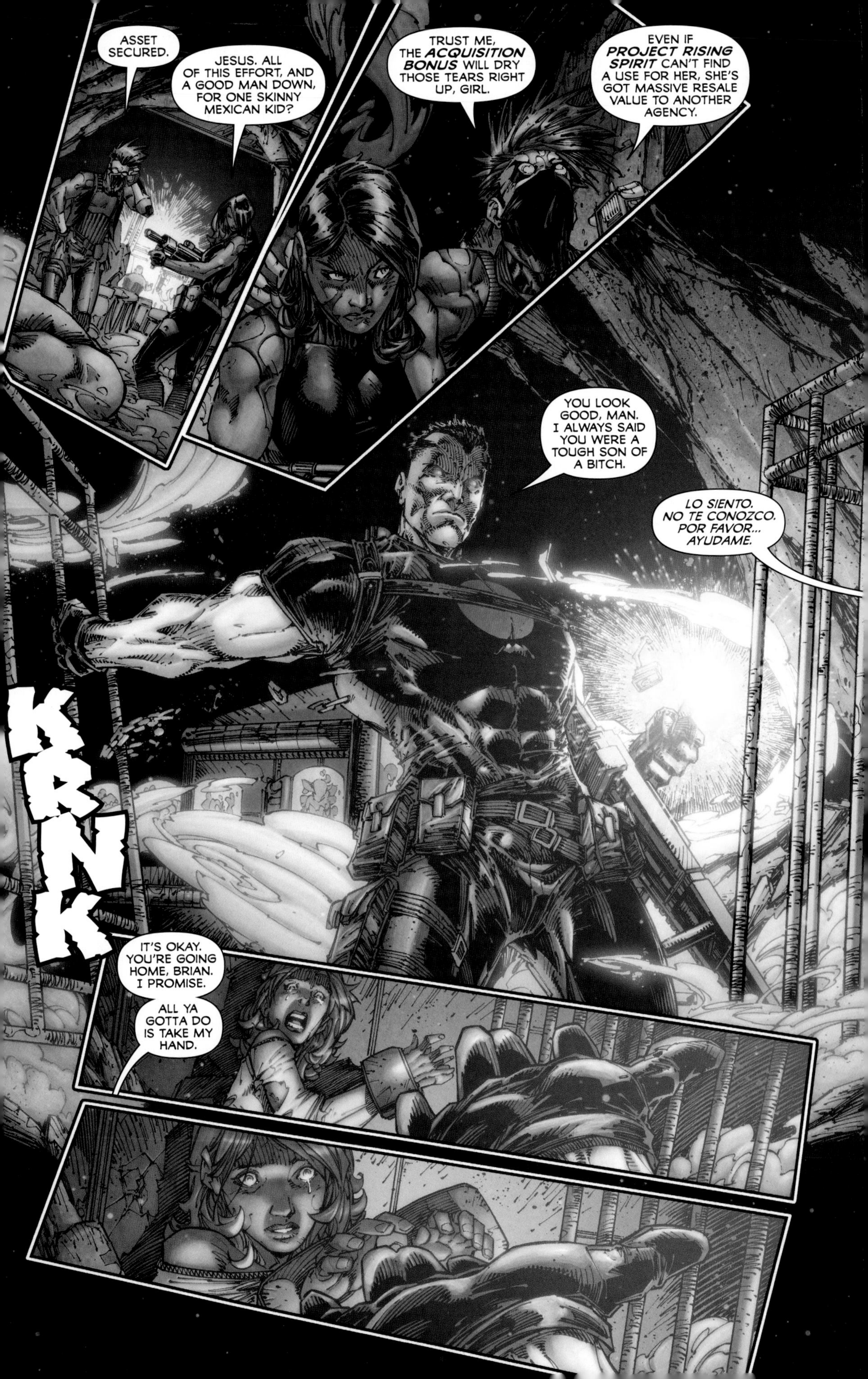
ASSET SECURED.
JESUS. ALL OF THIS EFFORT, AND A GOOD MAN DOWN, FOR ONE SKINNY MEXICAN KID?
TRUST ME, THE ACQUISITION BONUS WILL DRY THOSE TEARS RIGHT UP, GIRL.
EVEN IF PROJECT RISING SPIRIT CAN'T FIND A USE FOR HER, SHE'S GOT MASSIVE RESALE VALUE TO ANOTHER AGENCY.
YOU LOOK GOOD, MAN. I ALWAYS SAID YOU WERE A TOUGH SON OF A BITCH.
LO SIENTO. NO TE CONOZCO. POR FAVOR... AYUDAME.
KRNK
IT'S OKAY. YOU'RE GOING HOME, BRIAN. I PROMISE.
ALL YA GOTTA DO IS TAKE MY HAND.

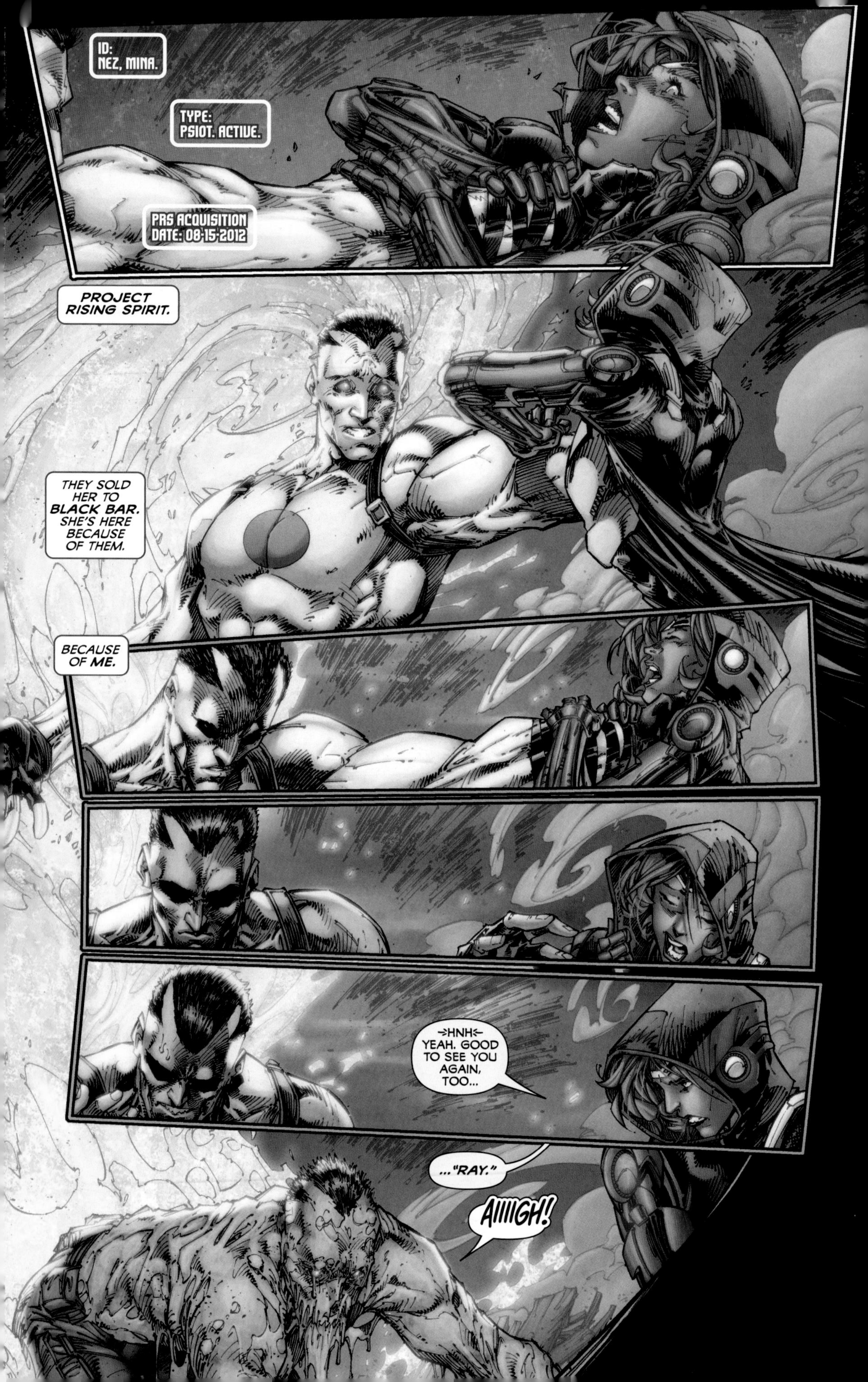
ID:
NEZ, MINA.
TYPE:
PSIOT. ACTIVE.
PRS ACQUISITION
DATE: 08-15-2012
PROJECT RISING SPIRIT.
THEY SOLD HER TO BLACK BAR. SHE'S HERE BECAUSE OF THEM.
BECAUSE OF ME.
-HNH- YEAH. GOOD TO SEE YOU AGAIN, TOO...
..."RAY."
AIIIIGH!

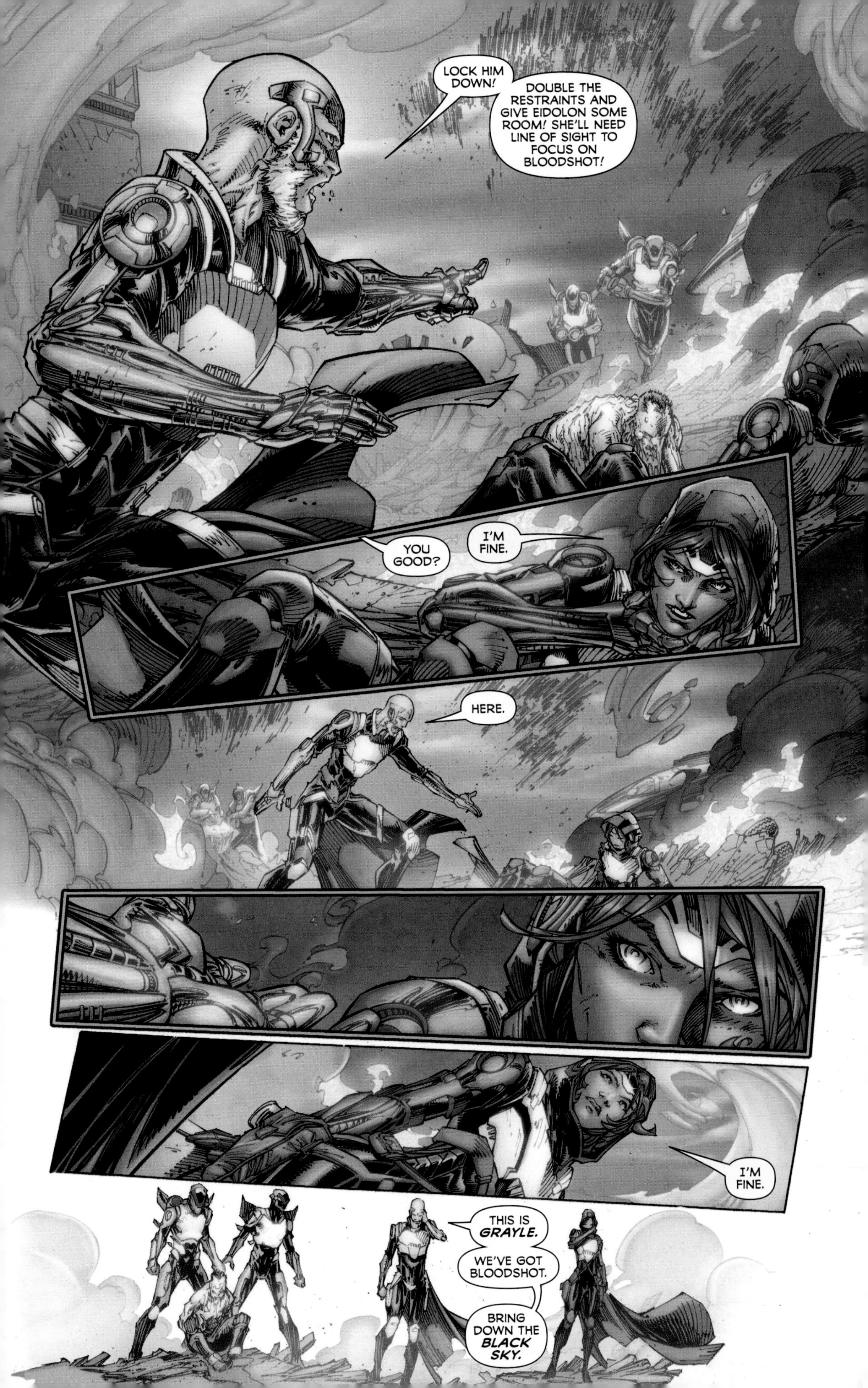
LOCK HIM DOWN!
DOUBLE THE RESTRAINTS AND GIVE EIDOLON SOME ROOM! SHE'LL NEED LINE OF SIGHT TO FOCUS ON BLOODSHOT!
YOU GOOD?
I'M FINE.
HERE.
I'M FINE.
THIS IS GRAYLE.
WE'VE GOT BLOODSHOT.
BRING DOWN THE BLACK SKY.

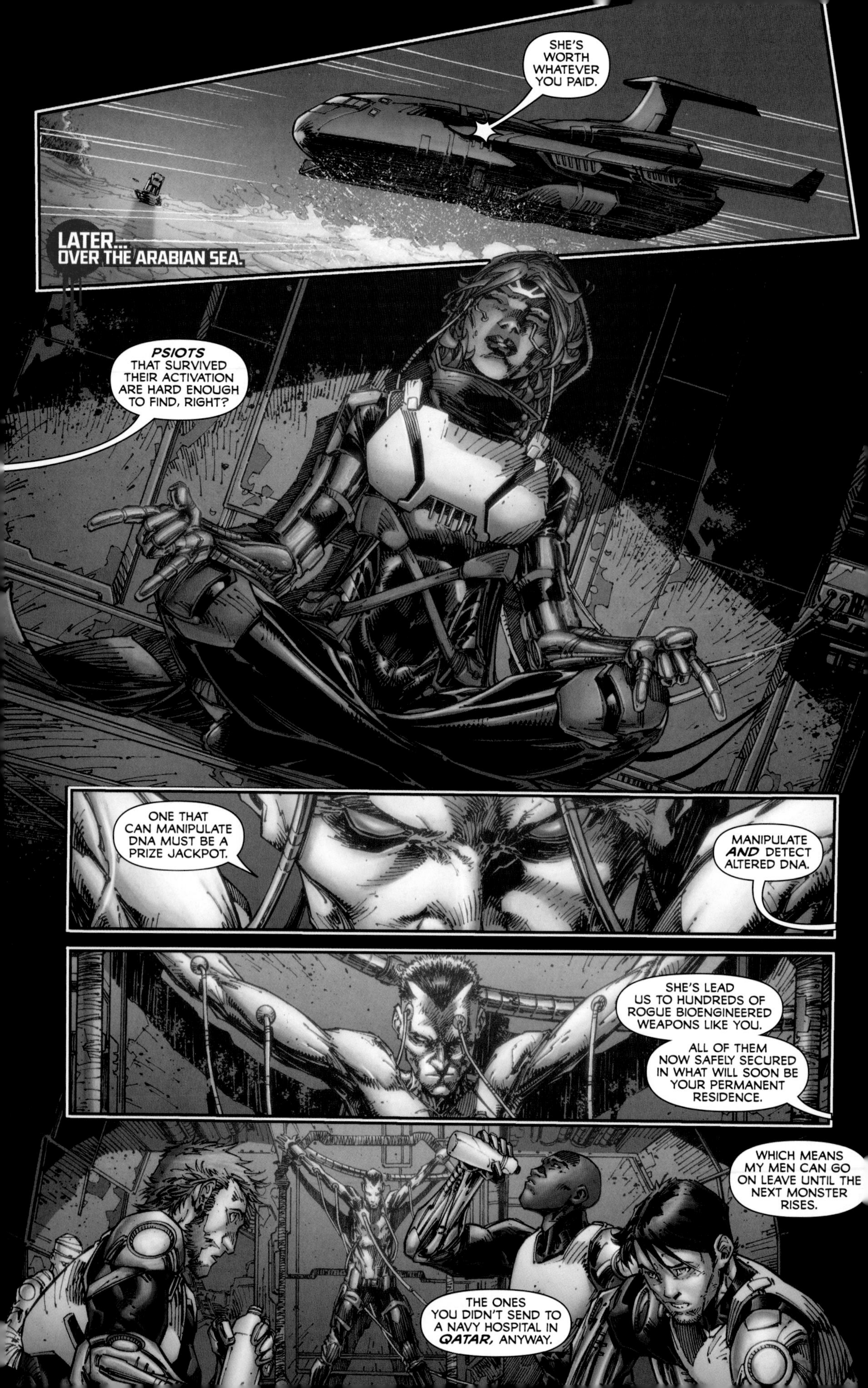
SHE'S WORTH WHATEVER YOU PAID.
LATER... OVER THE ARABIAN SEA.
PSIOTS THAT SURVIVED THEIR ACTIVATION ARE HARD ENOUGH TO FIND, RIGHT?
ONE THAT CAN MANIPULATE DNA MUST BE A PRIZE JACKPOT.
MANIPULATE AND DETECT ALTERED DNA.
SHE'S LEAD US TO HUNDREDS OF ROGUE BIOENGINEERED WEAPONS LIKE YOU.
ALL OF THEM NOW SAFELY SECURED IN WHAT WILL SOON BE YOUR PERMANENT RESIDENCE.
WHICH MEANS MY MEN CAN GO ON LEAVE UNTIL THE NEXT MONSTER RISES.
THE ONES YOU DIDN'T SEND TO A NAVY HOSPITAL IN QATAR, ANYWAY.

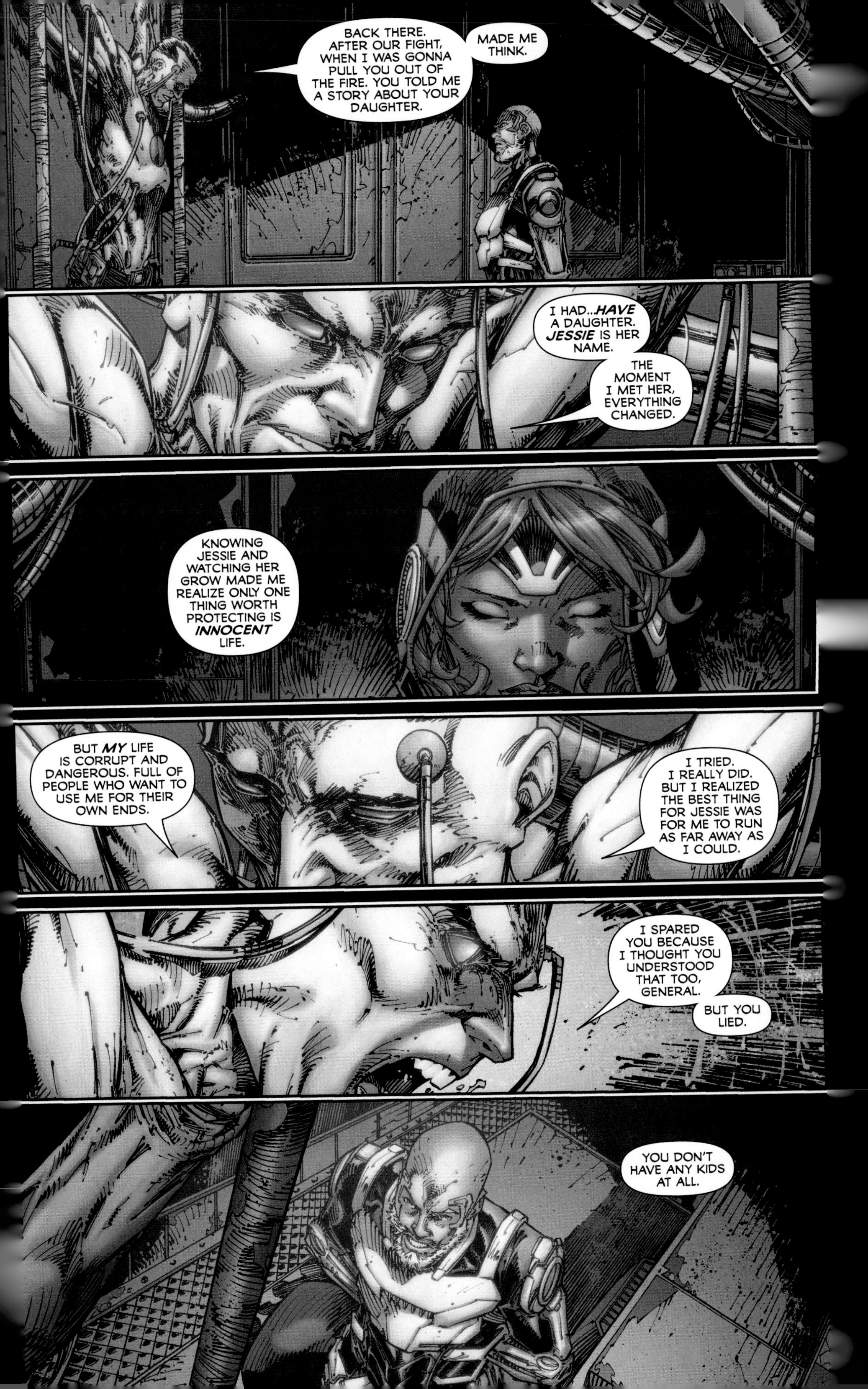

BACK THERE. AFTER OUR FIGHT, WHEN I WAS GONNA PULL YOU OUT OF THE FIRE. YOU TOLD ME A STORY ABOUT YOUR DAUGHTER.
MADE ME THINK.
I HAD...*HAVE* A DAUGHTER. *JESSIE* IS HER NAME.
THE MOMENT I MET HER, EVERYTHING CHANGED.
KNOWING JESSIE AND WATCHING HER GROW MADE ME REALIZE ONLY ONE THING WORTH PROTECTING IS *INNOCENT* LIFE.
BUT *MY* LIFE IS CORRUPT AND DANGEROUS. FULL OF PEOPLE WHO WANT TO USE ME FOR THEIR OWN ENDS.
I TRIED. I REALLY DID. BUT I REALIZED THE BEST THING FOR JESSIE WAS FOR ME TO RUN AS FAR AWAY AS I COULD.
I SPARED YOU BECAUSE I THOUGHT YOU UNDERSTOOD THAT TOO, GENERAL.
BUT YOU LIED.
YOU DON'T HAVE ANY KIDS AT ALL.

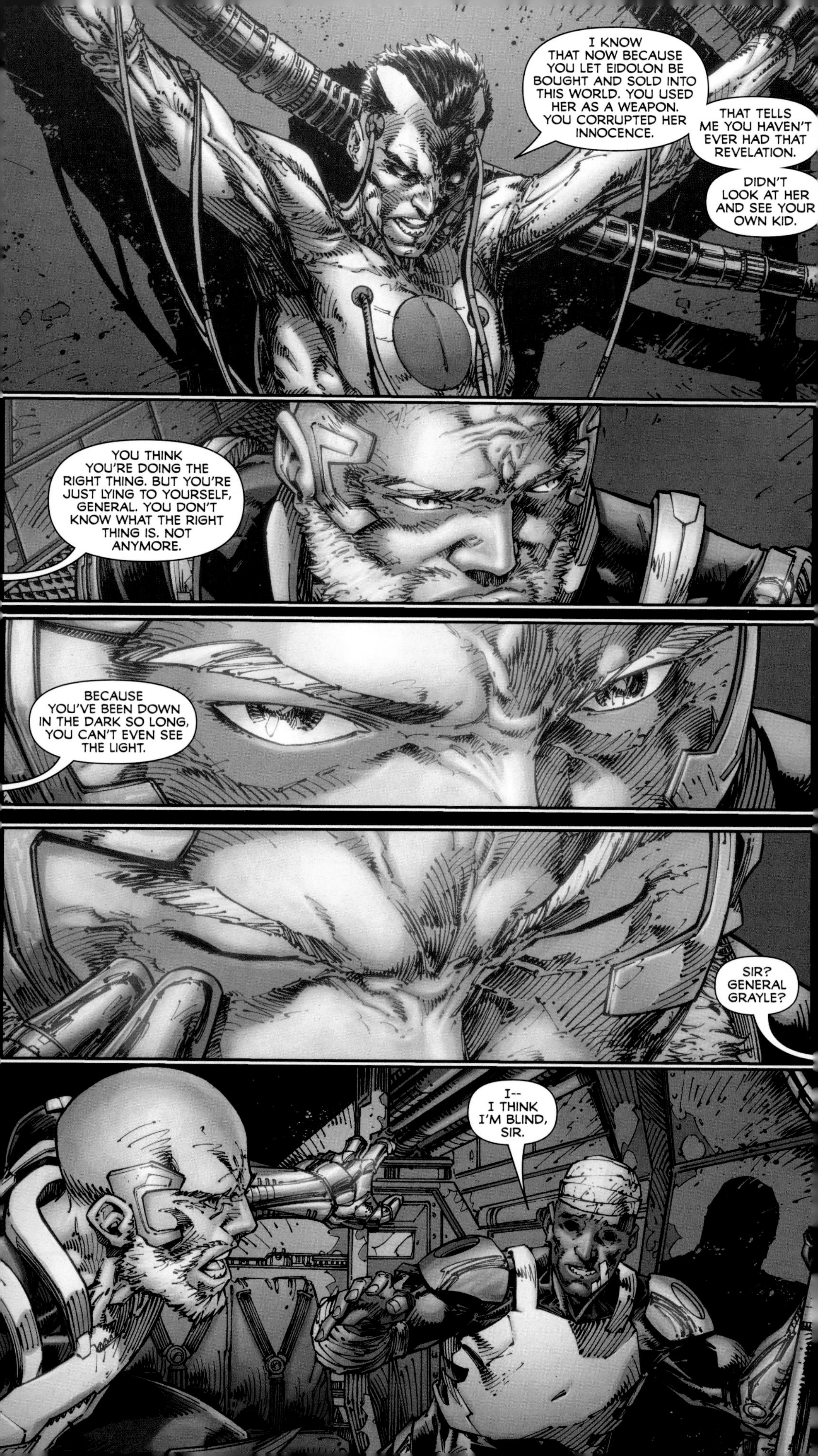
I KNOW THAT NOW BECAUSE YOU LET EIDOLON BE BOUGHT AND SOLD INTO THIS WORLD. YOU USED HER AS A WEAPON. YOU CORRUPTED HER INNOCENCE.
THAT TELLS ME YOU HAVEN'T EVER HAD THAT REVELATION.
DIDN'T LOOK AT HER AND SEE YOUR OWN KID.
YOU THINK YOU'RE DOING THE RIGHT THING. BUT YOU'RE JUST LYING TO YOURSELF, GENERAL. YOU DON'T KNOW WHAT THE RIGHT THING IS. NOT ANYMORE.
BECAUSE YOU'VE BEEN DOWN IN THE DARK SO LONG, YOU CAN'T EVEN SEE THE LIGHT.
SIR? GENERAL GRAYLE?
I-- I THINK I'M BLIND, SIR.

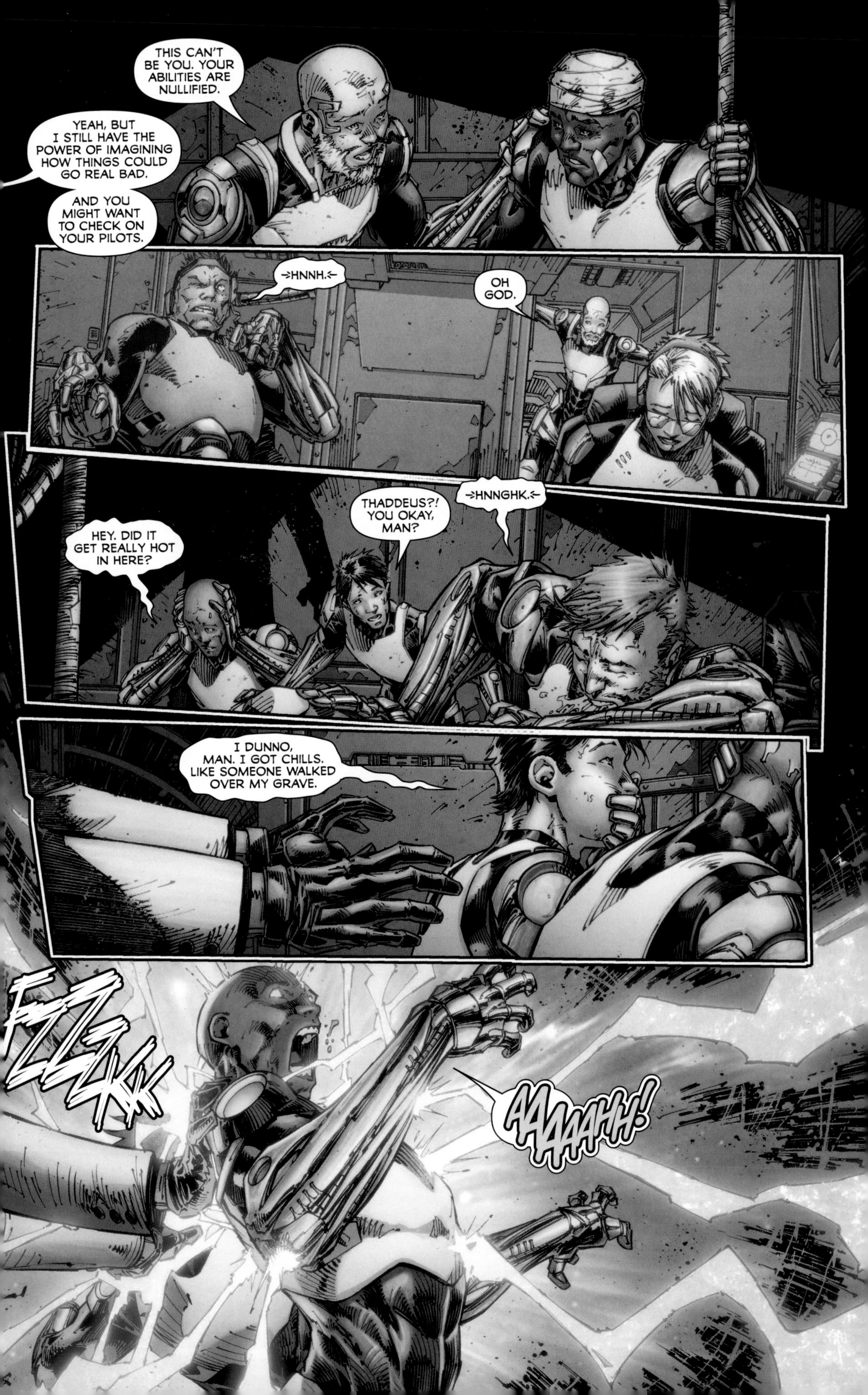
THIS CAN'T BE YOU. YOUR ABILITIES ARE NULLIFIED.
YEAH, BUT I STILL HAVE THE POWER OF IMAGINING HOW THINGS COULD GO REAL BAD.
AND YOU MIGHT WANT TO CHECK ON YOUR PILOTS.
HNNH.
OH GOD.
HEY. DID IT GET REALLY HOT IN HERE?
THADDEUS?! YOU OKAY, MAN?
HNNGHK.
I DUNNO, MAN. I GOT CHILLS. LIKE SOMEONE WALKED OVER MY GRAVE.
FZZZKKK
AAAAAHH!

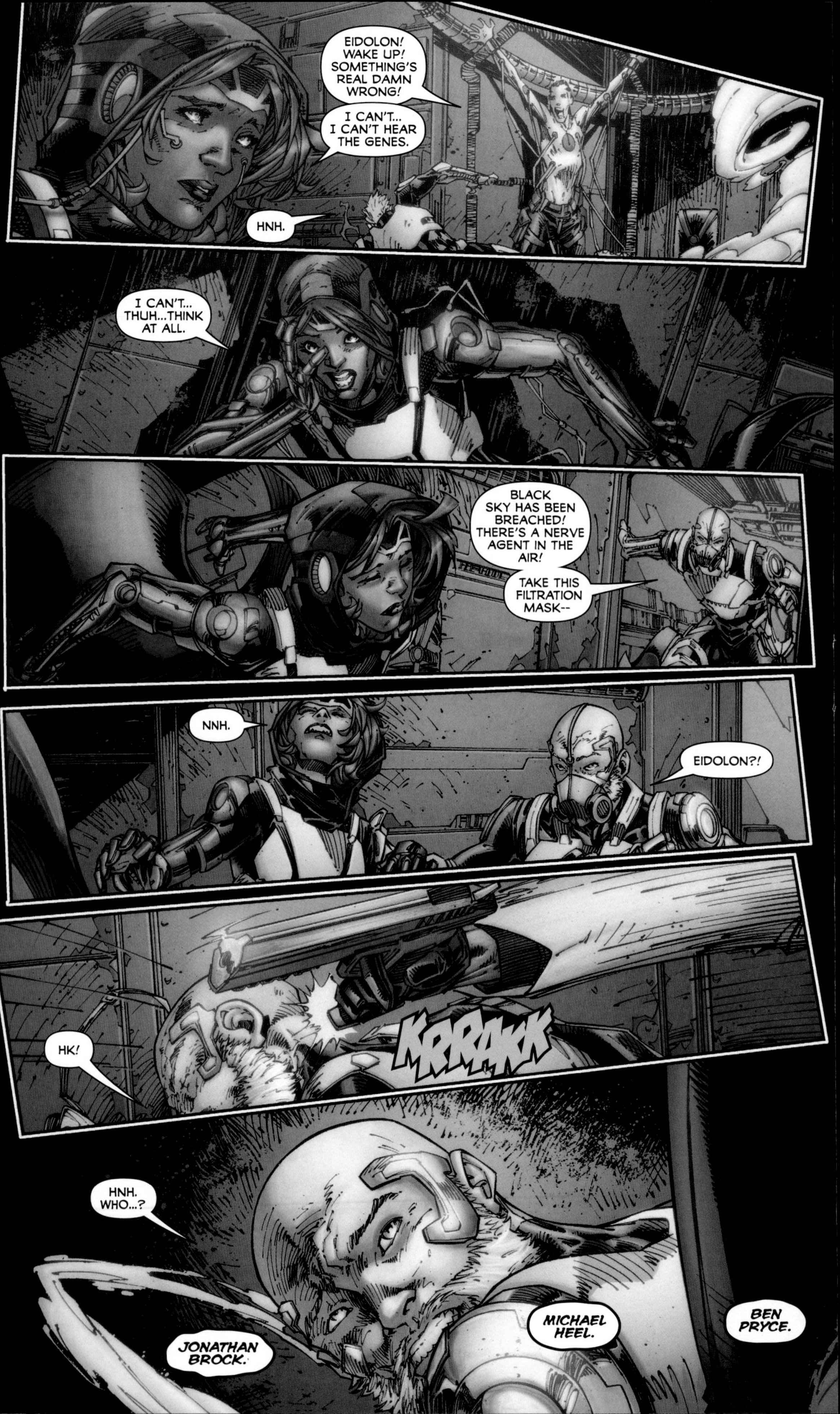
EIDOLON! WAKE UP! SOMETHING'S REAL DAMN WRONG!
I CAN'T... I CAN'T HEAR THE GENES.
HNH.
I CAN'T... THUH...THINK AT ALL.
BLACK SKY HAS BEEN BREACHED! THERE'S A NERVE AGENT IN THE AIR!
TAKE THIS FILTRATION MASK--
NNH.
EIDOLON?!
KRRAKK
HK!
HNH. WHO...?
JONATHAN BROCK.
MICHAEL HEEL.
BEN PRYCE.

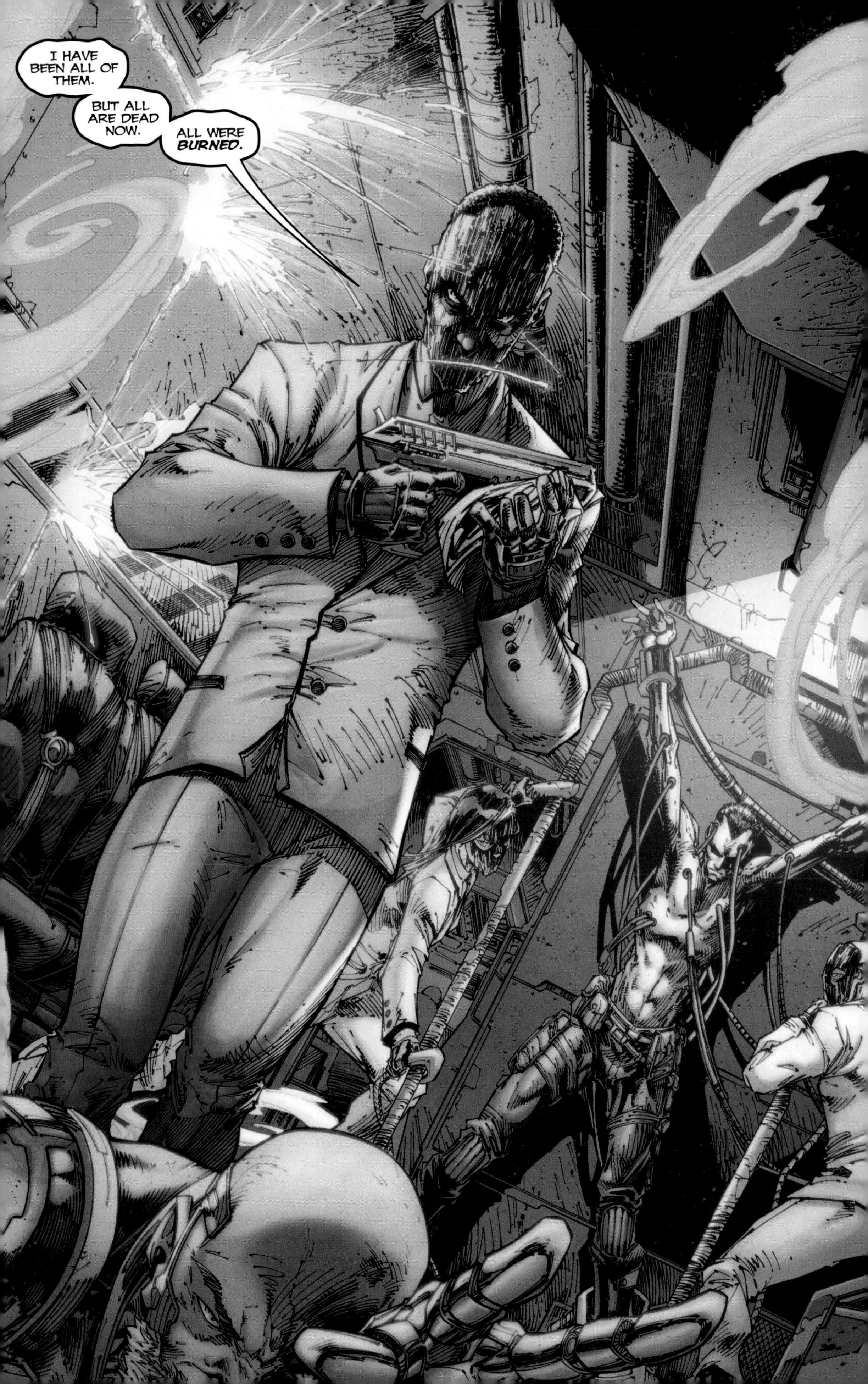
I HAVE BEEN ALL OF THEM.
BUT ALL ARE DEAD NOW.
ALL WERE *BURNED.*

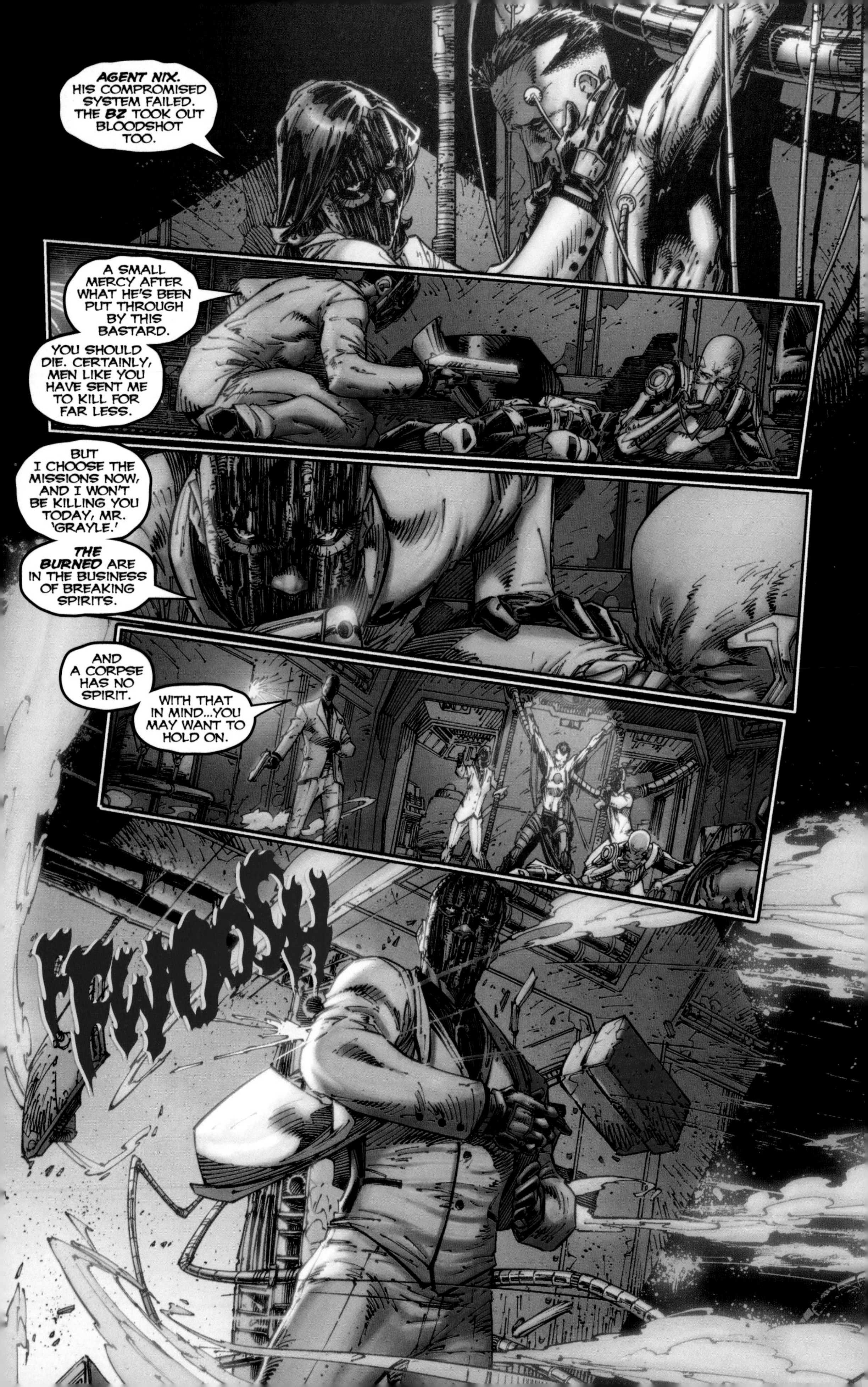
AGENT NIX. HIS COMPROMISED SYSTEM FAILED. THE B2 TOOK OUT BLOODSHOT TOO.
A SMALL MERCY AFTER WHAT HE'S BEEN PUT THROUGH BY THIS BASTARD.
YOU SHOULD DIE. CERTAINLY, MEN LIKE YOU HAVE SENT ME TO KILL FOR FAR LESS.
BUT I CHOOSE THE MISSIONS NOW, AND I WON'T BE KILLING YOU TODAY, MR. 'GRAYLE.'
THE BURNED ARE IN THE BUSINESS OF BREAKING SPIRITS.
AND A CORPSE HAS NO SPIRIT.
WITH THAT IN MIND...YOU MAY WANT TO HOLD ON.
FFWOOSH

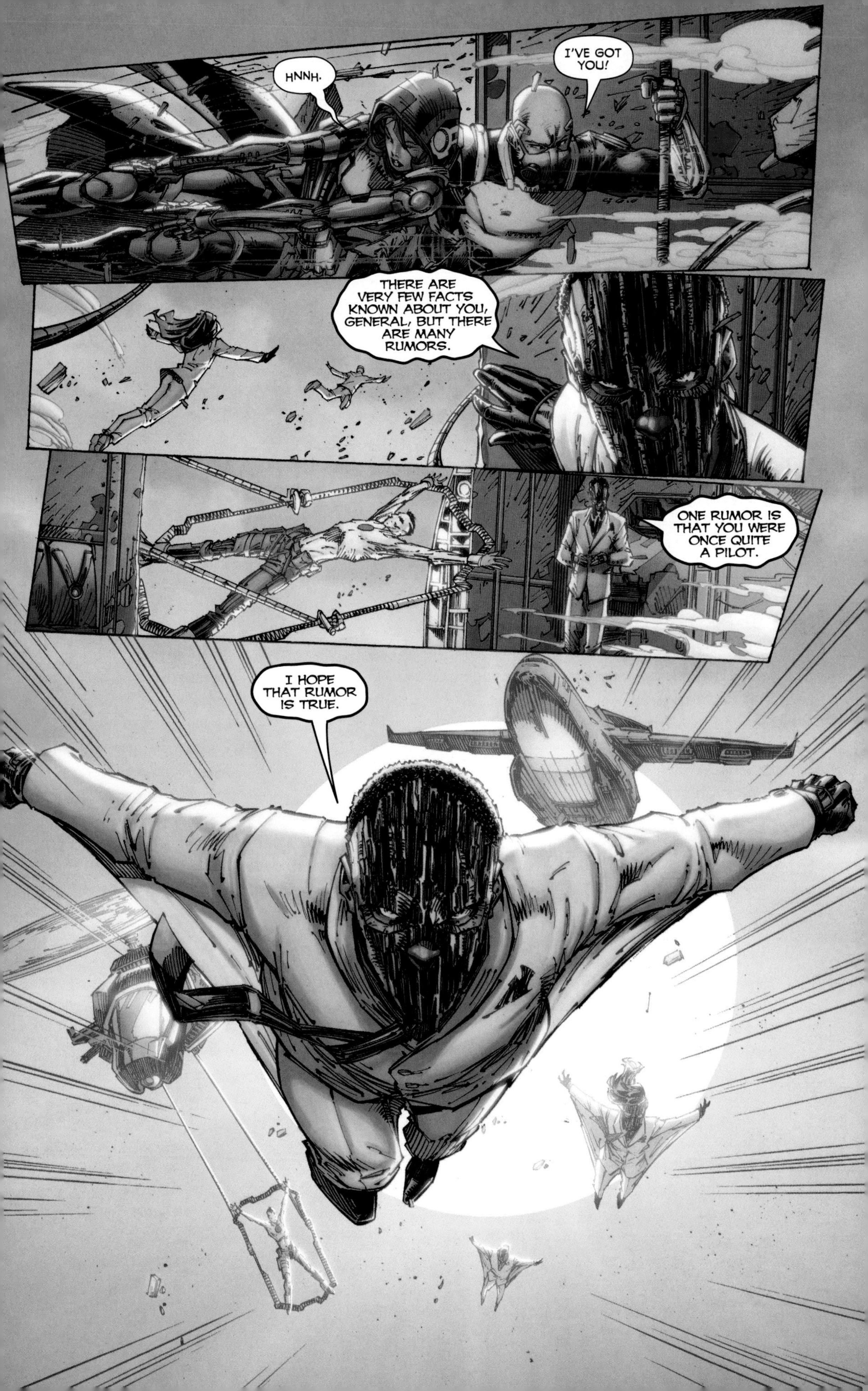
HNNH.
I'VE GOT YOU!
THERE ARE VERY FEW FACTS KNOWN ABOUT YOU, GENERAL, BUT THERE ARE MANY RUMORS.
ONE RUMOR IS THAT YOU WERE ONCE QUITE A PILOT.
I HOPE THAT RUMOR IS TRUE.

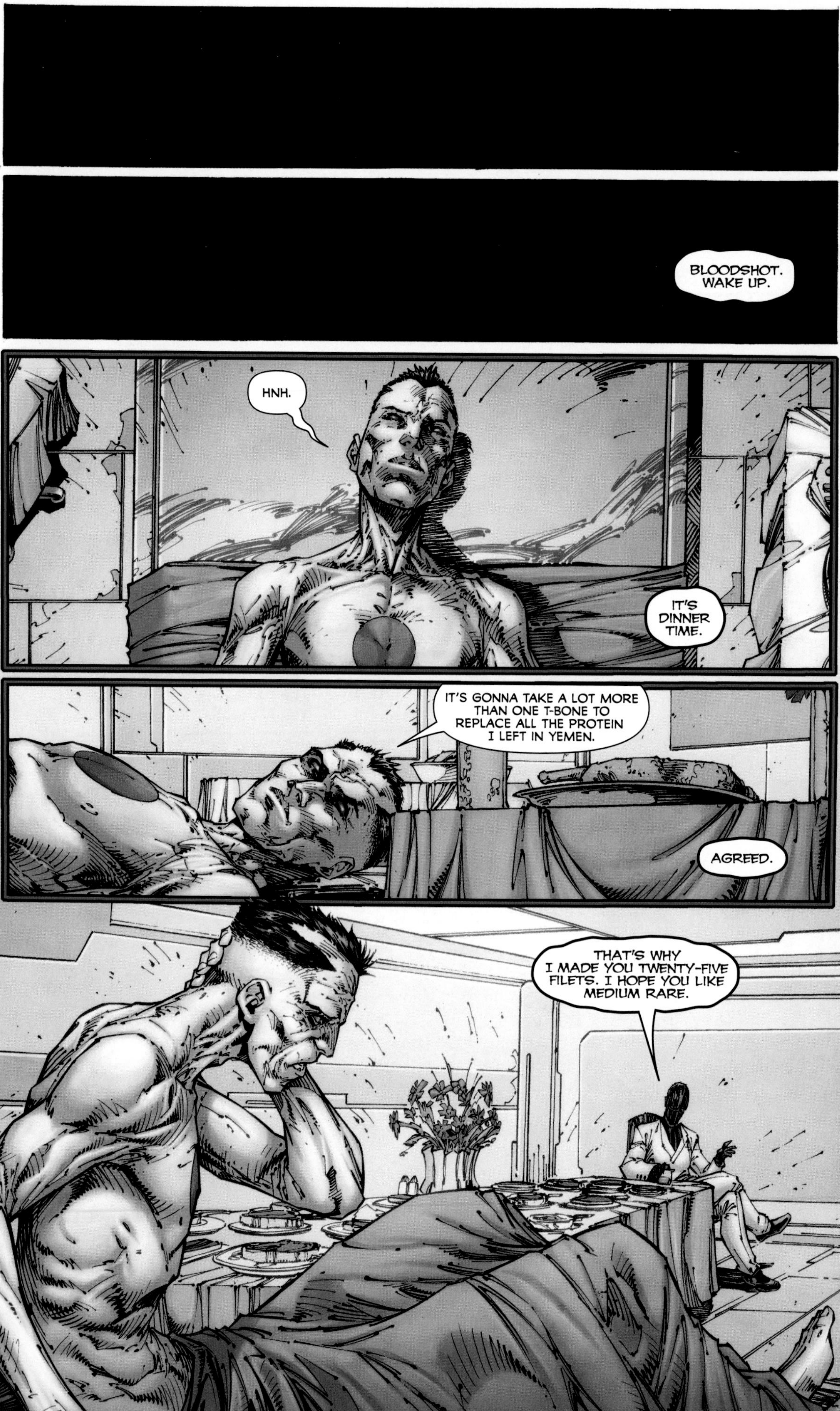
BLOODSHOT. WAKE UP.
HNH.
IT'S DINNER TIME.
IT'S GONNA TAKE A LOT MORE THAN ONE T-BONE TO REPLACE ALL THE PROTEIN I LEFT IN YEMEN.
AGREED.
THAT'S WHY I MADE YOU TWENTY-FIVE FILETS. I HOPE YOU LIKE MEDIUM RARE.

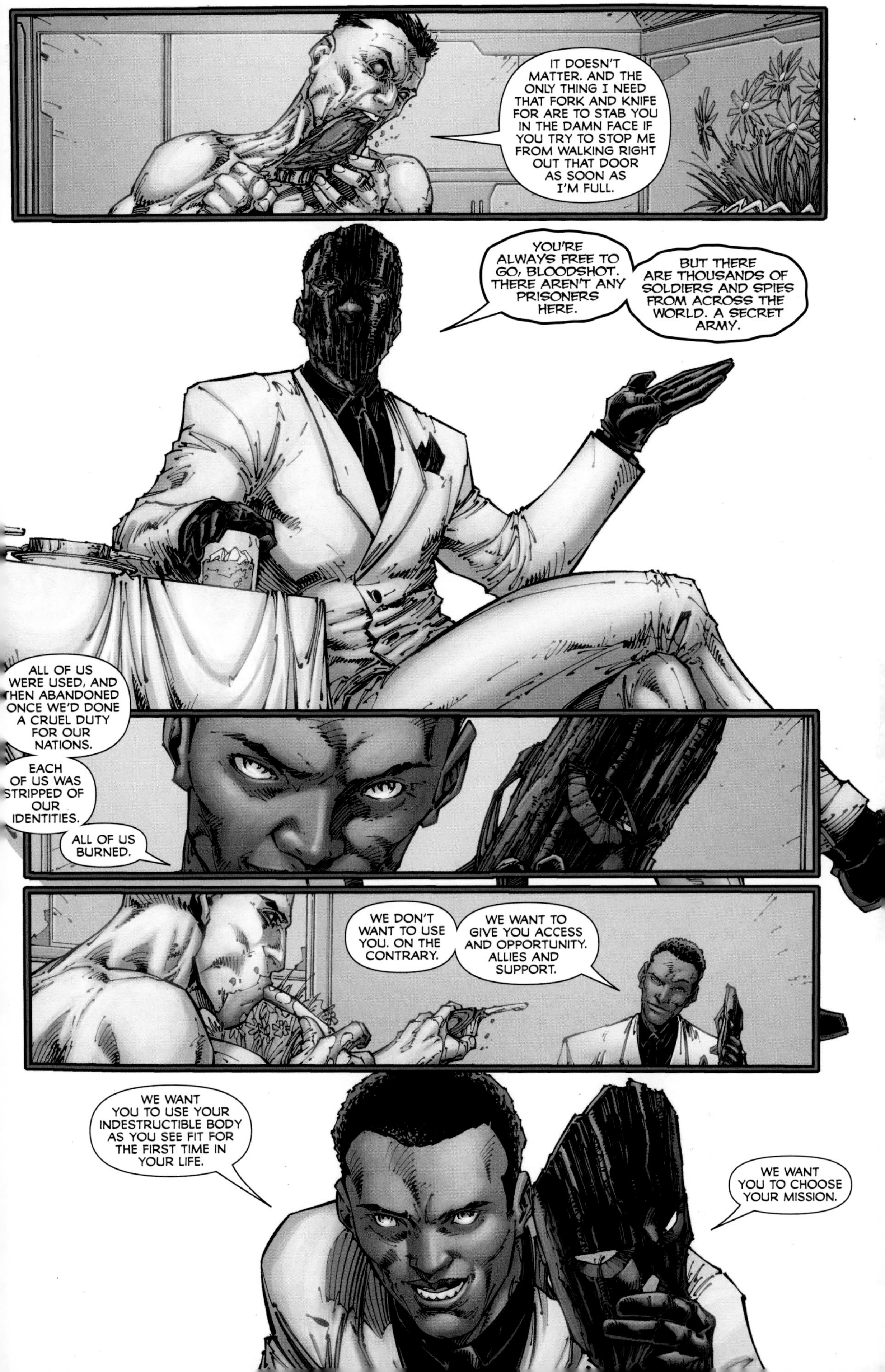
IT DOESN'T MATTER. AND THE ONLY THING I NEED THAT FORK AND KNIFE FOR ARE TO STAB YOU IN THE DAMN FACE IF YOU TRY TO STOP ME FROM WALKING RIGHT OUT THAT DOOR AS SOON AS I'M FULL.
YOU'RE ALWAYS FREE TO GO, BLOODSHOT. THERE AREN'T ANY PRISONERS HERE.
BUT THERE ARE THOUSANDS OF SOLDIERS AND SPIES FROM ACROSS THE WORLD. A SECRET ARMY.
ALL OF US WERE USED, AND THEN ABANDONED ONCE WE'D DONE A CRUEL DUTY FOR OUR NATIONS.
EACH OF US WAS STRIPPED OF OUR IDENTITIES.
ALL OF US BURNED.
WE DON'T WANT TO USE YOU. ON THE CONTRARY.
WE WANT TO GIVE YOU ACCESS AND OPPORTUNITY. ALLIES AND SUPPORT.
WE WANT YOU TO USE YOUR INDESTRUCTIBLE BODY AS YOU SEE FIT FOR THE FIRST TIME IN YOUR LIFE.
WE WANT YOU TO CHOOSE YOUR MISSION.

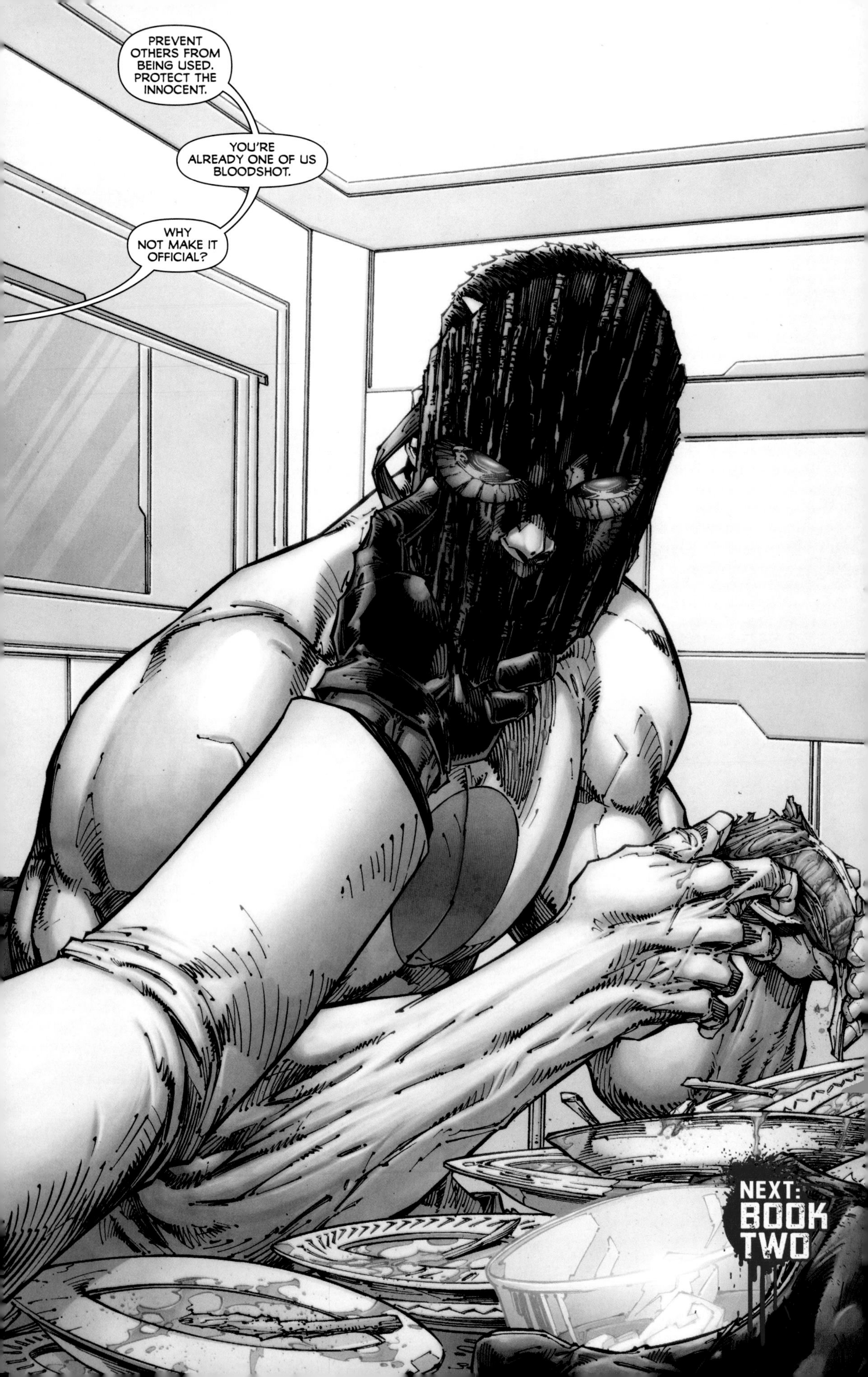
PREVENT OTHERS FROM BEING USED. PROTECT THE INNOCENT.
YOU'RE ALREADY ONE OF US BLOODSHOT.
WHY NOT MAKE IT OFFICIAL?
NEXT: BOOK TWO

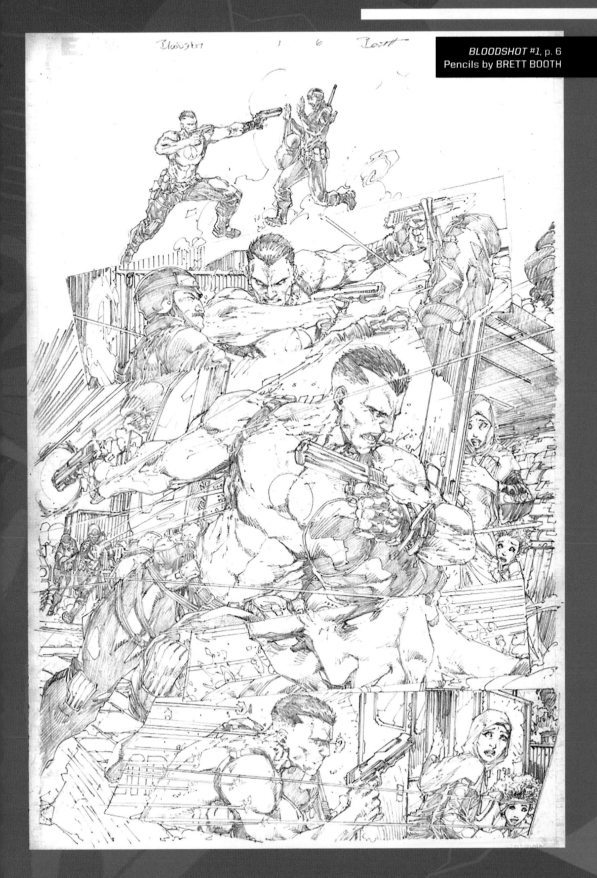

BLOODSHOT #1, p. 6
Pencils by BRETT BOOTH

TAKING HIS SHOT

This Fall, writer Tim Seeley takes on Bloodshot in a brand-new ongoing series and promises not to get too much into the supersoldier's head

By Ernie Estrella - SyFy Wire

We hope you enjoyed this brand-new Bloodshot story created especially for Free Comic Book Day. It's a sneak peek into writer Tim Seeley's upcoming BLOODSHOT series launching this Fall. Here, Ernie Estrella from Syfy Wire talks with Seeley about working on Valiant's unstoppable supersoldier.

SYFY WIRE: What did you want to set out and establish with Bloodshot in this new series and the present-day Valiant Universe?

TIM SEELEY: I wanted to figure out a way to take ol' Bloodshot back to his core concept, and make the series really feel unique and very specific. This is Bloodshot. This is what he does. This is why. This is his world. But on top of that, I

wanted to add lots of big action and ideas – this is an unlimited-budget action movie. So, what I hope you get is an action comic that's clear and simple and spare, but also LOADED WITH IDEAS.

SYFY WIRE: Will your ongoing series refer back to what is going on in Bloodshot Rising Spirit, which has been unpacking his early days and origins?

SEELEY: Not necessarily. There are a lot of toys in the chest, but this series is looking to focus on the shiny new ones.

SYFY WIRE: In this Free Comic Book Day story, we see a lot of people reacting to Bloodshot and those lives affected by him, and while we do hear him speak, we don't get into his head. Are you deliberately choosing to stay out of his point of view?

ART BY **TOMÁS GIORELLO** WITH **DIEGO RODRIGUEZ**

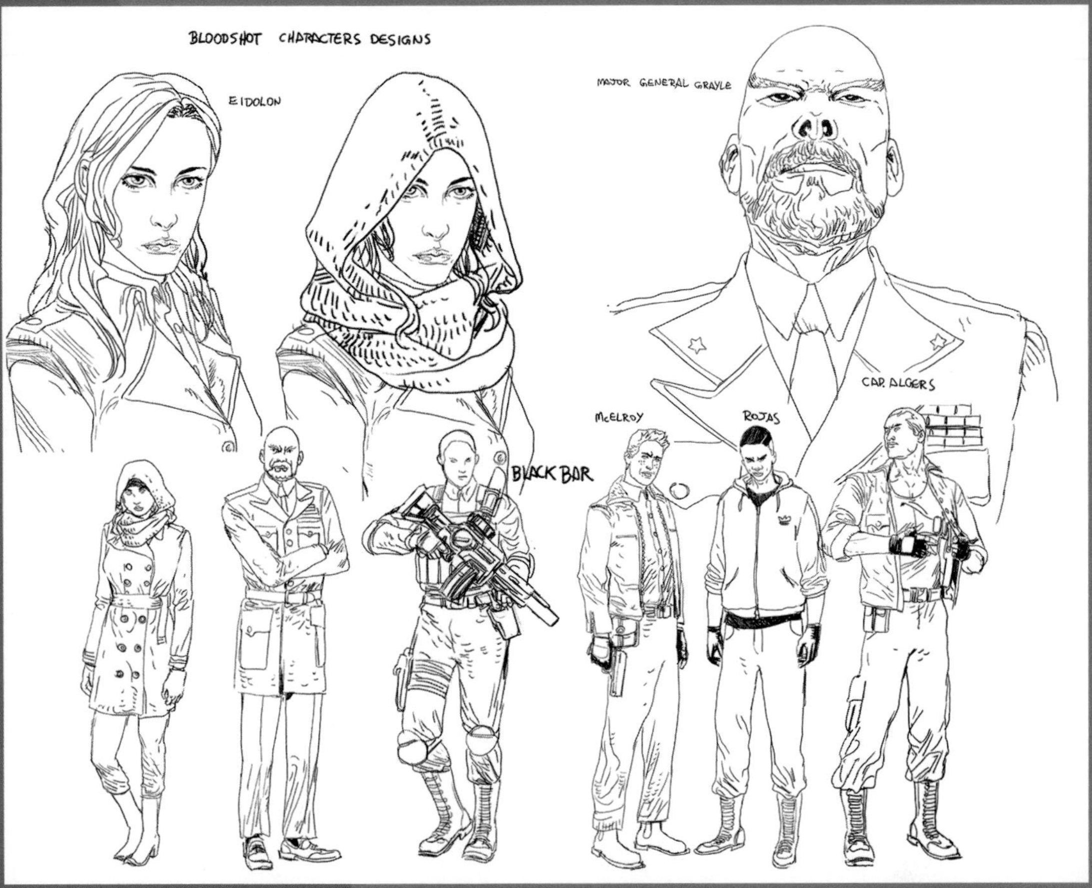
BLOODSHOT CHARACTERS DESIGNS
EIDOLON
MAJOR GENERAL GRAYLE
CAP. ALGERS
McELROY
ROJAS
BLACK BAR

CHARACTER DESIGNS BY AMILCAR PINNA

SEELEY: Yes! I kind of hate writing first-person narration. I want you to see what these people think by what they do and how they react to others. And, with Bloodshot especially, we're talking about a character who is somewhat of a mystery, and I think spending too much time in his head might ruin that a bit.

SYFY WIRE: I enjoyed a lot of the panels in the Free Comic Book Day story where it was absent dialogue but he was this imposing, almost Terminator-like presence. How much do you play with scenes like this?

SEELEY: As often as possible! And I think what you're seeing there is [artist] Tomás [Giorello's] ability to make anything and everything look super badass.

SYFY WIRE: We see these guys calling themselves the Last Sons of the Flesh, and they're disposed of quickly, but are they part of a larger story?

SEELEY: Not immediately, but I'm the kind of guy who lays down a lot of groundwork to pick up later. Plantin' seeds, I say. So, there are plenty of ways to bring those dudes back in.

SYFY WIRE: What did you enjoy about working with Tomás?

SEELEY: He's a storyteller above all. All his choices are made in service to the story, and he doesn't cheat the reader to get a cool drawing. He just happens to make everything cool!

SYFY WIRE: Are there any other major characters from the Valiant Universe that you're looking to play with, that you can tell or tease us about?

SEELEY: We won't be bringing in too many titular heroes in the beginning, but I have some ideas down the road. I'm not doing this right if I don't have Bloodshot tangle with X-O [Manowar] at some point. ■

Special thanks to Ernie Estrella of Syfy Wire. For his full interview with Tim Seeley, visit www.syfy.com.

Originally published in *VALIANT: BLOODSHOT FCBD 2019 SPECIAL*.

BLOODSHOT #1
OASAS COMICS
RETAILER VARIANT COVER
Art by JAE LEE

BLOODSHOT #1
MIDTOWN COMICS
NYCC RETAILER VARIANT COVER
Art by FRANCESCO MATTINA

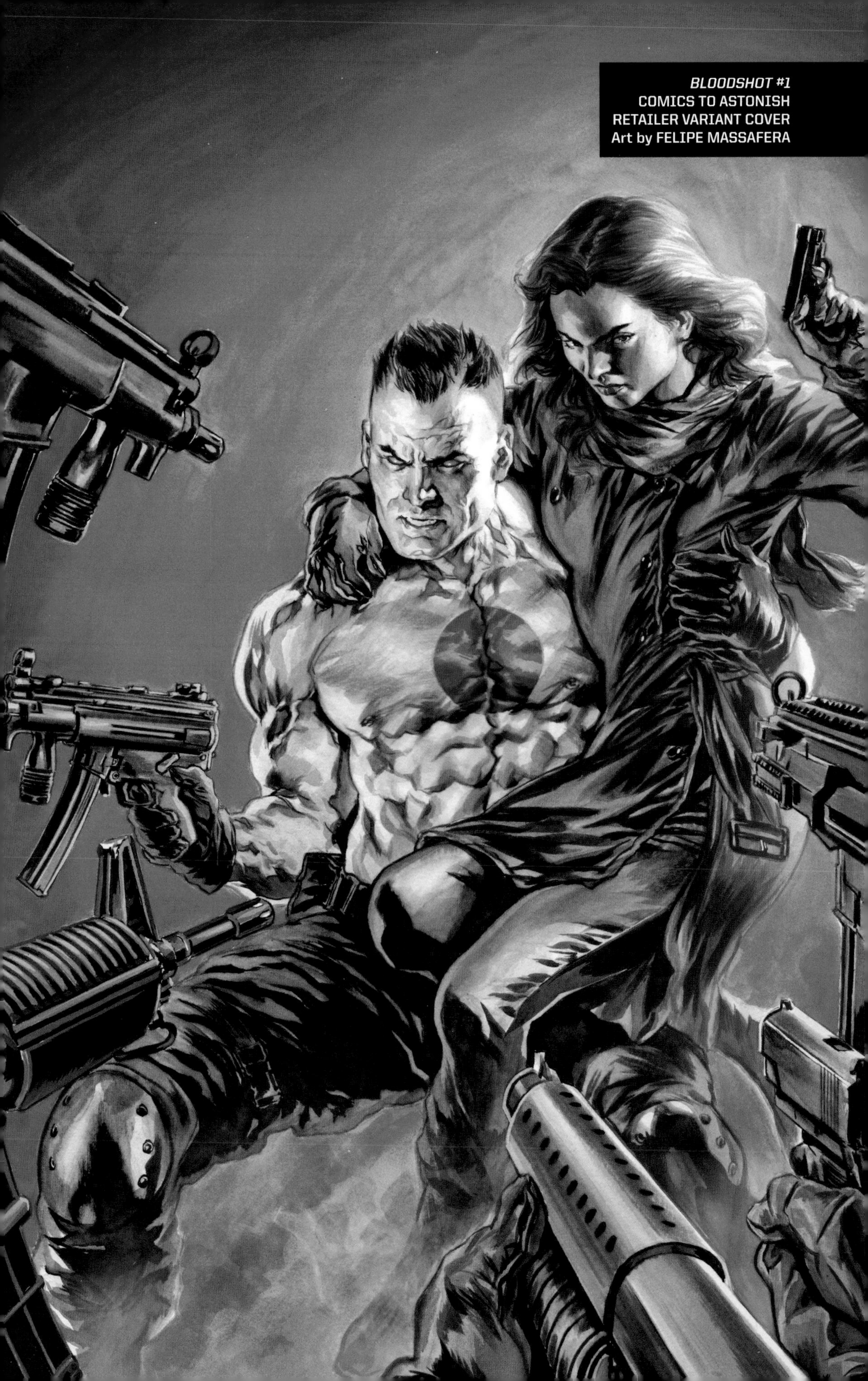

BLOODSHOT #1
COMICS TO ASTONISH
RETAILER VARIANT COVER
Art by FELIPE MASSAFERA

BLOODSHOT #2 COVER B
Art by DAVE JOHNSON

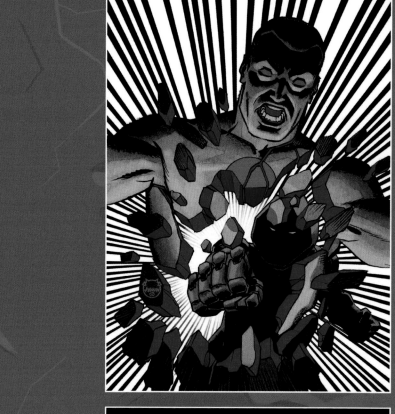

BLOODSHOT #3 COVER B
Art by DAVE JOHNSON

BLOODSHOT #2 COVER C
Art by SIMON BISLEY

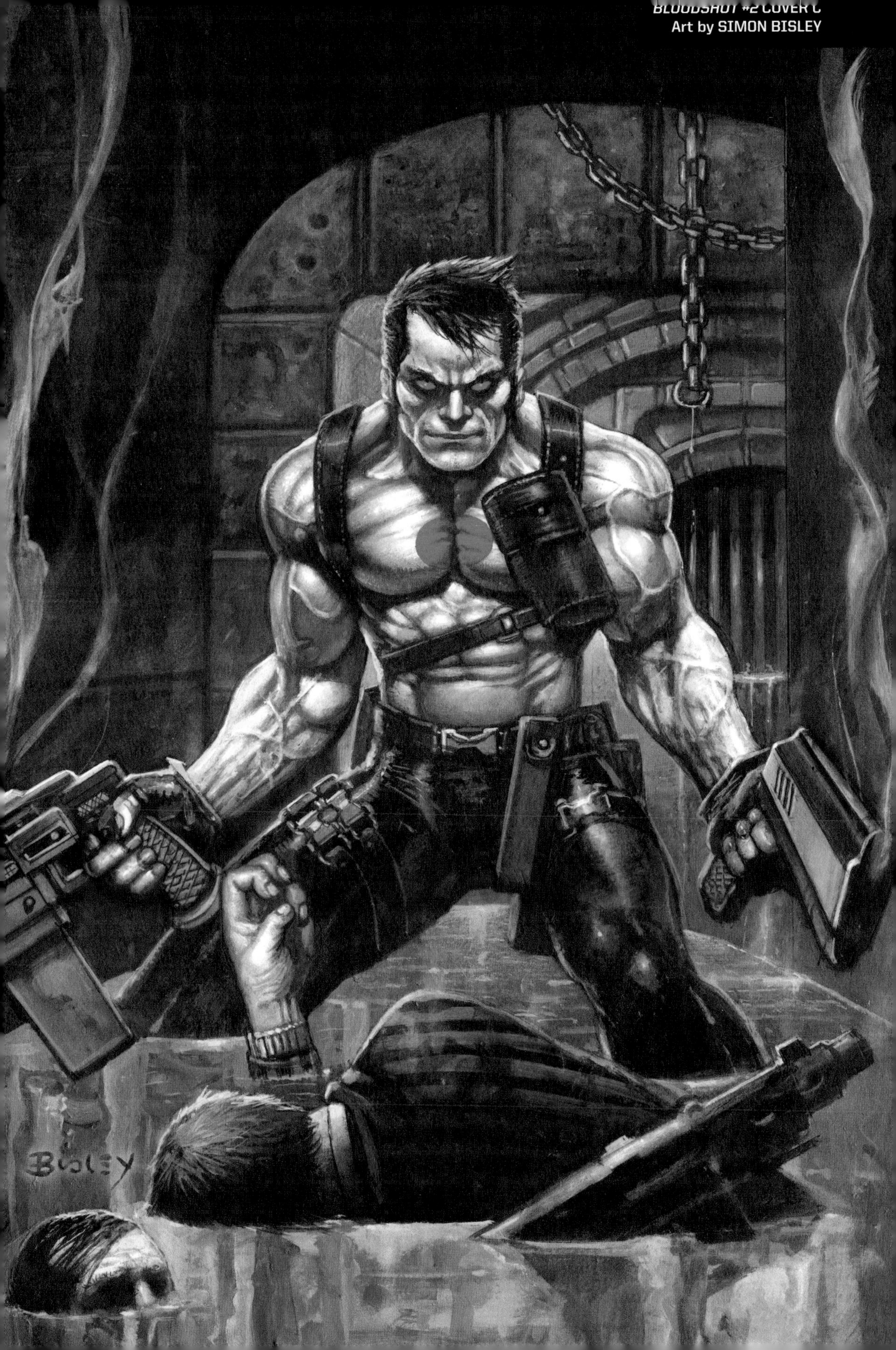
BISLEY

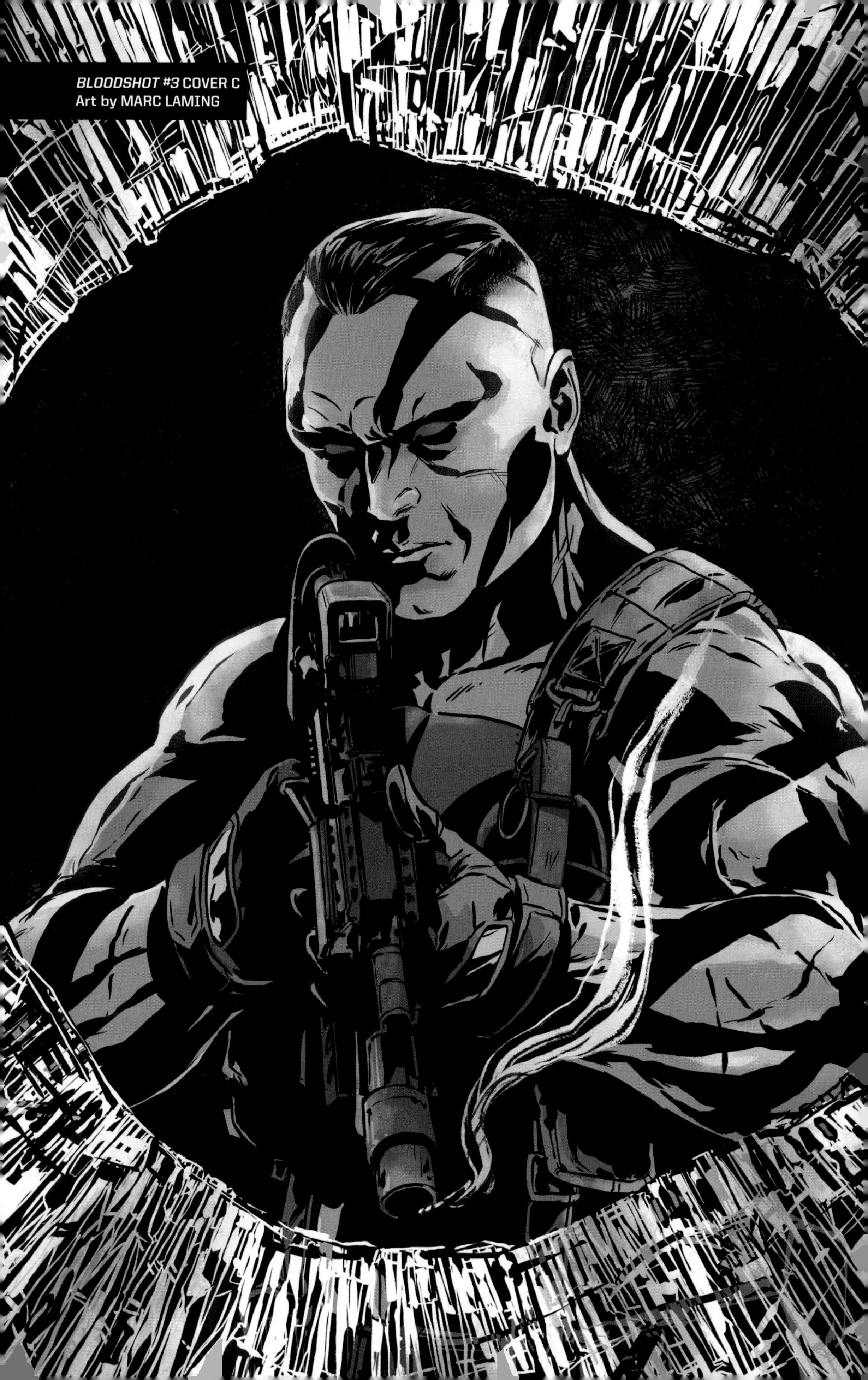

BLOODSHOT #3 COVER C
Art by MARC LAMING

CHARACTER INTRODUCTIONS WITH SERIES WRITER TIM SEELEY

THE BURNED – These guys are all ex-spies and intelligence agents from all over the world. Diverse races, nationalities and genders. They wear white suits, and masks that look to be made out of burned wood...charcoal in texture. They use a variety of spy weapons taken from their old jobs, the majority of which have been deemed too dangerous or too unethical for other agencies. These guys are CREEPY...they're the spookiest of spooks....spies of spies.

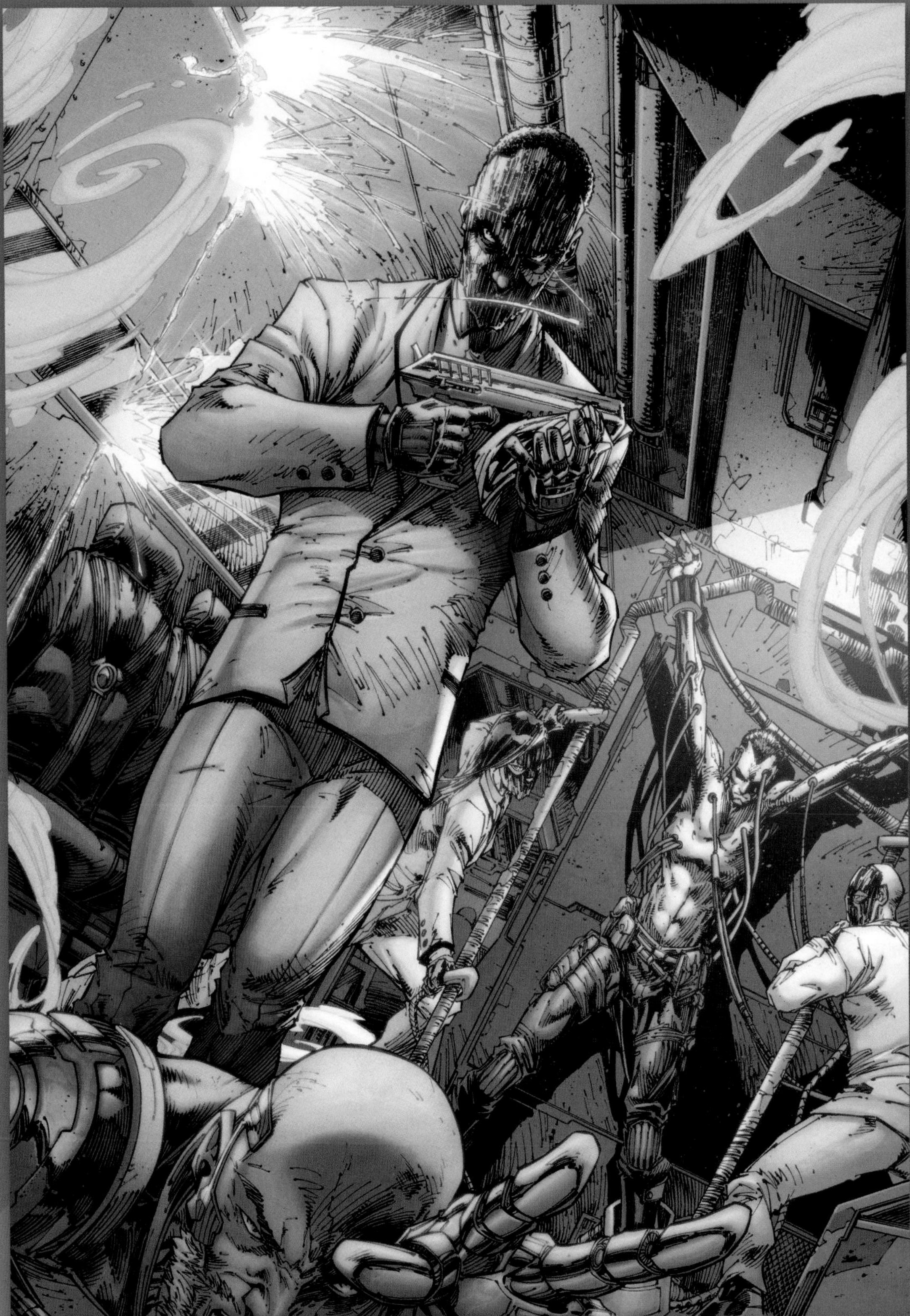

ARTWORK BY **BRETT BOOTH** WITH **ADELSO CORONA** AND **ANDREW DALHOUSE**
Originally published in ***BLOODSHOT #3 PRE-ORDER EDITION.***

"BLOODSHOT: Prelude" pages 2, 3, and (facing) 4
VALIANT: BLOODSHOT FCBD 2019 SPECIAL
Pencils by TOMÁS GIORELLO

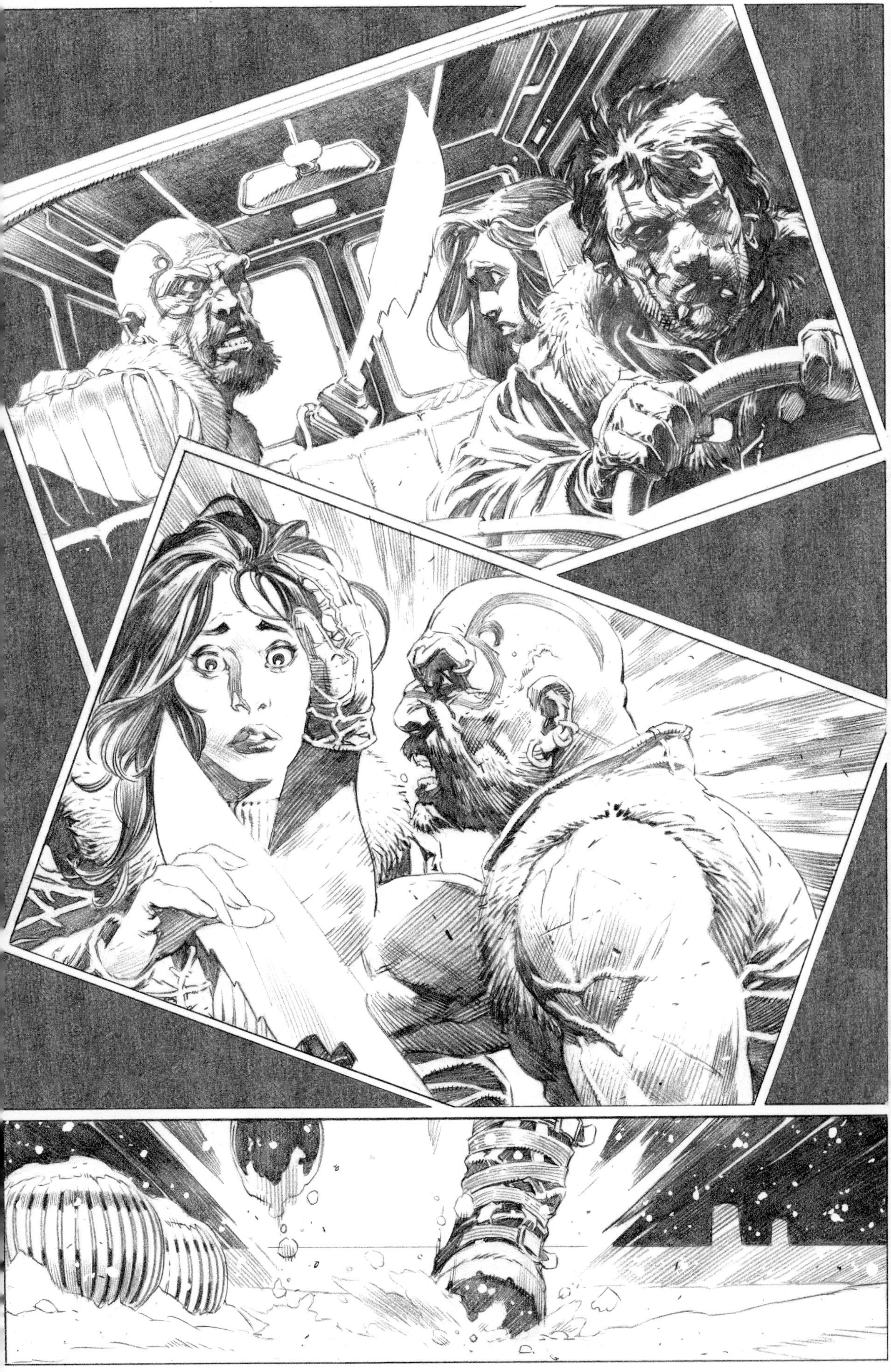

BLOODSHOT #1, pages 9, 10, and (facing) 11
Pencils by BRETT BOOTH
Inks by ADELSO CORONA

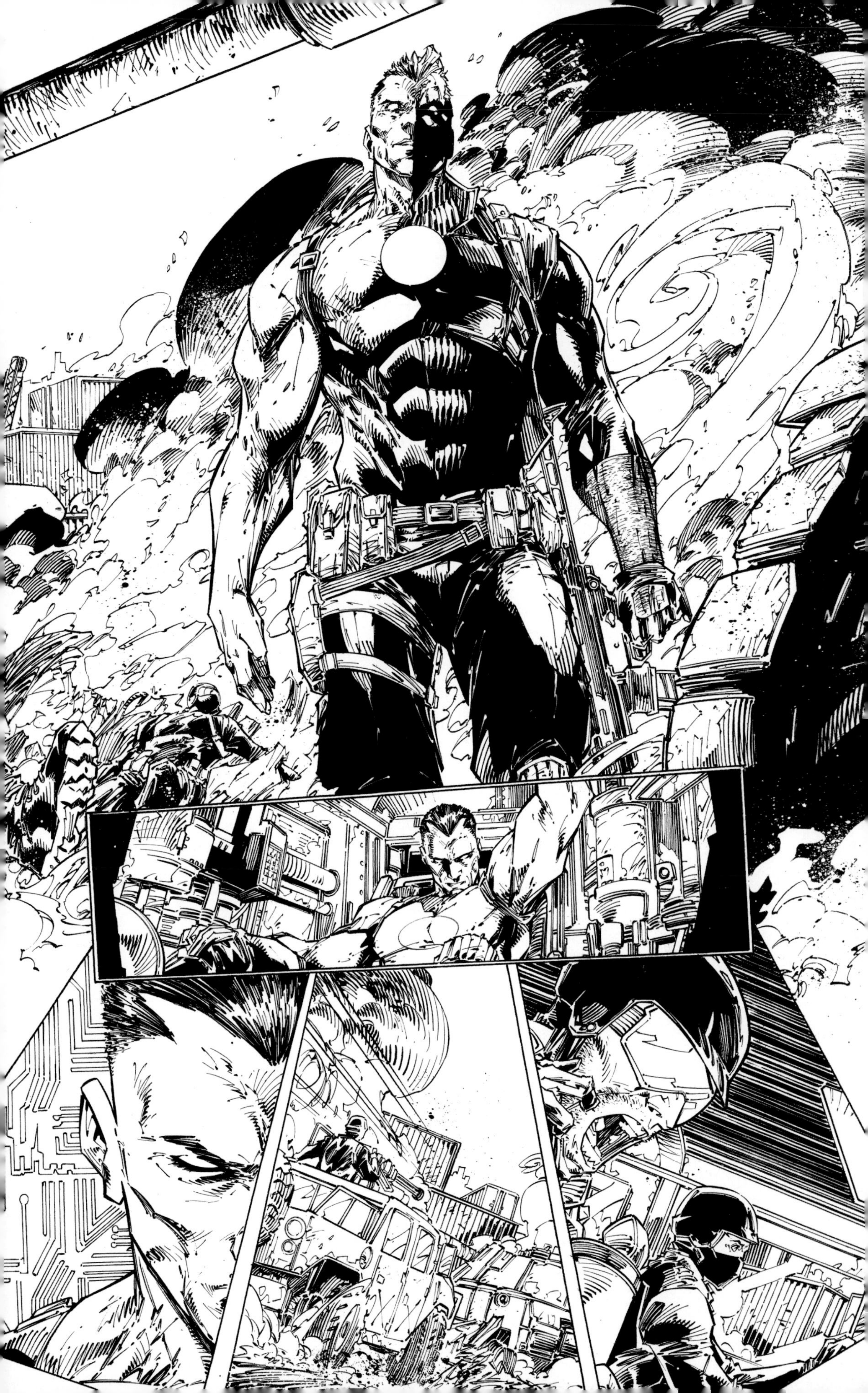

BLOODSHOT #1, pages 16, 17, and (facing) 18
Pencils by BRETT BOOTH
Inks by ADELSO CORONA

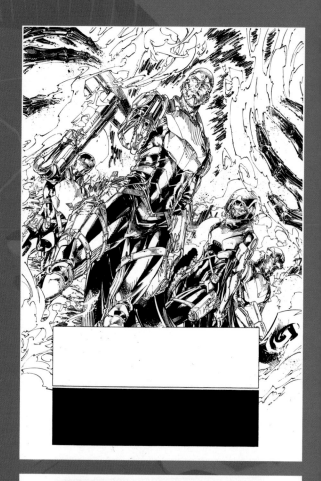

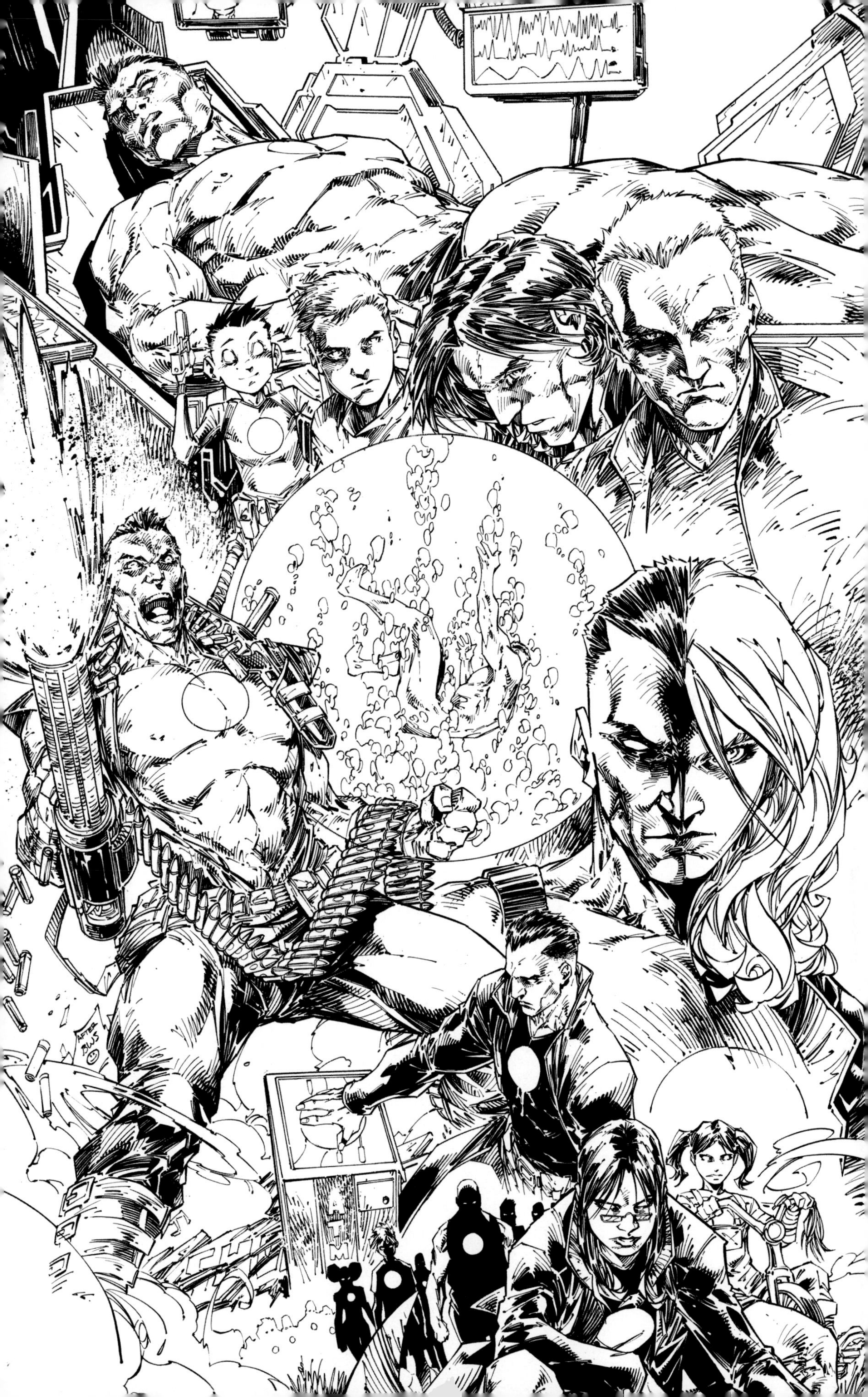

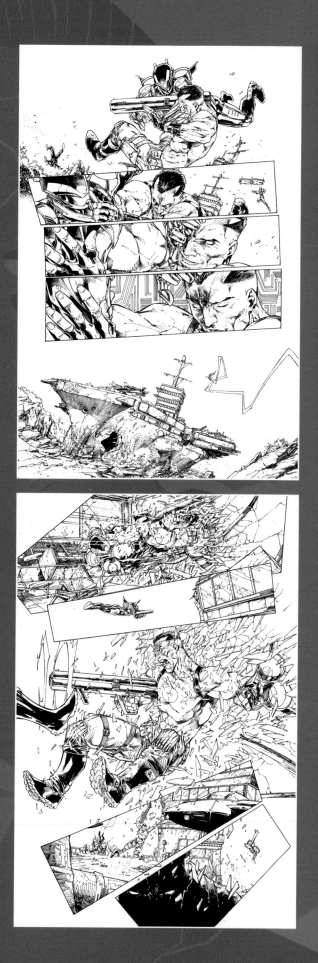

BLOODSHOT #2, pages 9, 10, and (facing) 11
Pencils by BRETT BOOTH
Inks by ADELSO CORONA

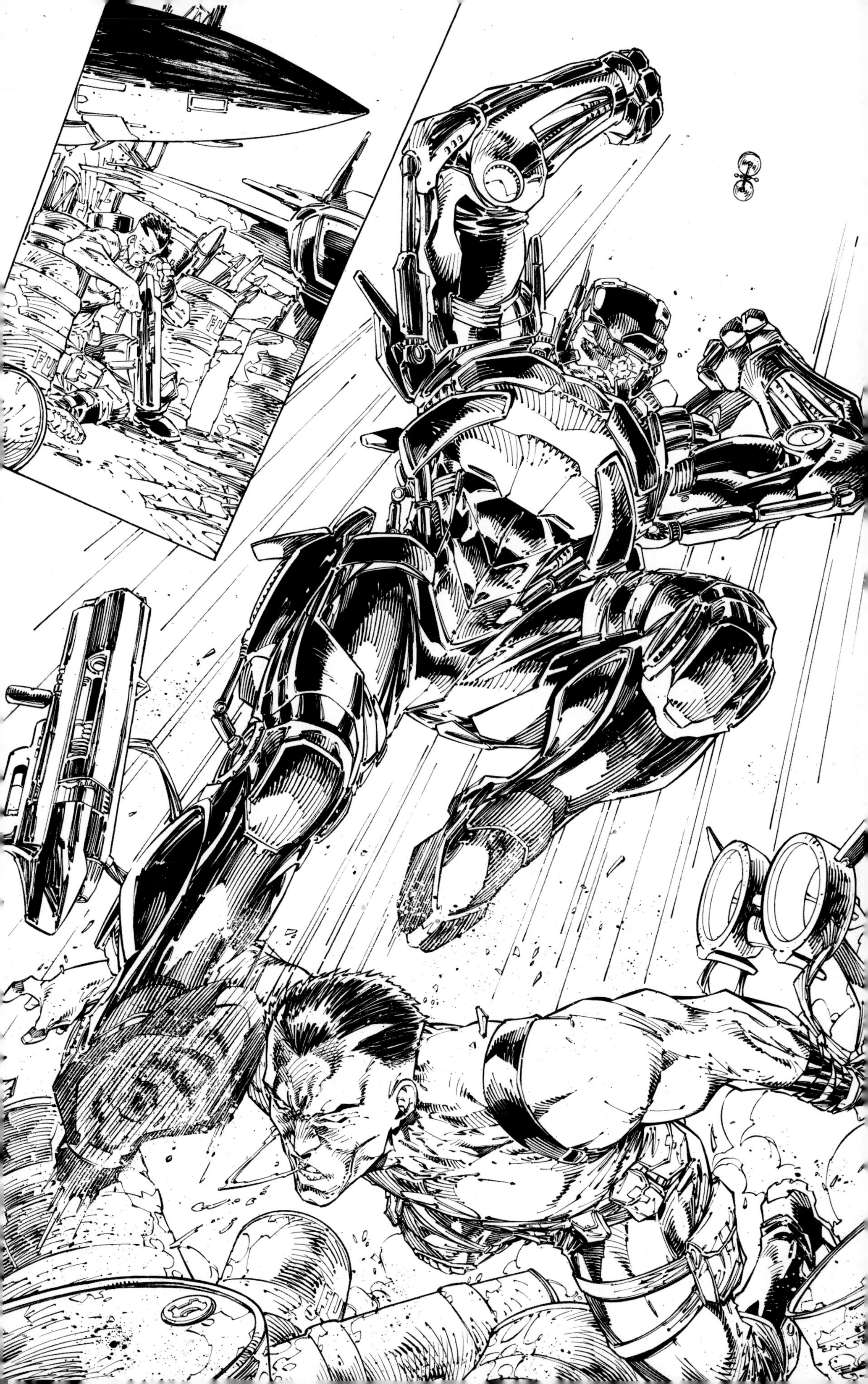

BLOODSHOT #2, pages 18, 19, and (facing) 20
Pencils by BRETT BOOTH
Inks by ADELSO CORONA

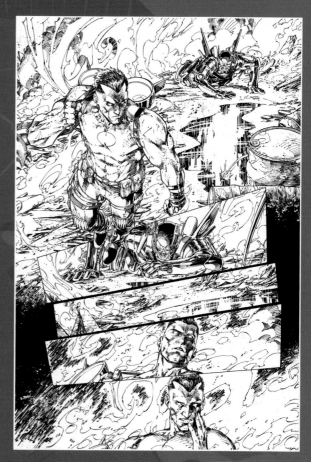

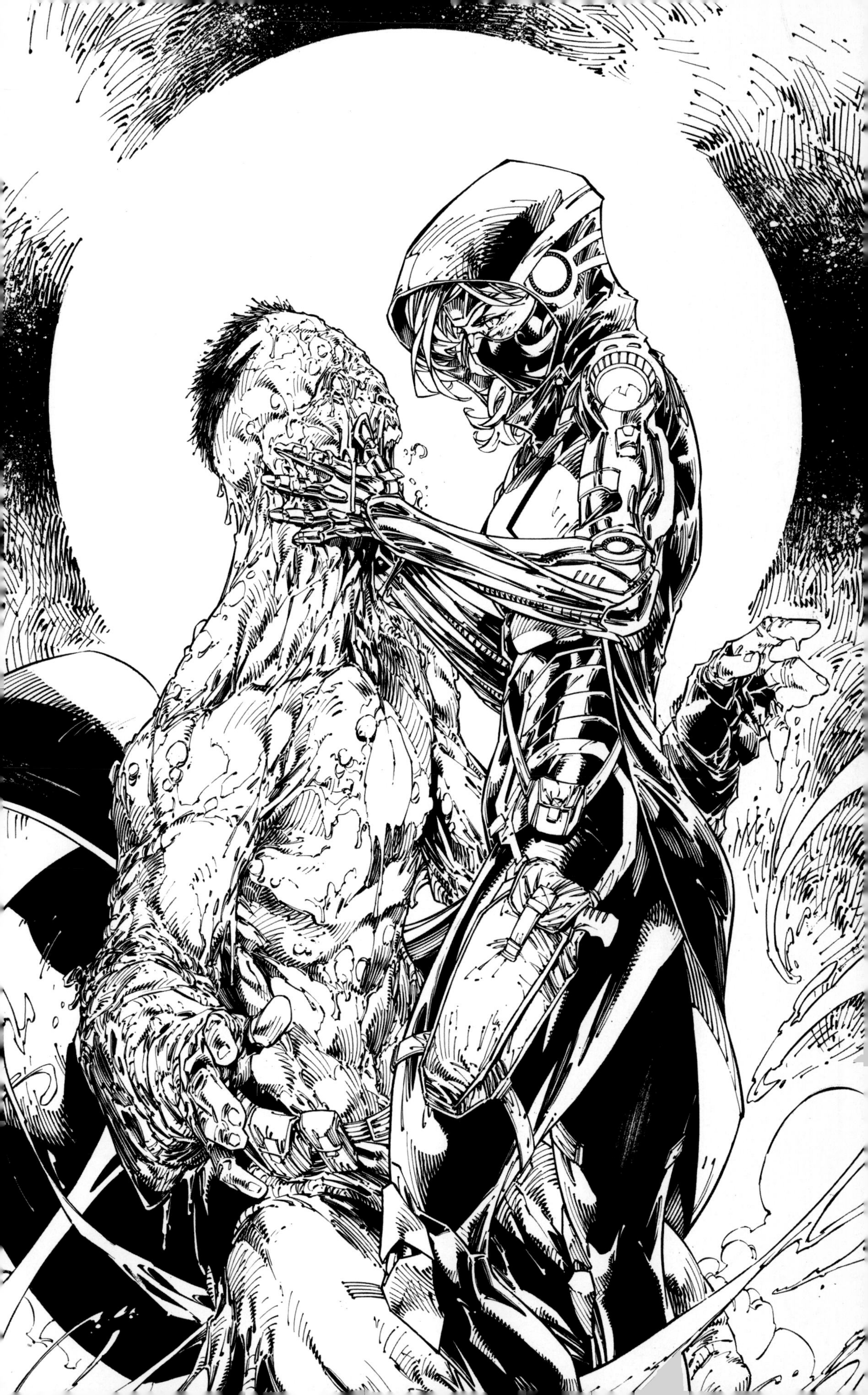

BLOODSHOT #3, pages 1, 2, and (facing) 3
Pencils by BRETT BOOTH
Inks by ADELSO CORONA

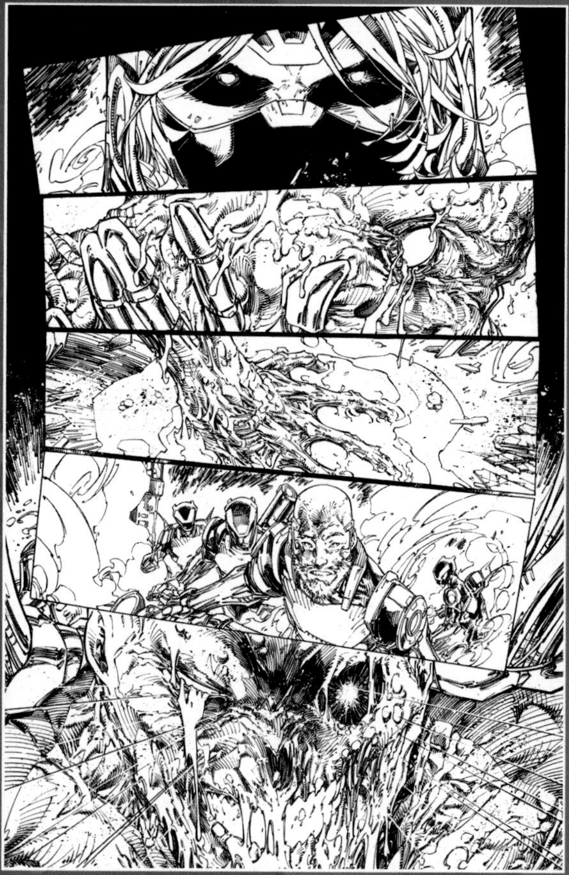

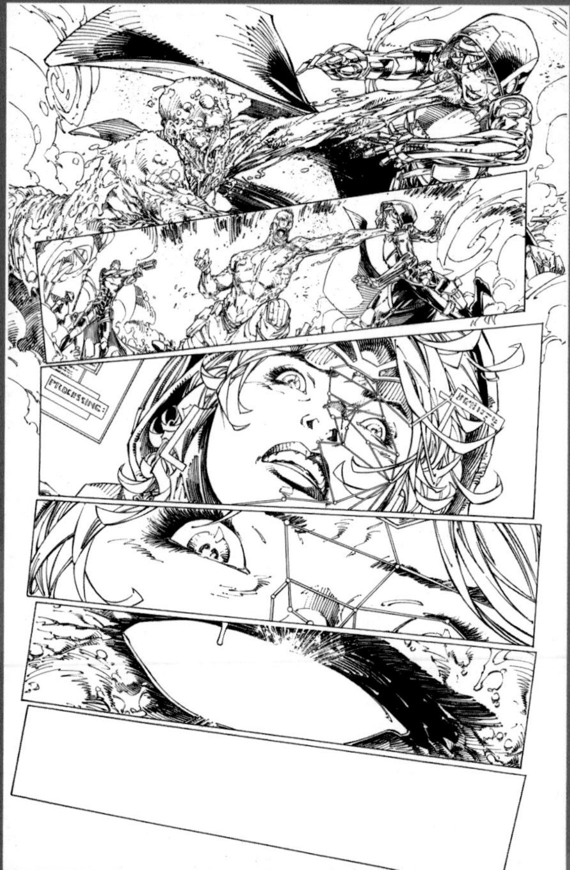
PROCESSING:

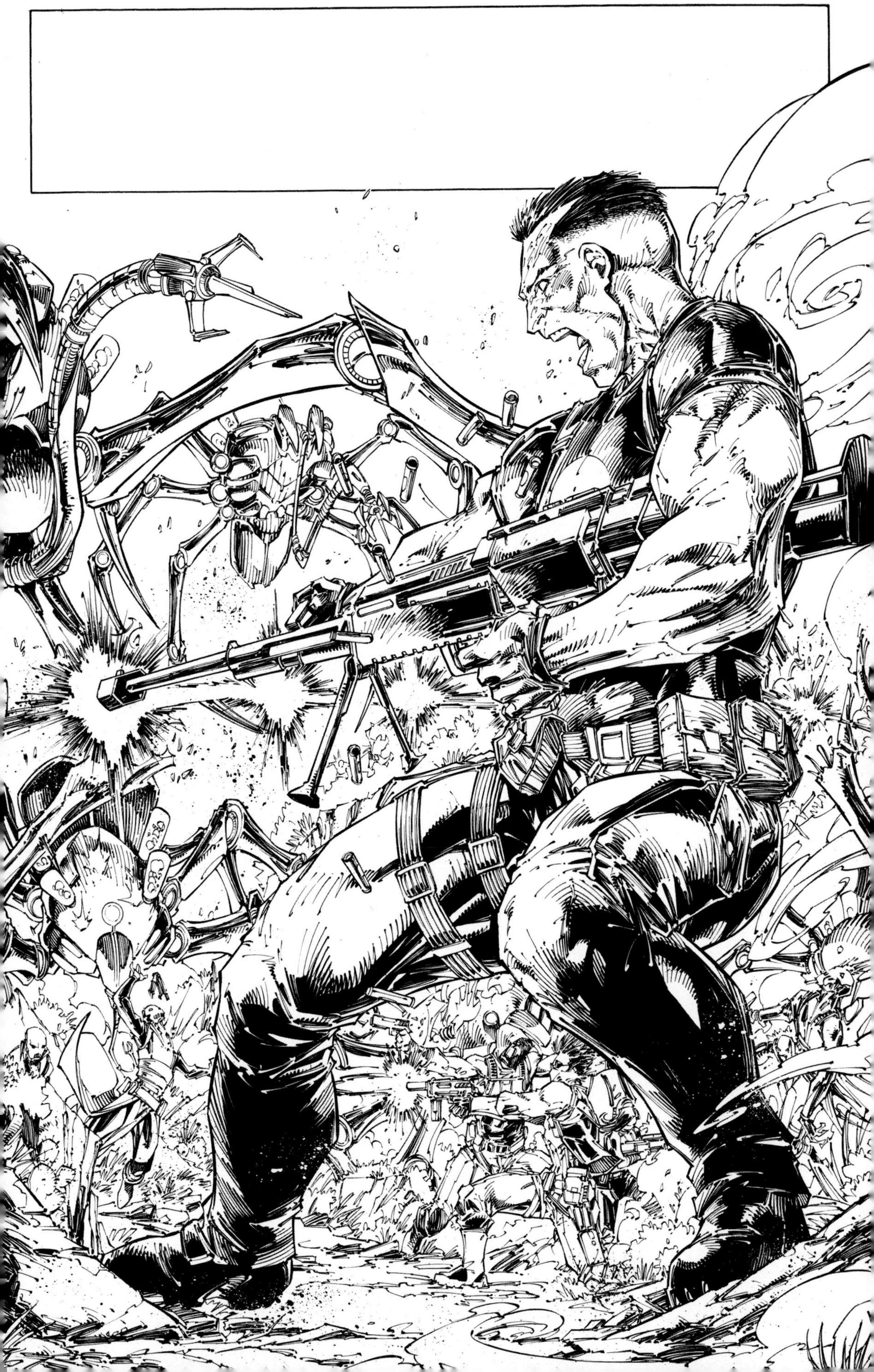

BLOODSHOT #3, pages 13, 14, and (facing) 15
Pencils by BRETT BOOTH
Inks by ADELSO CORONA

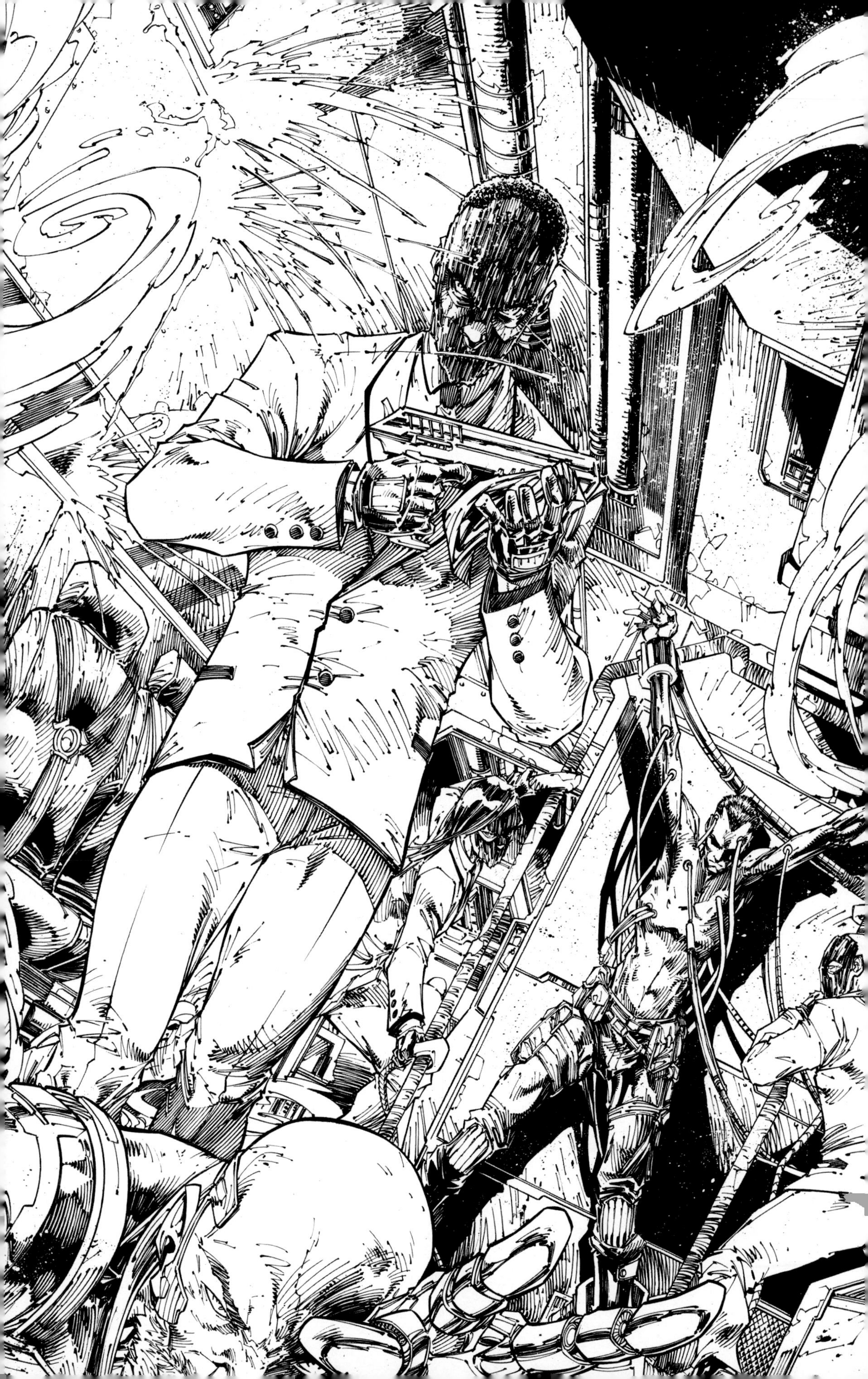

BLOODSHOT #3, pages 18, 19, and (facing) 20
Pencils by BRETT BOOTH
Inks by ADELSO CORONA

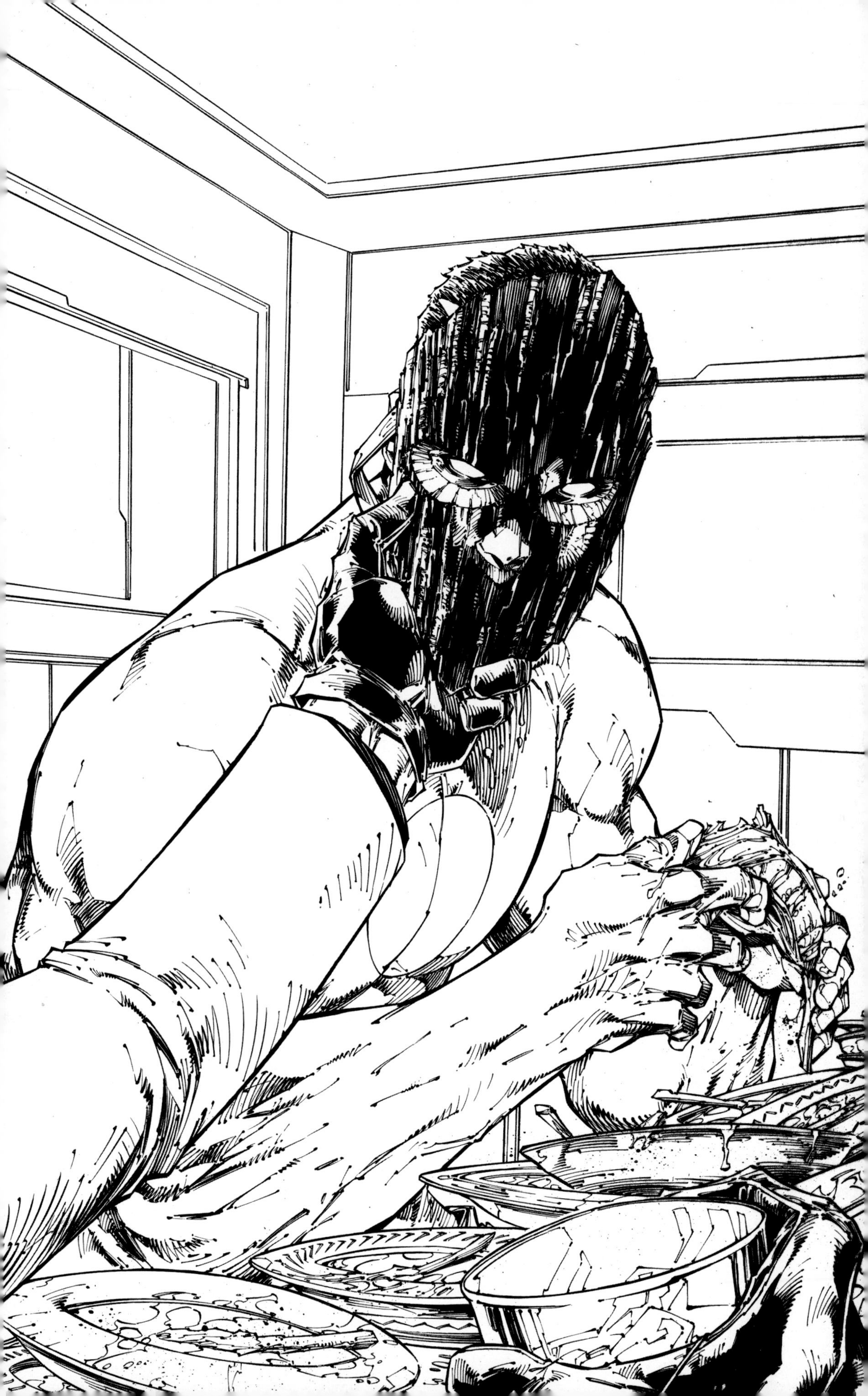

EXPLORE THE VALIANT

ACTION & ADVENTURE

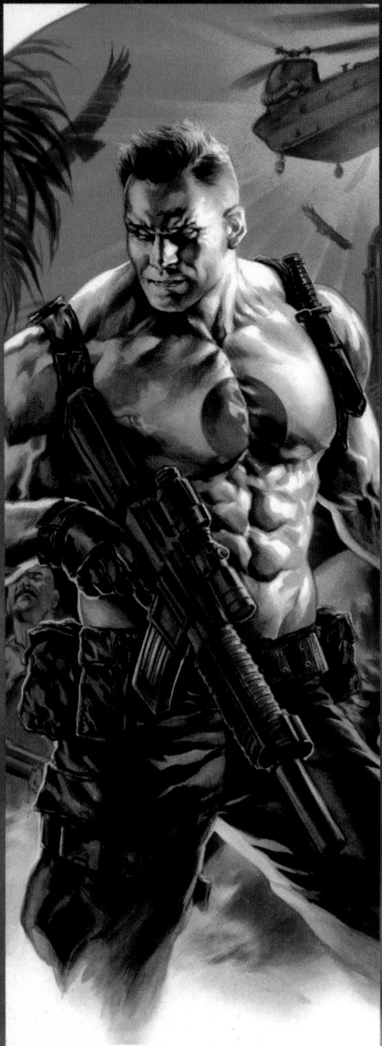

BLOODSHOT BOOK ONE
ISBN: 978-1-68215-342-0
NINJA-K VOL. 1: THE NINJA FILES
ISBN: 978-1-68215-259-1
SAVAGE
ISBN: 978-1-68215-189-1
WRATH OF THE ETERNAL WARRIOR VOL. 1: RISEN
ISBN: 978-1-68215-123-5
X-O MANOWAR (2017) VOL. 1: SOLDIER
ISBN: 978-1-68215-205-8

BLOCKBUSTER ADVENTURE

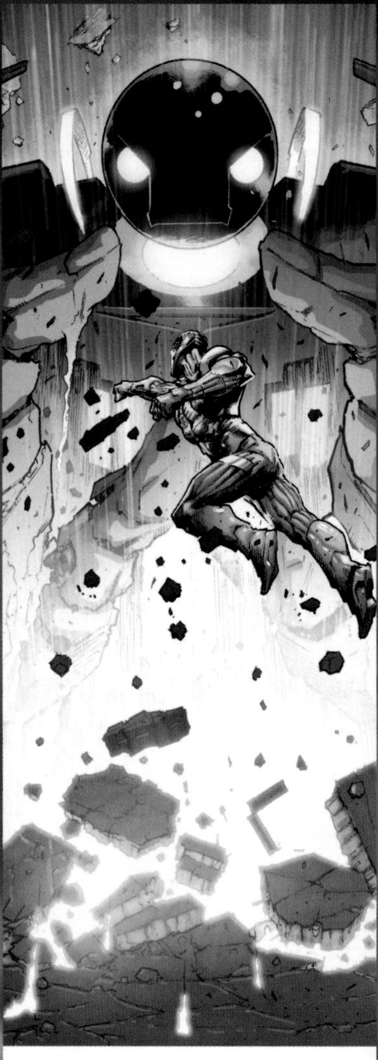

4001 A.D.
ISBN: 978-1-68215-143-3
ARMOR HUNTERS
ISBN: 978-1-939346-45-2
BOOK OF DEATH
ISBN: 978-1-939346-97-1
HARBINGER WARS
ISBN: 978-1-939346-09-4
THE VALIANT
ISBN: 978-1-939346-60-5

COMEDY

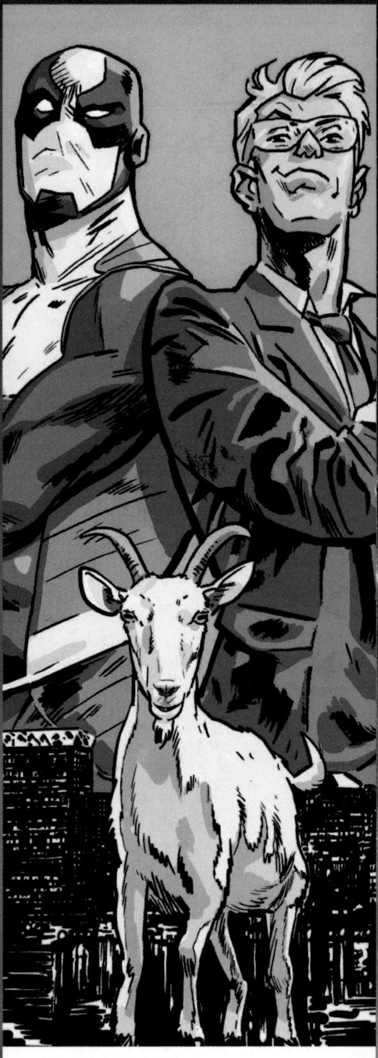

A&A: THE ADVENTURES OF ARCHER & ARMSTRONG VOL. 1: IN THE BAG
ISBN: 978-1-68215-149-5
THE DELINQUENTS
ISBN: 978-1-939346-51-3
QUANTUM AND WOODY! (2017) VOL. 1: KISS KISS, KLANG KLANG
ISBN: 978-1-68215-269-0

  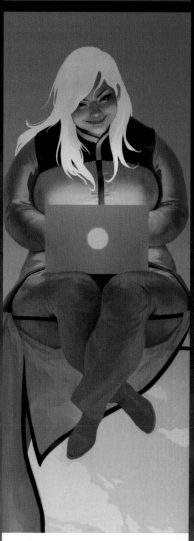

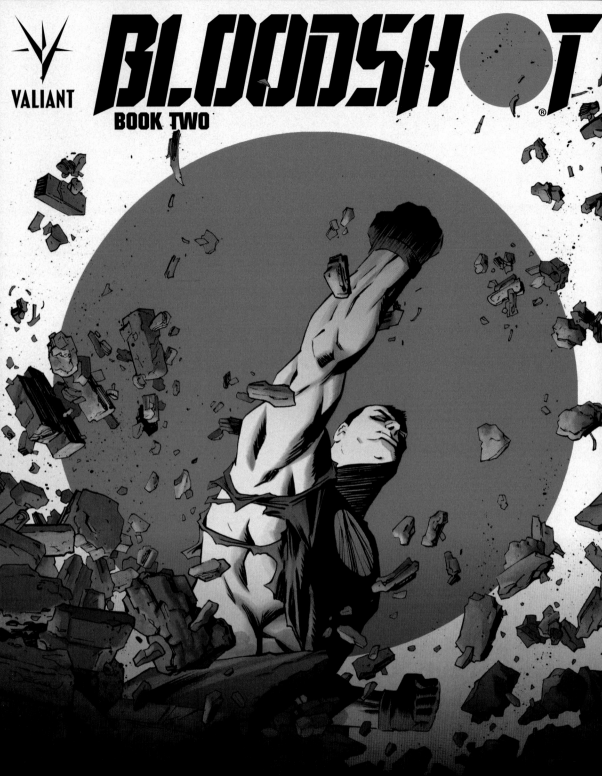

VALIANT

BLOODSHOT

BOOK TWO

FROM THE FIRST SHOT TO THE LONG SHOT...

Bloodshot faces off against the secret global task force known as Black Bar side by side with a coalition of former agents that call themselves the Burned. From a monster-filled bullet train through the heart of darkness to the homegrown terrors of Miami, high-speed thrills and blood-curdling chills lurk behind every turn in the next volume of the year's best new action series!

Witness the Valiant supersoldier unleashed as *New York Times* bestselling writer Tim Seeley (*Grayson*) and comics icon Brett Booth (*Titans*) let loose another can't-miss chapter of BLOODSHOT!

Collecting BLOODSHOT (2019) #4–6.

TRADE PAPERBACK
ISBN: 978-1-68215-350-5